Our Churches and Chapels

THEIR PARSONS, PRIESTS, & CONGREGATIONS; BEING A CRITICAL AND HISTORICAL ACCOUNT OF EVERY PLACE OF WORSHIP IN PRESTON.

Atticus

Our Churches and Chapels

Atticus (A. Hewitson)

PO Box 2211
Fairfield, IA 52556
www.1stworldlibrary.org
First Edition

LCCN: 2004091164

Softcover ISBN: 1-59540-610-7
eBook ISBN: 1-59540-710-3

Purchase *"Our Churches and Chapels"*
as a traditional bound book at:
www.1stWorldLibrary.org/purchase.asp?ISBN=1-59540-610-7

1st World Library Literary Society is a nonprofit organization dedicated to promoting literacy by:

- Creating a free internet library accessible from any computer worldwide.
- Hosting writing competitions and offering book publishing scholarships.

Readers interested in supporting literacy through sponsorship, donations or membership please contact:
literacy@1stworldlibrary.org
Check us out at: www.1stworldlibrary.org

Our Churches and Chapels

contributed by the Mahaney Family

in support of

1st World Library Literary Society

'T is pleasant through the loopholes of retreat to peep at such a world.

- Cowper.

INDEX

TO THE READER.

The general satisfaction given by the following sketches when originally printed in the Preston Chronicle, combined with a desire, largely expressed, to see them republished, in book form, is the principal excuse offered for the appearance of this volume. Into the various descriptions of churches, chapels, priests, parsons, congregations, &c., which it contains, a lively spirit, which may be objectionable to the phlegmatic, the sad-faced, and the puritanical, has been thrown. But the author, who can see no reason why a "man whose blood is warm within" should "sit like his grandsire cut in alabaster," on any occasion, has a large respect for cheerfulness, and has endeavoured to make palatable, by a little genial humour, what would otherwise have been a heavy enumeration of dry facts. Those who don't care for the gay will find in these sketches the grave; those who prefer vivacity to seriousness will meet with what they want; those who appreciate all will discover each. The solemn are supplied with facts; the facetious with humour; the analytical with criticism. The work embodies a general history of each place of worship in Preston - fuller and more reliable than any yet published; and for reference it will be found valuable, whilst for general reading it will be instructive. The author has done his best to be candid and impartial. If he has failed in the attempt, he can't help it; if he has succeeded, he is thankful. No writer can suit everybody; and if an angel had compiled these sketches some men would have croaked. To the generality of the Church of England, Catholic, and Dissenting clergymen, &c., in the town, the author tenders his warmest thanks for the generous manner they have assisted him, and the kindly way in which they have supplied him with information essential to the completion of the work.

Preston, Dec. 24th, 1869.

OUR CHURCHES AND CHAPELS: THEIR PARSONS, PRIESTS, AND CONGREGATIONS.

It is important that something should be known about our churches and chapels; it is more important that we should be acquainted with their parsons and priests; it is most important that we should have a correct idea of their congregations, for they show the consequences of each, and reflect the character and influence of all. We have a wide field before us. The domain we enter upon is unexplored. Our streets, with their mid-day bustle and midnight sin; our public buildings, with their outside elaboration and inside mysteries; our places of amusement, with their gilded fascinations and shallow delusions; our clubs, bar parlours, prisons, cellars, and workhouses, with their amenities, frivolities, and severities, have all been commented upon; but the most important of our institutions, the best, the queerest, the solemnest, the oddest - the churches and chapels of the town - have been left out in the cold entirely. All our public functionaries have been viewed round, examined closely, caressed mildly, and sometimes genteely maltreated; our parochial divinities, who preside over the fate of the poor; our municipal Gogs and Magogs who exhibit the extreme points of reticence and garrulity in the council chamber; our brandy drinkers, chronic carousers, lackered swells, pushing shopkeepers , otiose policemen , and dim-looking cab-drivers have all been photographed, framed, and hung up to dry long ago; our workshops and manufactories, our operatives and artisans, have likewise been duly pictured and exhibited; the Ribble has had its praises sung in polite literary strains; the parks have had their beauties depicted in rhyme and blank verse; nay - but this is hardly necessary - the old railway station, that walhallah of the gods and paragon of the five orders of architecture, has had its delightful peculiarities set forth; all our public places and public bodies have been thrown upon the canvas, except those of the more serious type - except places of worship and those belonging them. These have been neglected; nobody has thought it worth while to give them either a special blessing or a particular anathema.

There are about 45 churches and chapels and probably 60 parsons and priests in Preston; but unto this hour they have been treated, so far as they are individually concerned, with complete silence. We purpose remedying the defect, supplying the necessary criticism, and filling up the hiatus. The whole lot must have either something or nothing in them, must be either useful or useless; parsons must be either sharp or stupid, sensible or foolish; priests must be either learned or illiterate, either good, bad, or indifferent; in all, from the rector in his silken gown to the back street psalm-singer in his fustian, there must be something worth praising or condemning. And the churches and chapels, with their congregations, must likewise present some points of beauty or ugliness, some traits of grace or godlessness, some features of excellence, dignity, piety, or sham. There must be either a good deal of gilded gingerbread or a great let of the genuine article, at our places of worship. But whether there is or there is not, we have decided to say something about the church and the chapel, the parson and the priest, of each district in the town. This is a mere prologue, and we shall but hint at the general theme " on this occasion."

Churches and chapels are great institutions in the land. Nobody knows the exact time when the first was thought of; and it has not yet transpired when the last will be run up. But this is certain, we are not improving much in the make of them. The Sunday sanctums and Sabbath conventicles of today may be mere ornate, may be more flashy, and show more symptoms of polished bedizenment in their construction; but three-fourths of them sink into dwarflings and mediocrities when compared with the rare old buildings of the past. In strength and beauty, in vastness of design and skill of workmanship, in nobility of outline and richness of detail, the religious fabrics of these times fall into insignificance beside their grand old predecessors; and the manner in which they are cut up into patrician and plebeian quarters, into fashionable coteries for the perfumed portion of humanity, and into half-starved benches with the brand of poverty upon them for the poor, is nothing to the credit of anybody.

All the churches and chapels of the land may profess Christianity; but the game of the bulk has a powerful reference to money. Those who have got the most of the current coin of the realm receive the blandest smile from the parson, the politest nod from the beadle, the promptest attention from that strange mixture of piety and pay called "the chapel-keeper;" those who have not got it must take what they can get, and accept it with Christian resignation, as St. Paul tells them. This may be all right; we have not said yet that it is wrong; but it looks suspicious, doesn't it? - shows that in the arena of conventional Christianity, as in the seething maelstrom of ordinary life, money is the winner. Our parsons and priests, like our ecclesiastical architecture and general church management, do not seem to have improved upon their ancestors. Priests are not as jolly as they once were. In olden days "holy fathers" could wear horse-hair shirts and scarify their epidermis with a finer cruelty than their modern successors, and they could, after all that, make the blithest songs, sing the merriest melodies, and quaff the oldest port with an air of jocund conscientiousness, making one slyly like them, however much inclined to dispute the correctness of their theology. And the parsons of the past were also a blithesome set of individuals. They were perhaps rougher than those mild and refined gentlemen who preach now-a-days; but they were straightforward, thorough, absolutely English, well educated, and stronger in the brain than many of them. In each Episcopalian, Catholic, and Dissenting community there are new some most erudite, most useful men; but if we take the great multitude of them, and compare their circumstances - their facilities for education , the varied channels of usefulness they have - with those of their predecessors, it will be found that the latter were the cleverer, often the wiser, and always the merrier men. Plainness, erudition, blithesomeness, were their characteristics. Aye, look at our modern men given up largely to threnody-chiming and to polishing off tea and muffin with elderly females, and compare them, say, for instance, with -

> The poet Praed's immortal Vicar,
> Who wisely wore the cleric gown,
> Sound in theology and liquor;
> Quite human, though a true divine,
> His fellow-men he would not libel;

He gave his friends good honest wine,
And drew his doctrine from the Bible.

Institute a comparison, and then you will say that whilst modern men may be very aesthetic and neatly dressed, the ancient apostolic successors, though less refined, had much more metal in them, were more kindly, genial; and told their followers to live well, to eat well, and to mind none of the hair-splitting neological folly which is now cracking up Christendom. In old times the Lord did not "call" so many parsons from one church to another as it is said He does now; in the days which have passed the bulk of subordinate parsons did not feel a sort of conscientious hankering every three years for an "enlarged sphere of usefulness," where the salary was proportionately increased. We have known multitudes of parsons, in our time, who have been "called" to places where their salaries were increased; we know of but few who have gravitated to a church where the salary was less than the one left. "Business" enters largely into the conceptions of clergymen. As a rule, no teachers of religion, except Catholic priests and Methodist ministers, leave one place for another where less of this world's goods and chattels predominate; and THEY are COMPELLED to do so, else the result might be different. When a priest gets his mittimus he has to budge; it is not a question of "he said or she said," but of - go; and when a Wesleyan is triennially told to either look after the interests of a fresh circuit or retire into space, he has to do so. It would be wrong to say that lucre is at the bottom of every parsonic change; but it is at the foundation of the great majority - eh? If it isn't, just make an inquiry, as we have done. This may sound like a deviation from our text - perhaps it is; but the question it refers to is so closely associated with the subject of parsons and priests, that we should have scarcely been doing justice to the matter if we had not had a quiet "fling" at the money part of it. In the letters which will follow this, we shall deal disinterestedly with all - shall give Churchmen, Catholics, Quakers, Independents, Baptists, Wesleyans, Ranters, and Calathumpians, fair play. Our object will be to present a picture of things as they are, and to avoid all meddling with creeds. People may believe what they like, so far as we are concerned, if they behave themselves, and pay their debts. It is utterly impossible to get all to be of the same opinion; creeds, like faces, must differ, have differed, always will differ; and the best plan is to let people have their own way so long as it is consistent with the general welfare of social and civil life. It being understood that "the milk of human kindness is within the PALE of the Church," we shall begin there. The Parish Church of Preston will constitute our first theme.

I

PRESTON PARISH CHURCH.

It doesn't particularly matter when the building we call our Parish Church was first erected; and, if it did, the world would have to die of literary inanition before it got the exact date. None of the larger sort of antiquaries agree absolutely upon the subject, and the smaller fry go in for all sorts of figures, varying as to time from about two years to one hundred and fifty. This may be taken as a homoeopathic dose in respect to its history:- built about 900 years since by Catholics, and dedicated to St. Wilfrid; handed over to Protestants by somebody, who was perhaps acting on the very generous principle of giving other folk's property, in the 16th century; rebuilt in 1581, and dedicated to St. John; rebuilt in 1770; enlarged, elaborated, and rejuvenised in 1853; plagued with dry rot for a considerable time afterwards; in a pretty good state of architectural health now; and likely to last out both this generation and the next. It looks rather genteel and stately outside; it has a good steeple, kept duly alive by a congregation of traditional jackdaws; it has a capital set of bells which have put in a good deal of overtime during the past five months, through a pressure of election business; and in its entirety, as Baines once remarked, the building looks like "a good ordinary Parish Church." There is nothing either snobbish or sublime about it; and, speaking after Josh Billings, "it's a fair even-going critter," capable of being either pulled down or made bigger. That is about the length and breadth of the matter, and if we had to appeal to the commonwealth as to the correctness of our position it would be found that the "ayes have it." We don't believe in the Parish Church; but a good deal of people do, and why shouldn't they have their way in a small fight as well as the rest of folk? All, except Mormons and Fenians, who honestly believe in anything, are entitled to respect.

Our Parish Church has a good contour, and many of its exterior architectural details are well conceived and arranged; but, like other buildings of the same order, it has got a multiplicity of strange hobgoblin figure-heads about it which serve no purpose either earthly or heavenly, and which are understood by hardly one out of five million. We could never yet make it out why those grotesque pieces of masonry - gargoyles, we believe, they are called-were fixed to any place of worship. Around our Parish Church and half-way up the steeple, there are, at almost every angle and prominence, rudely carved monstrosities, conspicuous for nothing but their ineffable and heathenish ugliness. Huge eyes, great mouths, immense tooth, savage faces and distorted bodies are their prime characteristics. The man who invented this species of ecclesiastical decoration must have been either mad or in "the horrors." An evenly balanced mind could never have thought of them, and why they should he specially tacked to churches is a mystery in accordance with neither King Solomon nor Cocker. The graveyard of our Parish Church is, we dare say, something which very few people think of. We have seen many such places in our time; but that in connection with our

Parish Church is about the grimmest specimen in the lot. It has a barren, cold, dingy, unconsecrated look with it; and why it should have we can't tell. Either ruffianism or neglect must at some time have done a good stroke of business in it; for many of the gravestones are cracked in two; some are nearly broken to pieces; and a considerable number of those in the principal parts of the yard are being gradually worn out. We see no fun, for instance, in "paving" the entrances to the church with gravestones. Somebody must, at some time, have paid a considerable amount of money in getting the gravestones of their relatives smoothed and lettered; and it could never have been intended that they should be flattened down, close as tile work, for a promiscuous multitude of people to walk over and efface. The back of the churchyard is in a very weary, delapidated and melancholy state. Why can't a few shrubs and flowers be planted in it? Why is not the ground trimmed up and made decent? From the time when the Egyptians worshipped cats and onions down to the present hour, religious folk have paid some special attention to their grave spaces, and we want to see the custom kept up. Our Parish Church yard has a sad, forsaken appearance; if it had run to seed and ended in nothing, or had been neglected and closed up by an army of hypochondriacs, it could not have been more gloomy, barren, or disheartening. The ground should be looked after, and the stones preserved as much as possible. It is a question of shoes v. gravestones at present, and, if there is not some change of position, the shoes will in the end win.

About the interior of our Parish Church there is nothing particularly wonderful; it has a respectable, substantial, reverential appearance, and that is quite as much as any church should have. There is no emblematic ritualistic moonshine in any part of it; we hope there never may be; we are sure there never will be so long as the men now at the helm are in office. But let us start at the beginning. The principal entrance is through a massive and somewhat dimly-lighted porch, which, in its time, has necessarily, like all church porches, been the scene of much pious gossip, superstition, and sanctimonious scandal. It is rather a snug place to halt in. If you stand on one side of the large octagonal font, which is placed in the centre of the inner perch, and patronised by about 20 of the rising race every Sunday afternoon, you will be able to see everybody, whilst nobody can distinctly see you. As a rule, many people are too fired, or too ill, or too idle, to go to a place of worship on a Sunday morning, and at our Parish Church one may plainly notice this. A certain number always put in a regular appearance. If they did not attend the Parish Church twice a day they would become apprehensive as to both their temporal respectability awl spiritual welfare. They are descendants of the old long-horned stock, and have a mighty notion of the importance of church-going. Probably they don't care very profoundly for the sermons; but they have got into a safe-sided, orthodox groove, and some of them have an idea that they will be saved as much by church-going as by faith. The members of this class have a large notion of the respectability of their individual pews and seats. If they belonged to a family of five hundred each, and if every one of them had to go to Church every Sunday, they would want their respective seats, Prayer Books, footstools, and all that sort of thing. They don't like to see strangers rambling about, in search of a resting place; they are particularly solemn-looking, and give symptoms of being on the border of some catastrophe, if an unknown being shows any disposition to enter their pews. And some of them would see a person a good deal beyond the ether side of Jordan before they would think of handing him a Prayer Book. We don't suppose any of them are so precise as the old gentleman who once, when a stranger entered his pew, doubled up the cushion, sat upon it in a two-fold state, and intimated that ordinary beards were good enough for interlopers; but after all there is much of the "number one" principle in the devotion of these goodly followers of the saints, and they have been so long at the game that a cure is impossible.

Taking the congregation of our Parish Church in the agregate it is a fair sample of every class of human life. You have the old maid in her unspotted, demurely-coloured moire antique, carrying a Prayer Book belonging to a past generation; you have the ancient bachelor with plenty of money and possessing a thorough knowledge as to the safest way of keeping it, his great idea being that the best way of getting to heaven is to stick to his coins, attend church every Sunday, and take the sacrament regularly; you have the magistrate, whose manner, if not his beard, is of formal cut; the retired tradesman, with his domestic looking wife, and smartly-dressed daughters, ten times finer than ever their mother was; the manufacturer absorbed in cotton and wondering when he will be able to do a good stroke of business on 'change again; the lawyer, who has carried on a decent business amongst fees during the week, and has perhaps turned up to join in the general confession; the doctor, ready to give emphasis to that part of it which says:- "And there is no health in us;" the pushing tradesman, who has to live by going to church, as well as by counter work; the speculating shopkeeper, who has a connection to make; the young finely-feathered lady, got up in silk and velvet and carrying a chignon sufficient to pull her cerebellum out of joint; the dandy buttoned up to show his figure, and heavily dosed with scent; the less developed young swell, who is always "talking about his pa and his ma," and has only just begun to have his hair parted down the middle; the broken down middle-aged man who was once in a good position, but who years since went all in a piece to pot; the snuff-loving old woman who curtsies before fine folk, who has always a long tale to tell about her sorrows, and who is periodically consoled by a "trifle;" the working man who is rather a scarce article, except upon special occasions; and the representative of the poorest class, living somewhere in that venal slum of slime and misery behind the church. A considerable number of those floating beings called "strags" attend the Parish Church. They go to no place regularly; they gravitate at intervals to the church, mainly on the ground that their fathers and mothers used to go there, and because they were christened there; but they belong a cunning race; they can scent the battle from afar, and they generally keep about three-quarters of a mile from the Parish Church when a collection has to be made. To the ordinary attendants, collections do not operate as deterrents; but to the "strags" they are frighteners. "What's the reason there are so few people here?" we said one day to the beadle, and that most potent, grave, and reverend seignior replied, with a Rogersonian sparkle in his rolling eye, "There's a collection and the 'strags' won't take the bait." It is the same more or less at every place of worship; and to tell the truth, there's a sort of instinctive dislike of collections in everybody's composition.

The congregation of our Parish Church is tolerably numerous, and embraces many fine human specimens.

Money and fashion are well represented at it; and as Zadkiel and the author of Pogmoor Almanac say those powers have to rule for a long time, we may take it for granted that the Parish Church will yet outlive many of the minor raving academies in which they are absent. There is touch more generalisation than there used to be as to the sittings in our Parish Church; but "birds of a feather flock together" still. The rich know their quarters; exquisite gentlemen and smart young ladies with morrocco-bound gilt-edged Prayer Books still cluster in special sections; and although it is said that the poor have the best part of the church allotted to them, the conspicuousness of its position gives a brand to it neither healthy nor pleasant. They are seated down the centre aisle; but the place is too demonstrative of their poverty. If half the seats were empty, situated excellently though they may be, you wouldn't catch any respectable weasle asleep on them. If some doctor, or magistrate, or private bib-and-tucker lady had to anchor here, supposing there were any spare place in any other part of the house, there would be a good deal of quizzing and wonderment afloat. If you don't believe it put on a highly refined dress and try the experiment; and if you are not very specially spotted we wild give a fifty dollar greenback on behalf of the society for converting missionary eaters in Chillingo-wullabadorie. We shall say nothing with regard to the ordinary service of the Parish Church, except this, that it would look better of three fourths of the congregation if they would not leave the responses to a paid choir. "Lor, bless yer," as Betsy Jane Ward would say, a choir will sing, anything put before them if it is set to music; and they think no more of getting through all that sad business about personal sinfulness, agonising repentance, and a general craving for forgiveness, than the odd woman did when she used to kiss her cow and say it was delicious. There was once a period when all Parish Church goers made open confession joined audibly in the prayers, and said "Amen" as if they meant it; although we are doubtful about even that. Now, the choir does all the work, and the congregation are left behind the distance post to think about the matter. But if it suits the people it's quite right.

There are three parsons at our Parish Church - Canon Parr, who is the seventeenth vicar in a regular line of succession since the Reformation and two curates. As to the curates we shall say nothing beyond this, that one has got a better situation and is going to it, and that the other would like one if he could get it - not that the present is at all bad, only that there are others better. We don't know how many curates there have been at the Parish Church since the Reformation; but it, may be safely said that in their turn they have, as a rule, accepted with calm and Christian resignation better paid places when they had a fair opportunity of getting them. We are not going to say very much about Cannon Parr, and let nobody suppose that we shall make an effort to tear a passion to tatters regarding any of his peculiarities. Canon Parr is an easy-going, genial, educated man kindly disposed towards good living, not blessed with over much money, fond of wearing a billycock, and strongly in love with a cloak. He has seen much of the world, is shrewd, has a long head, has both studied and travelled for his learning, and is the smartest man Preston Protestants could have to defend their cause. But he has a certain amount of narrowness in his mental vision, and, like the bulk of parsons, can see his own way best. He has a strong temper within him, and he can redden up beautifully all over when his equanimity is disturbed. If you tread upon his ecclesiastical bunions he will give you either a dark mooner or an eye opener - we use these classical terms in a figurative sense. He will keep quiet so long as you do; but if you make an antagonistic move be will punish you if possible. He can wield a clever pen; his style is cogent, scholarly, and, unless overburdened with temper, dignified. He can fling the shafts of satire or distil the balm of pathos; can be bitter, saucy, and aggravating; can say a hard thing in a cutting style; and if he does not go to the bone it's no fault of his. He can also tone down his language to a point of elegance and tenderness; can express a good thing excellently, and utter a fine sentiment well. His speaking is modelled after a good style; but it is inferior to his writing. In the pulpit he expresses himself easily, often fervently, never rantingly. The pulpit of the Parish Church will stand for ever before he upsets it, and he will never approach that altitude of polemical phrenitis which will induce him to smash any part of it. His pulpit language is invariably well chosen; some of his subjects may be rather commonplace or inappropriate, but the words thrown into their exposition are up to the mark. He seldom falters; he has never above one, "and now, finally, brethren," in his concluding remarks; he invariably gives over when he has done - a plan which John Wesley once said many parsons neglected to observe; and his congregation, whether they have been awake or fast asleep, generally go away satisfied. Canon Parr has been at our Parish Church nine and twenty years, and although we don't subscribe to his ecclesiastical creed, we believe he has done good in his time. He is largely respected; he would have been more respected if he had been less exacting towards Dissenters, and less violent in his hatred of Catholics. Neither his Church-rate nor Easter Due escapade improved his position ; and some of his fierce anti-Popery denunciations did not increase his circle of friends. But these things have gone by, and let them be forgotten. In private life Canon Parr is essentially social: he can tell a good tale, is full of humour; he knows a few things as well as the rest of men, and is charitably disposed - indeed he is too sympathetic and this causes hint to be pestered with rubbishy tales from all sorts of individuals, and sometimes to act upon them as if they were true. As a Protestant vicar - and, remembering that no angels have yet been born in this country, that everybody is somewhat imperfect, and that folk will differ - we look upon Canon Parr as above the average. He has said extravagant and unreasonable things in his time; but he has rare properties, qualities of sense and erudition, which are strangers to many pretentious men in his line of business; and, on the whole, he may be legitimately set down, in the language of the "gods," as "O.K."

II

ST. WILFRID'S CATHOLIC CHURCH.

It was at one time of the day a rather dangerous sort of thing for a man, or a woman, or a medium-sized infant, living in this highly-favoured land of ours, to show any special liking for Roman Catholicism. But the days of religious bruising have perished; and Catholics are now, in the main, considered to be human as well as other people, and to have a right to live, and put their Sunday clothes on, and go to their own places of worship like the rest of mortals. No doubt there are a few distempered adherents of the "immortal William" school who would like to see Catholics driven into a corner, banished, or squeezed into nothing; probably there are some of the highly sublimated "no surrender" gentlemen who would be considerably pleased if they could galvanise the old penal code and put a barrel able to play the air of "Boyne Water" into every street organ; but the great mass of men have learned to be tolerant, and have come to the conclusion that Catholics, civilly and religiously, are entitled to all the liberty which a free and enlightened constitution can confer - to all the privileges which fair-play and even-handed justice call give; and if these are not fully granted now, the day is coming when they will be possessed. Lancashire seems to be the great centre of Catholicism in England, and Preston appears to be its centre in Lancashire. This benign town of Preston, with its fervent galaxy of lecturing curates, and its noble army of high falutin' incumbents, is the very fulcrum and lever of northern Romanism. If Catholics are wrong and on the way to perdition and blisters there are 33,000 of them here moving in that very awkward direction at the present. A number so large, whether right or wrong cannot he despised; a body so great, whether good or evil, will, by its sheer inherent force, persist in living, moving, and having, a fair share of being. You can't evaporate 33,000 of anything in a hurry; and you could no more put a nightcap upon the Catholics of Preston than you could blacken up the eye of the sun. That stout old Vatican gentleman who storms this fast world of ours periodically with his encyclicals, and who is known by the name of Pius IX., must, if he knows anything of England, know something of Preston; and if he knows anything of it he will have long since learned that wherever the faith over which he presides may be going down the hill, it is at least in Preston "as well as can be expected," and likely, for a period longer than be will live, to bloom and flourish.

Our text is - St. Wilfrid's Catholic Church, Preston. This place of worship is situated in a somewhat sanctified place - Chapel-street; but as about half of that locality is taken up with lawyers' offices, and the centre of it by a police station, we fancy that this world, rather than the next, will occupy the bulk of its attention. It is to be hoped that St. Wilfrid's, which stands on the opposite side, will act as a healthy counterpoise - will, at any rate, maintain its own against such formidable odds. The building in Chapel-street, dedicated to the old Angle-Saxon bishop - St. Wilfrid-who was a combative sort of soul, fond of argumentatively knocking down obstreperous kings and ecclesiastics and breaking up the strongholds of paganism - was opened seventy-six years ago. It signifies little how it looked then. Today it has a large appearance. There is nothing worth either laughing or crying about so far as its exterior goes. It doesn't look like a church; it resembles not a chapel; and it seems too big for a house. There is no effort at architectural elaboration in its outer arrangements. It is plain, strong, large; and like big feet or leathern shirts has evidently been made more for use than ornament. But this style of phraseology only refers to the extrinsic part. Inside, the church has a vast, ornate, and magnificent appearance. No place of worship in Preston is so finely decorated, so skilfully painted, so artistically got up. In the world of business there is nothing like leather; in the arena of religion there seems to be nothing like paint. Every church in the country makes an effort to get deeply into the region of paint; they will have it upon either windows, walls, or ceilings. It is true that Dissenters do not dive profoundly into the coloured abyss; but weakness of funds combined with defective aesthetic cultivation may have something to do with their deficiency in this respect. Those who have had the management and support of St. Wilfrid's in their hands, have studied the theory of colour to perfection, and whilst we may not theologically agree with some of its uses, one cannot but admire its general effect. Saints, angels, rings, squares, floriations, spiralizations, and everything which the brain or the brush of the most devoted painter could fairly devise are depicted in this church, and there is such an array of them that one wonders how anybody could ever have had the time or patience to finish the work.

The high altar which occupies the southern end is, in

its way, something very fine. A magnificent picture of the crucifixion occupies the back ground; flowers and candles, in numbers sufficient to appal the stoutest Evangelical and turn to blue ruin such men as the editor of the "Bulwark" are elevated in front; over all, as well as collaterally, there are inscriptions in Latin; designs in gold and azure and vermilion fill up the details; and on each side there is a confessional wherein all members, whether large or diminutive, whether dressed in corduroy or smoothest, blackest broad cloth, in silk or Surat cotton, must unravel the sins they have committed. This confession must be a hard sort of job, we know, for some people; but we are not going to enter upon a discussion of its merits or demerits. Only this may be said, that if there was full confession at every place of worship in Preston the parsons would never get through their work. Every day, from an early hour in the morning until a late period of the evening, St. Wilfrid's is open to worshippers; and you may see them, some with smiling faces, and some with very elongated ones, going to or coming from it constantly. Like Tennyson's stream, they evince symptoms of constant movement and the only conclusion we can fairly come to is that the mass of them are singularly in earnest. There are not many Protestants - neither Church people, nor Dissenters, neither quiescent Quakers nor Revivalist dervishes - who would be inclined to go to their religious exercises before breakfast, and if they did, some of them, like the old woman who partook of Sacrament in Minnesota, would want to know what they were going to "get" for it. On Sundays, as on week days, the same business - laborious as it looks to outsiders - goes on. There are several services, and they are arranged for every class - for those who must attend early, for those who can't, for those who won't, and for those who stir when the afflatus is upon them. There are many, however, who are regular attendants, soon and late, and if precision and continuity will assist them in getting to heaven, they possess those auxiliaries in abundance.

The congregation attending on a Sunday is a mixed one - rags and satins, moleskins and patent kids, are all duly represented; and it is quite a study to see their wearers put in an appearance. Directly after entrance reverential genuflections and holy-water dipping are indulged in. Some of the congregation do the business gracefully; others get through it like the very grand-father of awkwardness. The Irish, who often come first and sit last, are solemnly whimsical in their movements. The women dip fast and curtsy briskly; the men turn their hands in and out as if prehensile mysticism was a saving thing, and bow less rapidly but more angularly than the females; then you have the slender young lady who knows what deportment and reverence mean; who dips quietly, and makes a partial descent gracefully; the servant girl who goes through the preliminary somewhat roughly but very earnestly; the smart young fellow, who dips with his gloves on - a "rather lazy kind of thing," as the cobbler remarked when he said his prayers in bed - and gives a sort of half and half nod, as if the whole bend were below his dignity; the business man, who goes into the water and the bowing in a matter-of-fact style, who gets through the ceremony soon but well, and moves on for the next comer; the youth, who touches the water in a come-and-go style, and makes a bow on a similar principle; the aged worshipper, who takes kindly but slowly to the hallowed liquid, and goes nearly upon his knees in the fulness of his reverence; and towards the last you have about six Sisters of Mercy, belonging St.

Wilfrid's convent, who pass through the formality in a calm, easy, finished manner, and then hurry along, some with veils down and others with veils up, to a side sitting they have. There is no religious shoddy amongst these persons. They may look solemn, yet some of them have finely moulded features; they may dress strangely and gloomily, yet, if you converse with them, they will always give indications of serener spirits. Whether their profession be right or wrong, this is certain: they keep one of the best schools in the town, and they teach children manners - a thing which many parents can't manage. They also make themselves useful in visiting; they have a certain respect for faith, but more for good works; and if other folk in Christendom held similar views on this point the good done would in the end be greater. All these Sisters of Mercy are accomplished - they are clever in the head, know how to play music, to paint, and to sew; can cook well if they like; and it's a pity they are not married. But they are doing more good single than lots of women are accomplishing in the married state, and we had better let them alone. Its dangerous to either command or advise the gentler sex, and as everything finds its own level by having its own way they will, we suppose, in the end.

One of the most noticeable features in connection with the services at St. Wilfrid's is the music. It is proverbial that Catholics have good music. You won't find any of the drawling, face-pulling, rubbishy melodies worked up to a point of agony in some places of worship countenanced in the Catholic Church. All is classical - all from the best masters. There is an enchantment in the music which binds you - makes you like it whether you will or not. At St. Wilfrid's there is a choir which can't be excelled by any provincial body of singers in the kingdom. The learned individual who blows the organ may say that the comparative perfection attained in the orchestra is through the very consummate manner in which he "raises the wind"; the gentleman who manipulates upon its keys may think he is the primum mobile in the matter; the soprano may fancy she is the life of the whole concern; the heavy bass or the chief tenor may respectively lay claim to the honour; but the fact is, its amongst the lot, so that there may be a general rubbing on the question of service, and a reciprocal scratching on the point of ability.

There are several priests at St. Wilfrid's; they are all Jesuits to the marrow; and the chief of them is the Rev. Father Cobb. Each of them is clever - far cleverer than many of the half-feathered curates and full-fledged incumbents who are constantly bringing railing accusations against them; and they work harder - get up sooner, go to bed later - than the whole of them. They jump at midnight if their services are required by either a wild Irishman in Canal-street or a gentleman of the first water in any of our mansions. It is not a question of cloth but of souls with them. They are afraid of neither plague, pestilence, nor famine; they administer spiritual consolation under silken hangings, as well as upon straw lairs; in the fever stricken garret as well as in the gilded chamber. Neither the nature of a man's position nor the character of his disease enters into their considerations. Duty is the star of their programme; action the object of their lives. They receive no salaries; their simple necessaries are alone provided for. Some of them perhaps get half-a-crown a month as pocket money; but that will neither kill nor cure a man. Sevenpence halfpenny per week is a big sum - isn't it? - big enough for a Jesuit priest, but calculated to disturb the Christian balance of any other class of clergymen. If it isn't, try them.

In reference to the priests of St. Wilfrid's, we shall only specially mention, and that briefly, the Rev. Father Cobb. No man in Preston cares less for fine clothes than he does. We once did see him with a new suit on; but neither before nor since that ever-memorable day, have we noticed him in anything more ethereal than a plain well-worn coat, waistcoat, and pair of trousers. He might have a finer exterior; but he cares not for this kind of bauble. He knows that trappings make neither the man nor the Christian, and that elaborate suits are often the synonym of elaborate foolery. He takes a pleasure in work; is happy inaction; and hates both clerical and secular indifference. Priests, he thinks, ought to do their duty, and men of the world ought to discharge theirs. In education, Father Cobb is far above the ordinary run of men. He has a great natural capacity, which has been well regulated by study; he is shrewd; has a strong intuitive sense; can't be got over; won't be beaten out of the field if you once get him into it; and is sure to either win or make you believe that he has. Like all strong Catholics he has much veneration - that "organ," speaking in the vernacular of phrenology, is at the top of the head, and you never yet saw a thorough Catholic who did not manifest a good development of it; he is strong in ideality; has also a fine, vein of humour in him; can laugh, say jolly as well as serious things; and is a positively earnest and practical preacher. He speaks right out to his hearers; hits them hard in reference to both this world and the next; tells them "what to eat, drink, and avoid;" says that if they get drunk they must drop it off, that if they stuff and gormandise they will be a long while before reaching the kingdom of heaven; that they must avoid dishonesty, falsehood, impurity, and other delinquencies; and, furthermore, intimates that they won't get to any of the saints they have a particular liking for by a round of simple religious formality - that they must be good, do good, and behave themselves decently, individually and collectively. We have never heard a more practical preacher: he will tell young women what sort of husbands to get, young men what kind of wives to choose, married folk how to conduct themselves, and old maids and bachelors how to reconcile themselves virtuously to their fate. There is no half-and-half ring in the metal he moulds: it comes out clear, sounds well, and goes right home. In delivery he is eloquent; in action rather brisk; and he weighs - one may as well come down from the sublime to the ridiculous - about thirteen stones. He is a jolly, hearty, earnest, devoted priest; is cogent in argument; homely in illustration; tireless in work; determined to do his duty; and, if we were a Catholic, we should be inclined to fight for him if any one stepped upon his toes, or said a foul word about him. Here endeth our "epistle to the Romans."

III

CANNON-STREET INDEPENDENT CHAPEL.

Forty-four years ago the Ebenezer of a few believers in the "Bird-of-Freedom" school, with a spice of breezy religious courage in their composition, was raised at the bottom of Cannon-street, in Preston; and to this day it abideth there. Why it was elevated at that particular period of the world's history we cannot say. Neither does it signify. It may have been that the spirit of an irrepressible Brown, older than the Harper's Ferry gentleman, was "marching on" at an extra speed just then; for let it be known to all and singular that it was one of the universal Brown family who founded the general sect. Or it may have been that certain Prestonians, with a lingering touch of the "Scot's wha ha'e" material in their blood, gave a solemn twist to the line in Burns's epistle, and decided to go in

> - for the glorious privilege
> Of being Independent.

Be that as it may, it is clear that in 1825 the Independents planted a chapel in Cannon-street. Places of worship like everything else, good or evil, grow in these latter days, and so has Cannon-street chapel. In 1852 its supporters set at naught the laws of Banting, and made the place bigger. It was approaching a state of solemn tightness, and for the consolation of the saints, the ease of the fidgety, and the general blissfulness of the neighbourhood it was expanded. Cannon-street Chapel has neither a bell, nor a steeple, nor an outside clock, and it has never yet said that it was any worse off for their absence. But it may do, for chapels like churches are getting proud things now-a-days, and they believe in both lacker and gilt. There is something substantial and respectable about the building. It is neither gaudy nor paltry; neither too good nor too bad looking. Nobody will ever die in a state of architectural ecstacy through gazing upon it; and not one out of a battalion of cynics will say that it is too ornamental. It is one of those well-finished, middle-class looking establishments, about which you can't say much any way; and if you could, nobody would be either madder or wiser for the exposition. Usually the only noticeable feature about the front of it - and that is generally the place where one looks for the virtues or vices of a thing - is a series of caged-up boards, announcing homilies, and tea parties, and collections all over the north Lancashire portion of Congregational Christendom. It is to be hoped that the sermons are not too dry, that the tea saturnalias are neither too hot nor too wet, and that the collections have more sixpenny than threepenny pieces in them.

The interior of Cannon-street Chapel has a spacious and somewhat genteel appearance. A practical business air pervades it. There is no "storied window," scarcely any "dim religious light," and not a morsel of extra colouring in the whole establishment. At this place, the worshippers have an idea that they are going to get to heaven in a plain way, and if they succeed, all the better - we were going to say that they would be so much the more into pocket by it. Freedom of thought, sincerity of heart, and going as straight to the point as possible, is what they aim at. There are many seats in Cannon-street Chapel, and, as it is said that hardly any of them are to let, the reverend gentleman who makes a stipulated descent upon the pew rents ought to be happy. It is but seldom the pews are well filled: they are not even crammed on collection Sundays; but they are paid for, and if a congenial wrinkle does not lurk in that fact-for the minister - he will find neither the balm of Gilead nor a doctor anywhere. The clerical notion is, that pew rents, as well as texts; must be stuck to; and if those who pay and listen quietly acquiesce, then it becomes a simple question of "so mote it be" for outsiders.

The congregation at Cannon-street Chapel is made up of tolerably respectable materials. It is no common Dissenting rendezvous for ill-clad screamers and roaring enthusiasts. Neither fanatics nor ejaculators find an abiding place in it. Not many poor people join the charmed circle. A middle-class, shopkeeping halo largely environs the assemblage. There is a good deal of pride, vanity, scent, and silk-rustling astir in it every Sunday, just as there is in every sacred throng; and the oriental, theory of caste is not altogether ignored. The ordinary elements of every Christian congregation are necessarily visible here - backsliders and newly-caught communicants; ancient women duly converted and moderately fond of tea, snuff, and charity; people who cough continually, and will do so in their graves if not closely watched; parties, with the Fates against them, who fly off periodically into fainting fits; contented individuals, whose gastric juice flows evenly, who can sleep through the most impassioned sermon with the utmost serenity; weather-beaten orthodox souls who have been recipients of ever so much daily grace for half a life time, and fancy they are particularly near paradise; lofty and isolated beings who have a fixed notion that they are quite as respectable if not as pious as other people; easy-going well-dressed creatures "whose life glides away in a mild and amiable conflict between the claims of piety and good breeding."

But the bulk are of a substantial, medium-going description - practical, sharp, respectable, and naturally inclined towards a free, well got up, reasonable theology. There is nothing inflamed in them - nothing indicative of either a very thick or very thin skin. Any of them will lend you a hymn book, and whilst none of them may be inclined to pay your regular pew rent, the bulk will have no objection to find you an occasional seat, and take care of you if there would be any swooning in your programme. Clear-headed and full of business, they believe with Binney in making the best of both worlds. They will never give up this for the next, nor the next for this. Into their curriculum there enters, as the American preacher hath it, a sensible regard for piety and pickles, flour and affection, the means of grace and good profits, crackers and faith, sincerity and onions, benevolence, cheese, integrity, potatoes, and wisdom - all remarkably good in their way, and calculated, when well shaken up and applied, to Christianise anybody. The genteel portion of the congregation principally locate themselves in the side seats running from one end of the chapel to the other; the every day mortals find a resting place in the centre and the galleries; the poorer portion are pushed frontwards below, where they have an excellent opportunity of inspecting the pulpit, of singing like nightingales, of listening to every articulation of the preacher, and of falling into a state of coma if they are that way disposed.

The music at this place of worship has been considerably improved during recent times; but it is nothing very amazing yet. There is a curtain amount of cadence, along with a fair share of power, in the orchestral outbursts; the pieces the choir have off go well; those they are new at rather hang fire; but we shall not parry with either the conductor or the members on this point. They all manifest a fairly-defined devotional feeling in their melody; turn their visual faculties in harmony with the words: expand and contract their pulmonary processes with precision and if they mean what they sing, they deserve better salaries than they usually get. They are aided by an organ which is played well, and, we hope, paid for.

The minister of Cannon-street chapel is the Rev. H. J. Martyn, who has had a good stay with "the brethren," considering that their fighting weight is pretty heavy, and that some of them were made to "have their way." Frequently Independents are in hot water concerning their pastors. In Preston they are very exemplary in this respect. The Grimshaw street folk have had a storm in a tea pot with one of their ministers; so have the Lancaster-road Christians; and so have the Cannon-street believers; and the beauty of it is, they generally win. Born to have their own way in sacred matters, they can turn off a parson, if they can't defeat him in argument. And that is a great thing. They hold the purse strings; and no parson can live unless he has a "call" to some other "vineyard," if they are closed against him. On the whole, the present minister of Cannon-street Chapel has got on pretty evenly with his flock. He has had odd skirmishes in his spiritual fold; and will have if he stays in it for ever; but the sheep have a very fair respect for the shepherd, and can "paint the lily" gracefully. A while since they gave him leave of absence - paying his salary, of course, whilst away - and on his return some of them got up a tea party on his behalf and made him a presentation. There might be party spirit or there might be absolute generosity in such a move; but the parson was no loser - he enjoyed the out, and accepted with Christian fortitude the gift. The Rev. H. J. Martyn is a small gentleman - considerably below the average of parsons in physical proportion; but he consoles himself with the thought that he is all right in quality, if not in quantity. Diminutive men have generally very fair notions of themselves; small men as a rule are smarter than those of the bulky and adipose school; and, harmonising with this regulation, Mr. Martyn is both sharp and kindly disposed towards himself. He is not of opinion, like one of his predecessors, that he assisted at the creation of the world, and that the endurance of Christianity depends upon his clerical pivot; but he believes that he has a "mission," and that on the whole he is quite as good as the majority of Congregational divines. There is nothing pretentious in his appearance; nothing ecclesiastical in his general framework; and in the street he looks almost as much like anybody else as like a parson. The education of Mr. Martyn is equal to that of the average of Dissenting ministers, and better than that of several. He is, however, more of a reader than a thinker, and more of a speaker than either. On the platform he can make as big a stir as men twice his size. His delivery is moderately even; his words clear; and he can throw a good dash of imagination into his language. In the pulpit, to the foot of which place he is led every Sunday, by certain sacred diaconal lamas, who previously "rub him down" and saddle him for action, in a contiguous apartment - in the pulpit, we say, he operates in a superior style , and he looks better there - more like a parson - than anywhere else. He is here above the ordinary level of his hearers; if it were not for the galleries, minute as may be his physiology, he would be the loftiest being present; and if he wishes to "keep up appearances," we would advise him to remain in the pulpit and have his meals there. Casting joking overboard - out of the pulpit if you like - it may be said that Mr. Martyn as a preacher has many fair qualities. It is true he has defects; but who has not? - unless it be a deacon; - still there is something in his style which indicates earnestness, something in his language, demonstrative of culture and eloquence. His main pulpit fault is that he "goes off" too soon and too frequently. In the course of a sermon he will give you three or four perorations, and sometimes wind up without treating you to one. There is nothing very metaphysical in his subjects; sometimes he wanders slightly into space; occasionally he exhausts himself in fighting out the mysteries of faith, and grace, and justification; but in the ordinary run of his talk you can get good pictures of practical matters. He is a lover of nature, is fond of talking about the sublime and the beautiful, conjointly with other things freely named in Burke's essay, can pile up the agony with a good deal of ability, and split the ears of the groundlings as the occasion requires. He can get into a white heat quickly, or blow his solemn anger gradually - wind it up by degrees, and make it burst at a given point of feeling. He is a better declaimer than reasoner - has a stronger flow of imagination than logic. There is nothing bitter or mocking in his tone. He seldom flings the shafts of ridicule or irony. He constructs calmly, and then sends up the rocket: he draws you slowly to a certain point, and then tells you to look out for "it's coming." His apparatus is well fixed; he can give you any kind of dissolving view. His ecstacies are rapid and, therefore, soon over. The level places in his sermons are rather heavy, and, at times, uninteresting. It is only when the thermometer is rising that you enjoy him, and only when he reaches the climax and explodes, that you fall back and ask for water and a fan. Taking him in the aggregate we are of opinion that he is a good preacher; that he goes through his ordinary duties easily and complacently. He gets well paid for what be does - last year his salary exceeded 340 pounds; and our advice to him is - keep on good terms with the bulk of "the brethren," hammer as much piety into them as possible, tickle the deacons into a genial humour, and look regularly after the pew-rents.

IV

LUNE-STREET WESLEYAN METHODIST CHAPEL.

Wesleyan Methodism first breathed and opened its eyes in or about the year 1729. It was nursed in its infancy at Oxford by two rare brothers and a few students; was christened at the same place by a keenly-observing, slightly-satirical collegian; developed itself gradually through the country; took charge of the neglected masses and gave them a new life; and today it is one of the great religious forces of the world. The first Wesleyan chapel in Preston was built in the year 1787, and its situation was in that consecrated and highly aromatic region of the town called Back-lane. There was nothing very prepossessing or polished, nothing particularly fashionable or attractive about the profession of Methodism in those days. It was rather an indication of honest fanaticism than of deliberate reasoning - rather a sign of being solemnly "on the rampage" than of giving way to careful conviction - and more symptomatic of a sharp virtuous rant, got up in a crack and to be played out in five minutes, than of a judicious move in the direction of permanent good. The orthodox looked down with a genteel contempt upon the preachers whose religion had converted Kingswood colliers, and turned Cornwall wreckers into honest men; and the formally pious spoke of the worshippers at this new shrine of faith with a serene sneer, and classed them as a parcel of fiercely ejaculating, hymn-singing nonentities. But there was vitality at the core of their creed, and its fuller triumphs were but a question of time. In 1817, Methodism became dissatisfied with its Back-lane quarters, and migrated into a lighter, healthier, and cleaner portion of the town - Lune-street - where a building was erected for its special convenience and edification. It was not a very elegant structure: it was, in fact, a plain, phlegmatic aggregation of brick and mortar, calculated to charm no body externally, and evidently patronised for absolute internal rapture.

In 1861 the chapel was rebuilt - enlarged, beautified, and made fine, so as to harmonise with the laws of modern fashion, and afford easy sitting room for the large and increasing congregation attending it. The frontispiece is of a costly character; but it has really been "born to blush unseen." It is so tightly wedged in between other buildings, is so evenly crammed into companionship with the ordinary masonry of the street, that the general effect of the tall arch and spacious porch is lost. Nothing can be distinctly seen at even a moderate distance. You have to get to the place before you become clearly aware of its existence; and if you wish to know anything of its appearance, you have either to turn the head violently off its regular axis, or cross the street and ask somebody for a step ladder. The facade of the building is not very prepossessing; the large arch, which has given way at some of the joints considerably, and has been doing its best to fall for about six years, does not look well - it is too high and too big for the place; the stonework within is also hid; and the whitewashed ceiling above ought to be either cleaned or made properly black. At present it is neither light nor dark, and is rather awkwardly relieved at intervals with cobwebs. There is something humorous and incongruous in the physical associations of this chapel. It is flanked with a doctor's shop and a money-lending establishment; with a savings bank and a solicitor's office. The bank nestles very complacently under its lower wing, and in the ratio of its size is a much better looking building. The text regarding the deposit of treasure in that place where neither moth nor rust operate may be well worked in the chapel; but it is rather at a discount in the immediate neighbourhood.

A great work in the business of spreading Wesleyan Methodism has been done by the people and parsons of Lune-street chapel. We know of no place in the town whose religious influence has been more actively radiated. Its power, a few years ago, spread into the northern part of the town, and the result was a new chapel with excellent schools there; it then moved eastward, and the consequence was a school chapel in St. Mary-street. In Croft-street, Canal-street, and on the Marsh, it has also outposts, whose officers are fighting the good fight with lung, and head, and heart, in a sprightly and vigorous fashion. Originally, what is termed the "circuit" of Lune-street embraced places 18 or 20 miles from Preston; but the area of the sacred circumbendibus was subsequently reduced; and its servants now find that they have as much on hand as they can fairly get through by looking after half of the town and a few of the contiguous villages. There are none of those solemn milkmen called deacons in connection with Wesleyanism; still, there are plenty of medicine men, up; up the ears in grace and business, belonging it. At Lune-street Chapel, as at all similar places, there are class-leaders, circuit stewards, chapel stewards, and smaller divinities, who find a niche in the general pantheon of duty. The cynosure of the inner circle is personal piety, combined with a "penny a week and a shilling a quarter." All members who can pay this have to do so.

Beneath the chapel there is a Sunday school, which operates as a feeder. When the scholars - there are 500 or 600 of them altogether - show certain symptoms of inherent rectitude and facial exactness, when they answer particular questions correctly and pass through the crucial stages of probation consistently, they are drafted into "the church," and presented with licences of perennial happiness if they choose to exercise them. The school is well supervised, and if some of the teachers are as useful and consoling at home as they are in their classes their general relatives will be blissful.

The congregation of Lune-street Chapel is moderately numerous; but it has been materially thinned at intervals by the establishment of other Wesleyan chapels. In its circuit there are now between 800 and 900 persons known as members, who are going on their way rejoicing; at the chapel itself there are between 300 and 400 individuals similarly situated. Viewed in the aggregate, the congregation is of a middle class character both in regard to the colour of the hair and the clothes worn. There are some exceedingly poor people at the place, but the mass appear to be individuals not particularly hampered in making provision for their general meals. Lune-street chapel is the fashionable Wesleyan tabernacle of Preston; the better end of those whose minds have been touched, through either tradition or actual conviction, with the beauties of Methodism, frequent it. There is more silk than winsey, more cloth than hodden grey, and a good deal more false hair and artificial teeth in the building on a Sunday than can be found by fair searching at any other Wesleyan chapel in the town. A sincere desire to "flee from the wrath to come and be saved from their sins" - the only condition which John Wesley insisted upon for admission into his societies - does not prevent some of the members from attending determinedly to the bedizenments, conceits, and spangles of this very wicked speck in the planetary system.

In the congregation there are many most excellent, hardworking, thoroughly sincere men and women, who would be both useful and ornamental to any body of Christians under the sun; but there are in addition, as there are in every building set apart for the purposes of piety, several who have "more frill than shirt," and much "more cry than wool" about them - rectified, beautifully self-righteous, children who would "sugar over" a very ugly personage ten hours out of the twelve every day, and then at night thank the Lord for all his mercies. In Lune-street Chapel faction used to run high and wilfulness was a gem which many of the members wore very near their hearts; but much of the old feudal spirit of party fighting has died out, and there are signs of pious resignation and loving kindness in the flock, which would at one time have been rare jewels. A somewhat lofty isolation is still manifested here and there; a few regular attenders appear heavily oppressed with the idea that they are not only as good as anybody else but much better. Still this is only human nature and no process of convertibility to the most celestial of substances can in this world entirely subdue it. The bruising deacon who said that grace was a good thing, but that that knocking down an impertinent member was a better didn't miss the bull's eye of natural philosophy very far. The observation was not redolent of much Christian spirit; but it evinced that which many of the saints are troubled with - human nature.

Lune-street chapel contains standing, sitting, and sleeping room, for about 1,400 people. The bulk who attend it take fair advantage of the accomodation afforded for the first and second positions; a moderate number avail themselves of the privileges held out for the whole three postures. The chapel is not often crowded; it is moderately filled as a rule; and there is no particular numeric difference in the attendance at either morning or evening service on a Sunday. The singing is neither loftily classic nor contemptibly common-place. It is good, medium, well modulated melody, heartily got up; and thoroughly congregational. In some places of worship it is considered somewhat vulgar for members of the congregation to give specimens of their vocalisation; and you can only find in out-of-the-way side and back pews odd persons warbling a mild falsetto, or piping an eccentric tenor, or doing a heavy bass on their own responsibility; but at Lune-street Chapel the general members of the congregation go into the work with a distinct determination to either sing or make a righteous noise worthy of the occasion. They are neither afraid nor ashamed of the job; and we hope they draw consolation from it. The more genteel worshippers take up their quarters mainly on the ground floor - at the back of the central seats and at the sides. The poor have resting places found for them immediately in front of the pulpit and at thc rear of the galleries. Very little of that unctuous spasmodic shouting, which used to characterise Wesleyanism, is heard in Lune-street Chapel. It has become unfashionable to bellow; it is not considered "the thing" to ride the high horse of vehement approval and burst into luminous showers of "Amens" and "Halleleujahs." Now and then a few worshippers of the ancient type drop in from some country place, and explode at intervals during the course of some impulsive prayer, or gleeful hymn, or highly enamelled sermon. You may occasionally at such a time, hear two or three in distant pews having a delightful time of it. At first they only stir gently, as if some on were mildly pinching or tickling them. Gradually they become more audible, and as the fire of their zeal warms up, and the eloquence of the minister enflames, they get keener, fiercer, more rapturous; the intervals of repose are shorter, the moments of ecstacy are more rapid and fervent; and this goes on with gathering desperation, until the speaker reaches his - climax, and stops to either breathe or use his handkerchief. But hardy a scintilla of this is perceived on ordinary occasions; indeed it has become so unpopular that an exhibition of it seems to quietly amuse - to evoke mild smiles and dubious glances - rather than meet with reciprocity of approval. It must be some great man in the region of Wesleyanism; some grand, tearing, pathetic, eloquent preacher who can stir to a point of moderate audibility the voices of the multitude of worshippers. In Lune-street Chapel, the Ten Commandments occupy a prominent position, and that is a good thing. It would be well if they were fastened up in every place of worship, and better still if the parsons referred to them more frequently.

Respecting the ministers of the chapel in question, we way say that there are three. None of them can stay less than one, nor more than three, years. It is a question of "Hey, presto - quick change," every third year. The names of the triumvirate at Lune-street are, the Rev. W. Mearns, M.A., who is the superintendent;

the Rev. W. H. Tindall, second in command; and the Rev. F. B. Swift, the general clerical servant of all work. Mr. Mearns is a calm, rather bilious-looking, elderly man. There is nothing bewitching in his appearance; he looks like what he is - a quietly-disposed, evenly-tempered, Methodist minister. He is neither fussy, nor conceited, nor fond of brandishing the sword of superiority. He goes about his work steadily, and is as patient in harness as out of it. He has northern blood in his veins which checks impulsiveness and everything approaching that solemn ferocity sometimes displayed in Methodist pulpits. There is nothing oratorical in his style of delivery; it is calm, slow, and has a rather soporific influence upon his hearers. There is more practical than argumentative matter in his sermons; but, in the aggregate, they are hard and dry - lack lustre and passion; and this, combined with his stoical manner of delivery, has a chilling, rather than an attractive, influence. He always speaks in harmony with the rules of grammar. His sentences, although uttered extemporaneously, are invariably well finished and scholarly. His words are well chosen; they are fit in with cultivated exactitude and polished precision. They will stand reading; nay, they will read excellently - infinitely better than the burning rhapsody of more phrensied and eloquent men; but they fall with a long-drawn dulness upon the ear when first uttered, and don't, as Sam Slick would say, "get up one's steam anyhow." Mr. Mearns has a clear head and a good heart, but his spoken words want power and immediate brightness, and his style is deadened for the want of a little enthusiasm.

The Rev. Mr. Tindall comes up in a more polished, energetic, and fashionable garb. He is eloquent, argumentative, polemical. His literary capacity is good, and it has been well trained. He has read much and studied keenly. His sermons are well thought out; he has copious notes of them; and when he enters the pulpit they are made complete for action - are fully equipped in their Sunday clothes and ready for duty. His delivery is good; but physical weakness deprives it of potency; and his contempt of the clock before him renders people now and then uneasy. His manner is refined; his matter is select; but there is something in both at times which you don't altogether believe in digesting. A rather haughty, dictatorial ring is sometimes noticed in them. A large notion of the importance of the preacher occasionally peeps up. He has a perfect right to venerate Mr. Tindall, and if he is a little fashionable, what of that? - isn't it fashionable to be fashionable? Only this may be carried a little too far, even in men for whom pulpits are made and circuits formed, and it is not always safe to let organ "15" in phrenological charts get the upper hand. After all we admire Mr. Tindall's erudition and eloquence. He is free from vulgarity, and in general style miles ahead of many preachers in the same body, whose great mission is to maltreat pulpits and turn religion into a rhapsody of words.

The well-meaning and plodding Mr. Smith succeeds. He is a hard worker; but there does not appear to be over much in him at present. More thinking, and a greater experience of life, may cause him to germinate agreeably in a few years. His style is stereotyped and copied; there is a lack of original force in him; when he talks you know what's coming next - you can tell five minutes off what he is going to say, and that rather spoils the sensation of newness and surprise which one likes to experience when parsons are either pleasing or terrifying sinners. But Mr. Swift does his best, and, according to Ebenezer Elliot, he does well who does that. It would be wrong to deal harshly with a new beginner, and therefore we have decided to check our criticism - to be brief - with Mr. Swift and express a hope that in time he will be president of the Conference.

V

FISHERGATE BAPTIST CHAPEL.

The "right thing" in regard to baptism is a recondite point; but we are not going to enter into any controversy about it. We shall say nothing as to the defects or merits of aspersion or sprinkling, immersion or dipping, affusion or pouring. Opinions vary respecting each system; and one may fairly say that the words uttered in explanation of the general theme come literally to us in the "voice of many waters.", Jacob the patriarch was the first Baptist; the Jews kept up the rite moderately, but had more faith in its abstergent than spiritual influence; John turned it into an institution of Christianity; the Primitive Church carried on the business slowly, Turtullian kicking against and Cyprian lauding it; in the fifth century baptism became fully established amongst all Christian communities; then the Eastern and Western Churches quarrelled as to whether sprinkling or immersion constituted the proper ceremony; other small disputes concerning the modus operandi followed; and from that time to this the adherents of each scheme have spilled a great deal of water in piously working out their notions. There was once a time when nobody could undergo the ordinary process of baptism except at Easter or Whitsuntide; but children and upgrown people can now be put through the ceremony whenever it is considered necessary. In Preston, as elsewhere, the majority of people think well of water when it is required by children for engulphing or baptismal purposes; but they care little for its use when the teens have been trotted through. It may be right enough for the physical and religious comfort of babes and sucklings; but its virtues recede in the ratio of development. There are, however, some sections of men and women in the town who, symbolically at least, have a high regard for water at any time after the years of sense and reason have been reached.

These are the Baptists. There are four or five chapels set apart for their improvement in Preston, and the smartest of these is in Fishergate. In Leeming-street it was in the chrysalis state; in Fishergate the butterfly epoch has been reached. A dull, forlorn looking edifice, afterwards taken advantage of by the Episcopalian party, and now cleared off to make way for St. Saviour's church, once formed the sacred asylum of a portion of the Baptists; but a desire for better accomodation, combined with a wish for more fashionable quarters, induced a change. The dove was repeatedly sent out, and dry land was finally found for the Baptists in Fishergate. In 1858 a chapel was erected upon the spot, and thus far it has steadfastly maintained its position. It is a handsome building, creditable to both the architect and the congregation, and if its tower were less top heavy, it would, in its way, be quite superb. We never look at that solemn tower head without being reminded of some immense quadrangular pepper castor, fit for a place in the kitchen of the Titans. In every other respect the building is arranged smartly; if anything it is too ornamental, and in making a general survey one is nearly afraid of meeting with Panathenaic frieze work.

On the principle that you can't have the services of a good piper without paying proportionately dear for them, so you can't obtain a handsome chapel except by confronting a long bill. The elysium of antipedo-baptism in Fishergate cost the modest sum of 5,000 pounds, and of that amount about 800 pounds remains to be paid. Considering the greatness of the original sum, the debt is not very large; but if it were less the congregation would be none the worse; and if it didn't exist at all they would be somewhat nearer bliss in this general vale of tears. Fishergate Baptist Chapel is the only Dissenting place of worship in the town possessing an exterior clock; and it is one of the most orderly articles in the town, for it never strikes and has not for many months shown itself after dark. It used to exhibit signs of activity after sunset; but it was, considered a "burning shame" by some economists to light it up with gas when the Town Hall clock was got into working order, and ever since then it has been nightly kept in the dark.

Fishergate Baptist Chapel has an excellent interior, and it will accommodate about twice as many people as patronise it. Long stately side lights, neatly embellised with stained glass and opaque filigree work, give it a mild solemnity which is relieved by fine circular windows occupying the gables. The seats are arranged in the usual three-row style, and there is a touch of neat gentility about them indicative of good construction, whatever the parties they have been made for are like. Fashionably-conceived gas-stands shoot up and spread their branches at intervals down the chapel; and at the extreme end there is a broad gallery, set apart for the singers, who need be in no fear of breaking it down through either the weight of their melodious metal or the specific gravity of their physique. A new organ is much wanted, and if a few new singers were secured, or the old ones polished up slightly, the proceedings would be more lively and agreeable. Nearly three of the members of the choir are really good singers; the remainder are what may be termed only moderate. What Lune-street is to the Wesleyans, so Fishergate seems to be to the Baptists - the centre of gravity of the more refined and fashionable worshippers. Very few poor people visit it, and it is thought that if they don't come of their own accord they will never he seriously pressed on the subject. The free sittings are just within the door, on the left hand side, and we should fancy that not more than 25 really poor people use them. The higher order of Christians occupy the lower portion of the same range of seats, the central pews, and those on the right side thereof.

The congregation consists almost entirely of middle-class persons - people who have either saved money in business or who are making a determined effort to do so. Good clothes, quiet demeanour, and numerical smallness are the striking characteristics. Nothing approaching fervour ever takes possession of the general body. Religion with them is not a termagant, revered for her sauciness and loved for her violent evolutions. It is a reticent, even spirited, calmly orthodox affair, whose forerunner fed on locusts and wild honey, and whose principles are to be digested quietly. There may be a few very boisterous sheep in the fold, who get on fire periodically in the warmth of speaking and praying; who will express their willingness, when the pressure is up, to do any mortal thing for the good of "the cause;" but who will have to be caught there and then if anything substantial has to follow. Like buckwheat cakes and rum gruel they are best whilst hot. At a night meeting they may be generously disposed and full of universal sympathy; but they can sleep out their burning thoughts in a few hours, and waken up next morning like larks, with no recollection of their gushing promises.

There is accomodation in the chapel for about 400 persons, but the average attendance is not more than 200; and there are only about 90 "members." Not much difference between the morning and evening attendance is noticed. The baptismal Thermophylae is generally guarded by the sacred 90, and looked at by the fuller 200. The pew rents are very high; but this evil is compensated for by the comparative absence of those solemn gad flies which come in the shape of collections. At some places of worship contribution boxes and bags are seen floating about rapidly nearly every other Sunday, for either home expenses or perishing Indians; but at Fishergate Baptist Chapel incidental requirements are blended with the pew rents; and for other purposes about two collections annually suffice. That is all, and that ought to make attendance at such a place rather agreeable.

The primal government of the chapel is in the hands of four deacons; but they are not very officious like some pillars of the church: one of them is mild and obliging, the second is wise-looking and crotchety, the third is disposed to pious rampagiousness in his lucid intervals, and the fourth is a kindly sort of being, with a moderate respect for converted dancers and hallaleujah men. Some theological writers say that there are "evangelists" as well as deacons in connection with Baptist government. There may be some of this class at the Fishergate Chapel; but we have not yet seen their sacred personages. The place is highly favoured with clocks. Not only is there a specimen of horology outside, but there is one within, and it may be called a worldly-wise creature, for it never gets beyond No. I in its striking. Tradition hath it that once when there was no clock in the chapel, the preacher used to overshoot most uncomfortably the ordinary limits of time; that the congregation, whilst fond of sermons, did not like them stretched too violently; and that they resolved unanimously to purchase a clock. Probably this story is groundless; but it is a fact nevertheless that the clock is so situated as to be only fully and easily seen by the preacher. More than three-fourths of the people sit with their backs directly to it. And it is furthermore a fact that, whilst when there was no clock the usual time of deliverance was passed, the congregation are now released with scrupulous exactitude. They got into the open air one Sunday evening when we were there about 16 seconds before eight, and the preacher had abandoned the pulpit by the time the Town Hall clock gave its opinion on the question.

In winter there is a Sunday morning prayer meeting at the place; but in summer the members can't stand such a gathering, either because too much light is thrown upon the subject, or because the attendance is too small, or because early prayers are not required at that season of the year. A prayer meeting is, however, held all the year round, on a Wednesday night, and it is favoured, on an average, with about 20 earnest individuals, who sometimes create what might, if not properly explained, be considered a rather solemn disturbance. These parties meet in the Sunday school, which is beneath the chapel. The average attendance of scholars at this school is not very large. When buns and coffee are astir it may be computed at 200; when ordinary religious instruction is simply placed before the juvenile mind the attendance may be set down at about 100.

In the chapel and immediately before the pulpit, there is a square hole, usually covered, which in denominational phraseology goes by the name of the "baptistery." In the first ages of Christianity such places were made outside the church, and were either hexagonal or octagonal, then they became polygonal, then circular, and now they have got quadrangular. Two of the finest baptisteries in the world are at Florence and Pisa; that at the former, place being 100 feet in diameter, made of black and white marble, and surrounded with a gallery on granite columns; that at the latter being 116 feet wide, and beautifully ornamented. The biggest baptistery ever made is supposed to have been that at St. Sophia, in Constantinople, which, we are told, was so spacious as to have once served for the residence of the Emperor Basilicus. But there is no marble about the baptistery in Fishergate Chapel, and no one would ever think of transmuting it into a residence. It is used two or three times a year, and if outsiders happen to get a whisper of an intended dipping, curiosity leads them to the chapel, and they look upon the ceremony as a piece of sacred fun, right enough to look at, but far too wet for anything else. This dipping is, indeed, a quaint, cold piece of business. None except adults or youths who have, it is thought, come to sense and reason, are permitted to pass through the ordeal, and it is recognised by them as symbolic of their entrance into "the Church." Sometimes as many as six or seven are immersed. They put on old or special garments suitable for the occasion, and the work of baptism is then carried on by the minister, who stands in the figurative Jordan. He quietly ducks them overhead; they submit to the process without a murmur; they neither bubble, nor scream, nor squirm; and the elders look on solemnly, though impressed with thoughts that, excellent as the ceremony may be, it is a rather shivering sort of business after all. After being baptised, the new members retire into an adjoining room, strip their saturated cloths, rub themselves briskly with towels, or get the deacons to do the work for them, then re-dress, comb their hair, and receive liberty to rejoice with the general Israel of the flock. Such baptism as that we have described seems a rather curious kind of rite; but it is honestly believed in, and as those who submit to it have to undergo the greatest punishment in the case - have to be put right overhead in cold Longridge water - other persons may keep tolerably cool on the subject. People have a right to use water any way so long as they don't throw it unfairly upon others or drown themselves; and if three-fourths of the people who now laugh at adult baptism would undergo a dipping next Sunday, and then stick to water for the remainder of their lives, they would be better citizens, whatever might become of their theology.

The Rev. J. O'Dell is the pastor of Fishergate Baptist Chapel, and he is an exemplary man in his way, for be only receives a small salary and yet contrives to keep out of debt - a thing which a good deal of parsons, and which many of the ordinary children of grace, can't accomplish. He is well liked by his congregation, and we have heard of no fighting over either his virtues or defects. He has quite a clerical look, and, if he hadn't, his voice would give the cue to his profession. There is an earnest unctuous modulation about it, which, as a rule, is acquired after men have flung overboard the common idioms of secular life. The salary of Mr. O'Dell is about 160 pounds a year, and although he would like more, he can make himself and Mrs. O'Dell, and the younger branches of the house of O'Dell, comfortable on that sum. Some pastors gnash their teeth if their purse strings are opened for less than 300 pounds a year; Mr. O'Dell would purchase a pair of wings, and sing "'Tis like a little heaven below," if his stipend was raised to that figure. There is nothing very extraordinary in the preaching style of Mr. O'Dell. It lacks the cunning of that rare old Baptist bird, who once went by the name of Birney, and it is devoid of that learned and masterly eloquence so finely worked by the last minister of the chapel, who used to read some of his sermons over to the deacons, before trying them upon the other sinners in the chapel; still it is sincere, straight-forward, and theologically sound. It never reaches a point of raving, is never loudly pretentious, or ferocious in tone. Mr. O'Dell will never be a brilliant man; but he is now what is often much better - a good working minister. He will never occupy the position of a commander, will never even be a lieutenant, but he will always be a good soldier in the ranks. He has neither a lofty imaginative capacity nor a dashing ratiocinative faculty, but he has a clear sense of the importance of his pastoral duties, he goes easily and earnestly to work, makes neither much fuss nor smoke, and if he does now and then seem to pull queer faces in his sermons - give odd twists to some of his muscles - that does not debar him from preaching fair even-sounding sermons, soothing to his general hearers and pleasing to those who have to pay him. There are a few people whom Mr. O'Dell's sermons fail to keep awake; but as such parties are probably better asleep than in a full state of consciousness, no great harm is done. He has all sorts of folk to deal with - men who are pious, and smooth creatures quietly given to humbug; people who practice what they are taught, and a few so wonderfully good that if they called a meeting of their creditors they would begin the business by saying, "Let us pray;" individuals who follow their duties calmly, and make no show about their work; and respectable specimens of indifference, who go to chapel because it is fashionable to do so. But they seem all complacent, and the "happy family" element predominates. Mr. O'Dell suits them; they suit Mr. O'Dell; and if he had only a fuller chapel - a better salary, too, wouldn't be despised by him - he could send up his orisons with more courage, and preach to the sinners around him with the steam hammer force of a Gadsby.

VI

ST. GEORGE'S CHURCH.

"My respecks to St. George and the Dragoon," wrote the gay and festive showman, at the conclusion of an epistle - penned under the very shadow of "moral wax statters" - to the Prince of Wales. And there was no evil in such a benevolent expression of feeling. George, the particular party referred to, occupies a prominent position in our national escutcheonry, ant the "Dragoon" is a unique creature always in his company, which it would be wrong to entirely forget. The name of the saint sounds essentially English, and it has been woven into the country's history. The nation is fond of its Georges. We had four kings - not all of a saintly disposition - who rejoiced in that name; we sometimes swear by the name of George; and it plays as good a part as any other cognomen in our universal system of christening. Nobody can really tell who St. George was, and nobody will ever be able to do so. Gibbon fancies he was at one time an unscrupulous bacon dealer, and that he finally did considerable business in religious gammon. Butler, the Romish historian, thinks he was martyred by Diocletian for telling that amiable being a little of his mind; ancient fabulists make it out that be killed a dragon, saved a fair virgin's life, and then did something better than either - married her; medieval men, with a knightly turn of mind, transmuted him into the patron of chivalry; Edward III made him the patron of the Order of the Garter; the Eastern and Western churches venerate him yet; Britains have turned him into their country's tutelary saint; and many places of worship have been dedicated to this curiously mythologic individual. We have a church in Preston in this category; and it is of such church - St. George's - we shall speak now.

In 1723 it was erected. Up to that time the Parish Church was the only place of worship we had in connection with what is termed "the Establishment;" St. George's was brought into existence as a "chapel of ease" for it; and it is still one of the easiest, quietest, best behaved places in the town. It was a plain brick edifice at the beginning, but in 1843-4 the face of the church was hardened - it was turned into stone, and it continues to have a substantial petrified appearance. In 1848 a new chancel was built; and afterwards a dash of Christian patriotism resulted in a new pulpit and reading desk. The general building, which is of cruciform shape, has a subdued, solemn, half-genteel, half-quaint look. There is neither architectural maze nor ornamental flash in its construction. It is plain all round, and is characterised by a simplicity of style which could not be well reduced unless a severe plainness were adopted. Its position is not in a very imposing locality, and the roads to it are bad and irregular. Baines, the historian, says that St. George's Church is situated between Fishergate and Friargate - rather a wide definition applicable to about 500 other places ranging from billiard rooms to foundries, from brewing yards to bedstead warehouses in the same region. That brightest of all our historical blades, "P. Whittle , F.A.S. , " states that it is located on the south-west side of Friargate - a better, but still very mystical, exposition to all not actually acquainted with the place; whilst Hardwicke comes up to the rescue in the panoply of modern exactness, and tells us that it is on the south side of Fishergate. These historians must have missed their way in trying to find the place, and in their despair guessed at its real situation. There are many ways to St. George's - you can get to it from Fishergate, Lune-street, Friargate, or the Market place; but if each of those ways was thrown into one complete whole, the road would still be fifteenth rate. Tortuousness and dimness mark them, and a strong backyard spirit of adventure must operate largely in the minds of some who manage to reach the building.

The churchyard of St. George's has nothing interesting to the common mind about it. The great bulk of the grave stones are put flat upon the ground - arranged so that people can walk over them with ease and comfort, whatever may become of the letters; and if it were not for a few saplings which shoot out their bright foliage periodically, and one very ancient little tree which has become quite tired of that business, the yard would look very grave and monotonous. The principal entrance can be reached by way of Lune-street or Chapel-walks; but when you have got to it, there is nothing very peculiar to be seen. It is plain, rather gloomy, and in no way interesting.

The interior of the church wears a somewhat similar complexion; but it improves by observation, and in the end you like it for its thorough simplicity. No place of worship can in its internal arrangements be much plainer than St. George's. If it were not for three stained windows in the chancel, which you can but faintly make out at a distance, nothing which could by any possibility be termed ornamental would at first sight strike you. On reaching the centre of the place you get a moderately clear view of the pulpit which somewhat edifies the mind; and, on turning right round, you see a magnificent organ which compensates for multitudes of defects, and below it - in front of the orchestra - a rather powerful representation of the royal arms, a massive lion and unicorn, "fighting for the crown" as usual, and got up in polished wood work. We see no reason why there should not be something put up contiguously, emblematic of St. George and the dragon. It is very unfair to the saint and unjust to the dragon to ignore them altogether - The Ten Commandments are put on one side in this church-not done away with, but erected in a lateral position, very near a corner and somewhat out of the way. One of the historians previously quoted says that St. George's used to be "heated by what is commonly called a cockle" - some sort of a warmth radiating apparatus, which he describes minutely and with apparent pleasure. We have not inquired specially as to the fate of this cockle. It may still have an existence in the sacred edifice, or it may have given way, as all cockles must do in the end, whether in churches or private houses, to hot-water arrangements. The pews in St. George's are of the old, fashioned, patriarchal character. They are of all sizes an irregularity quite refreshing peculiarises them; there are hardly two alike in the building; and a study of the laws of variety must have been made by those who had the management of their construction. Private interests and family requirements have probably regulated the size of them. Some of the pews are narrow and hard to get into - a struggle has to be made before you can fairly take possession; others are broader and easier to enter: a few are very capacious and might be legitimately licensed to carry a dozen inside with safety; nearly all or them are lined with green baize, much of which is now getting into the sere and yellow leaf period of life; many of them are well-cushioned - green being the favourite colour; and in about the same number Brussels carpets may be found. There is a quiet, secluded coziness about the pews; the sides are high; the fronts come up well; nobody can see much of you if care is taken; and a position favourable to either recumbent ease or horizontal sleep may be assumed in several of them with safety. The general windows, excepting those in the chancel, are very plain; and if it were not for a rim of amber-coloured glass here and there and a fair average accumulation of dust on several of the squares, there would be nothing at all to relieve their native simplicity. The pillars supporting the nave are equally plain; the walls and ceiling are almost entirely devoid of ornament: and primitive white-wash forms the most prominent colouring material. The gas stands, often very elaborate in places of worship, have been made solely for use here. Simple upright pipes, surmounted by ordinary burners constitute their sum and substance. The pulpit lights are simpler. Gas has not yet reached the place where the law and the prophets are expounded. The orthodox mould candle reigns paramount on each side of the pulpit; and its light appears to give satisfaction.

There is no Sunday school in connection with St. George's. In some respects this may be a disadvantage to the neighbourhood; but it is a source of comfort to the congregation, for all the noise which irrepressible children create during service hours at every place where they are penned up, is obviated. Neither children nor babes are seen at St. George's. It is considered they are best at home, and that they ought to stay there until the second teeth have been fairly cut. The congregation of St. George's is specifically fashionable. A few poor people may be seen on low seats in the centre aisle; but the great majority of worshippers either represent, or are connected with, what are termed "good families." Young ladies wearing on just one hair the latest of bonnets, and elaborated with costly silks and ribbons; tender gentlemen of the silver-headed cane school and the "my deah fellah" region; quiet substantial looking men of advanced years, who believe in good breeding and properly brushed clothes; elderly matrons, "awfully spiff" as Lady Wortley Montague would say; and a few well-disposed tradespeople who judiciously mingle piety with business, and never make startling noises during their devotional moments - these make up the congregational elements of St. George's. They may be described in three words - few, serene, select. And this seems to have always been the case. Years since, the historian of Lancashire said that St. George's "has at all times had a respectable, though not a very numerous, congregation." The definition is as correct now as it was then. The worshippers move in high spheres; the bulk of them toil not, neither do they spin; and if they can afford it they are quite justified in making life genteel and easy, and giving instructions for other people to wait upon them. We dare say that if their piety is not as rampant, it is quite as good, as that of other people. Vehemence is not an indication of excellence, and people may be good without either giving way to solemn war-whoops or damaging the hearing faculties of their neighbours. Considering the situation of St. George's Church - its proximity to Friargate and the unhallowed passages running therefrom - there ought to be a better congregation. Churches like beefsteaks are intended to benefit those around them. It is not healthy for a church to have a congregation too select and too fashionable. Souls are of more value than either purses or clothes. More of the people living in the immediate neighbourhood of St. George's ought to regularly visit it; very few of them ever go near the place; but the fault may be their own, and neither the parson's, nor the beadle's.

The choir of St. George's is a wonderfully good one, and whether the members sing for love or money, or both, they deserve praise. Their melody is fine; their precision good; their expression excellent. They can give you a solemn piece with true abbandonatamente; they can observe an accelerando with becoming taste; they can get into a vigorosamente humour potently and on the shortest notice. They will never be able to knock down masonry with their musical force like the Jericho trumpeters, nor build up walls with their harmony like Amphion; but they will always possess ability to sing psalms, hymns, spiritual songs, and whatever may be contained in popular music books, with taste and commendable exactitude. We recommend them to the favourable consideration of the public. In St. George's Church there is an organ which may be placed in the "h c" category. It is a splendid instrument - can't be equalled in this part of the country for either finery or music - and is played by a gentleman whose name ranks in St. George's anthem book, with those of Beethoven, Handel, and Mozart. We have heard excellent music sung and played at St. George's; but matters would be improved if the efforts of the choir were seconded. At present the singers have some time been what we must term, for want of a better phrase, musical performers. They are tremendously ahead of the congregation. Much of what they sing cannot be joined in by the people. Many a time the congregation have to look on and listen - ecstacised with what is being sung, wondering what is coming next, and delightfully bewildered as to the whole affair.

The minister at St. George's is the Rev. C. H. Wood - a quiet, homely, well-built man, who is neither too finely dressed nor too well paid. His salary is considerably under 200 pounds a year. Mr. Wood is frank and unostentatious in manner; candid and calm in language; and of a temperament so even that he gets into hot water with nobody. You will never catch him with his virtuous blood up, theologically or politically. He has a cool head and a quiet tongue-two excellent articles for general wear which three-fourths of the parsons in this country have not yet heard of. He is well liked by the male portion of his congregation, and is on excellent terms with the fair sex. He is a batchelor, but that is his own fault. He could be married any day, but prefers being his own master. He may have an ideal like Dante, or a love phantom like Tasso, or an Imogene like the brave Alonzo; but he has published neither poetry nor prose on the subject yet, and has made no allusion to the matter in any of his sermons. No minister in Preston, with similar means, is more charitably disposed than Mr. Wood. He behaves well to poor people, and the virtue of that is worth more than the lugubriousness or eloquence of many homilies. Charity in purse as well as in speech is one of his characteristics; and if that doth not cover a multitude of ordinary defects nothing will. In the reading desk Mr Wood gets through his work quickly and with a good voice. There is no effort at elocution in his expression: he goes right on with the business, and if people miss the force of it they will have to be responsible for the consequences. In the pulpit he drives forward in the same earnest, matter-of-fact style. There is no hand flinging, hair-wringing, or dramatic raging in his style. The matter of his sermons is orthodox and homely - systematically arranged, innocently illustrated at intervals, and offensive to nobody. His manner is calculated to genially persuade rather than fiercely arouse; and it will sooner rock you to sleep than lash you to tears. There is a slight touch of sanctity at the end of his sentences - a mild elevation of voice indicative of pious oiliness; but, altogether, we like his quiet, straightforward, simple, English style. People fond of Church of England ideas could not have a more genial place of worship than St. George's: the seats are easy and well lined, the sermons short and placid, and the company good.

VII

ST. AUGUSTINE'S CATHOLIC CHURCH.

St. Augustine's Catholic Church, Preston, is of a retiring disposition; it occupies a very southern position; is neither in the town nor out of it; and unlike many sacred edifices is more than 50 yards from either a public-house or a beershop. Clean-looking dwellings immediately confront it; green fields take up the background; an air of quietude, half pastoral, half genteel, pervades it; but this ecclesiastical rose has its thorn. Only in its proximate surroundings is the place semi-rural and select. As the circle widens - townwards at any rate - you soon get into a region of murky houses, ragged children, running beer jugs, poverty; and as you move onwards, in certain directions, the plot thickens, until you get into the very lairs of ignorance, depravity, and misery. St. Augustine's "district" is a very large one; it embraces 8,000 or 9,000 persons, and their characters, like their faces, are of every colour and size. Much honest industry, much straight-forwardness and every day kindness, much that smells of gin, and rascality, and heathenism may be seen in the district. There is plenty of room for all kinds of reformers in the locality; and if any man can do any good in it, whatever may be his creed or theory, let him do it. The priests in connection with St. Augustine's Catholic Church are doing their share in this matter, and it is about them, their church, and their congregation that we have now a few words to say. The church we name is not a very old one. It was formally projected in 1836; the first stone of it was laid on the 13th of November, 1838; and it was opened on the 30th of July, 1840, by Dr. Briggs, afterwards first bishop of the Catholic diocese of Beverley. It has a plain yet rather stately exterior. Nothing fanciful, nor tinselled, nor masonically smart characterises it. Four large stone pillars, flanked with walls of the same material surmounted with brick, a flight of steps, a portico, a broad gable with massive coping, and a central ornament at the angle, are all which the facade presents. The doors are lateral, and are left open from morning till night three hundred and sixty-five days every year.

The interior of the church is spacious, wonderfully clean, and decorated at the high altar end in most tasteful style. We have not inquired whether charity begins at home or not in this place; perhaps it does not; but it is certain that painting does; for all the fine colouring, with its many formed classical devices, at the sanctuary was executed by one of the members of the congregation. The principal altar is a very fine one, and a fair amount of pious pleasure may be derived from looking at a tremendous pastoral candlestick which stands on one side. It is, when charged with a full-sized candle, perhaps five feet ten high, and it has a very patriarchal and decorous appearance - looks grave and authoritative, and seems to think itself a very important affair. And it has a perfect right to its opinion. We should like to see it in a procession, with Zaccheus, the sacristian, carrying it. Three fine paintings, which however seem to have lost their colour somewhat, are placed in the particular part of the church we are now at. The central one represents the "Adoration of the Magi," and was painted and given by Mr. H. Taylor Bulmer, who formerly resided in Preston. The second picture to the left is a representation of "Christ's agony in the Garden;" and the third on the opposite side is "Christ carrying the Cross." In front of the altar there is the usual lamp with a crimson spirit flame, burning day and night, and reminding one of the old vestal light, watched by Roman virgins, who were whipped in the dark by a wrathful pontifex if they ever let it go out. At the northern end of the church there is a large gallery, with one of the neatest artistic designs in front of it we ever saw. The side walls are surmounted with a chaste frieze, and running towards the base are "stations" and statues of saints. A small altar within a screen, surmounted with statuary, is placed on each side of the sanctuary, and not far from one of them there is a bright painting which looks well at a distance, but nothing extra two yards off. It represents Christ preaching out of a boat to some Galileans, amongst whom may be seen the Rev. Canon Walker. If the painting is correct, the worthy canon has deteriorated none by age, for he seems to look just as like himself now as he did eighteen hundred years since, and to be not a morsel fonder of spectacles and good snuff now than he was then. His insertion, however, into this picture, was a whim of the artist, whose cosmopolitan theory led him to believe that one man is, as a rule, quite as good as another, and that paintings are always appreciated best when they refer to people whom you know.

There are three of those very terrible places called confessionals at St. Augustine's, and one day not so long since we visited all of them. It is enough for an ordinary sinner to patronise one confessional in a week, or a month, or a quarter of a year, and then go home and try to behave himself. But we went to three in one forenoon with a priest, afterwards had the courage to get into the very centre of a neighbouring building wherein were two and twenty nuns, and then reciprocated compliments with an amiable young lady called the "Mother Superior." Terrible places to enter, and most unworldly people to visit, we fancy some of our Protestant friends will say; but we saw nothing very agonising or dreadful - not even in the confessionals. Like other folk we had heard grim tales about, such places - about trap doors, whips, manacles, and all sorts of cruel oddities; but in the confessionals visited we beheld nothing of any of them. Number one is a very small apartment, perhaps two yards square, with a seat and a couple of sacred pictures in it. In front there is an aperture filled in with a slender grating and backed by a curtain which can be removed at pleasure by the priest who officiates behind. On one side of the grating there is a small space like a letter-box slip, and through this communications in writing, of various dimensions, are handed. Everything is plain and simple where the penitent is located; and the apartment behind, occupied by the priest who hears confession, is equally simple. There is no weird paraphernalia, no mysterious contrivances, no bolts, bars, pullies, or strings for either working miracles, or making the hair of sinners stand on end. Number two confessional is similarly arranged and equally plain. We examined this rather more minutely than the other, and whilst we could find nothing dreadful in the penitents' apartment, we fancied, on entering the priest's side, that, we had met with something belonging the realm of confessional torture as depicted by the Hogans, Murphys, and Maria Monk showmen, and which the officials had forgot to put by in some of their secret drawers. It was hung upon a nail, had a semi-circular, half viperish look, and was cupped at each end as if intended for some curious business of incision or absorption. We were relieved on getting nearer it and on being informed that it was merely an ear trumpet through which questions have to be put to deaf penitents who now and then turn up for general unravelment and absolution. The two confessionals described are contiguous to a passage at the rear of the church; the third we are now coming to is near one of the subsidiary altars, nod looks specifically snug. It is a particularly small confessional, and a very stout penitent would find it as difficult to get into it as to reveal all his sins afterwards. There is nothing either harrowing or cabalistic in the place; and you can see nothing but two forms, a screen, and a crucifix.

There are many services at St. Augustine's. On Monday mornings at a quarter past seven, and again at half-past eight, mass is said; on Tuesdays and Thursdays there is benediction at half-past seven; on Fridays and Saturdays and on the eve of holidays there is confession; on Sundays there is mass at half-past seven, half-past eight, half-past nine, and at 11, when regular service takes place; on Sunday afternoons, at three, the children are instructed, and at half-past six in the evening there are vespers, a sermon, and benediction. The church has a capacity for about 1,000 persons, without crushing. The average number hearing mass on a Sunday is 3,290. On four consecutive Sundays recently - from February 14 to March 14 - upwards of 13,100 heard mass within the walls of the church.

The congregation is almost entirely made up of

working people. A few middle class and wealthy persons attend the place - some sitting in the gallery, and others at the higher end of the church - but the general body consists of toiling every-day folk. The poorest section, including the Irish - who, in every Catholic Church, do a great stroke of business on a Sunday with holy water, beads and crucifixes - are located in the rear. It is a source of sacred pleasure to quietly watch some of these poor yet curious beings. They are all amazingly in earnest while the fit is on them; they bow, and kneel, and make hand motions with a dexterity which nothing but long years of practice could ensure; and they drive on with their prayers in a style which, whatever may be the character of its sincerity, has certainly the merit of fastness. How to get through the greatest number of words in the shortest possible time may be a problem which they are trying, to solve. The great bulk of the congregation are calm and unostentatious, evincing a quiet demeanour in conjunction with a determined devotion. There are several very excellent sleepers in the multitude of worshippers; but they are mainly at the entrance end where they are least seen. We happened to be at the church the other Sunday morning and in ten minutes after the sermon had been commenced about 16 persons, all within a moderate space, were fast asleep. Their number increased slowly till the conclusion. Several appeared to be struggling very severely against the Morphean deity dining the whole service; a few might be seen at intervals rescuing themselves from his grasp - getting upon the very edge of a snooze, starting suddenly with a shake and waking up , dropping down their heads to a certain point of calmness and then retracing their steps to consciousness.

There are five men at St. Augustine's called collectors - parties who show strangers, &c., their seats, and look after the pennies which attendants have to pay on taking them. Not one of these collectors has officiated less than 11 years; three of them have been at the work for 27; and what is still better they discharge their duties, as the sacristan once told us, "free gracious." That is a philanthropic wrinkle for chapel keepers and other compounders of business and piety which we commend to special notice. The singers at St. Augustine's are of more than ordinary merit. Two or three of them have most excellent voices; and the conjoint efforts of the body are in many respects capital. Their reading is accurate, their time good, and their melody frequently constitutes a treat which would do a power of good to those who hear the vocalisation of many ordinary psalm-singers whose great object through life is to kill old tunes and inflict grevious bodily harm upon new ones. There is a very good organ at St. Augustine's, and it is blown well and played well.

Usually there are three priests at the mission; but on our visit there were only two - the Rev. Canon Walker, and the Rev. J. Hawkesworth; and if you had to travel from the lowest point in Cornwall to the farthest house in Caithness you wouldn't find two more kindly men. We Protestants talk volubly about the grim, grinding character of priests, about their tyrannous influence, and their sinister sacerdotalism; but there is a good deal of extra colouring matter in the picture. Whatever their religion may be, and however much we may differ from it, this at least we have always found amongst priests - excellent education, amazing devotion to duty, gentlemanly behaviour, and in social life much geniality. They have studied all subjects;

they know something about everything; their profession necessarily makes them acquainted with each phase and feeling of life. The Rev. Canon Walker is a good type of a thoroughly English priest and of a genuine Lancashire man. He is unassuming, obliging in manner, careful in his duties, fonder of a good pinch of snuff than of warring about creeds, much more in love with a quiet chat than of platform violence, and would far sooner offer you a glass of wine, and ask you to take another when you had done it, than fight with you about piety. He is a man of peace, of homely, disposition, of kindly thought, unobtrusive in style, sincere in action, with nothing bombastic in his nature, and nothing self-righteous in his speech. His sermons are neither profound nor simple - they are made up of fair medium material; and are discharged rapidly. There is no effort at rhetorical flourish in his style; a simple lifting of the right hand, with an easy swaying motion, is all the "action" you perceive. Canon Walker speaks with a rapidity seldom noticed. Average talkers can get through about 120 words in a minute; Canon Walker can manage 200 nicely, and show no signs of being out of breath.

The Rev. Mr. Hawkesworth - a bright-eyed, rubicund-featured gentleman, with a slight disposition to corporeal rotundity - is the second priest. He is a sharp, kindly-humoured gentleman, and does not appear to have suffered in either mind or body by a four years residence in Rome. Mr. Hawkesworth is a practical priest, a good singer, and a hard worker. He resides with Canon Walker in a spacious house adjoining St. Augustine's. No unusual sounds have ever been heard to proceed from the residence, and it may fairly be inferred that they dwell together to harmony. The house is substantially furnished. The library within it is not very large, but what it lacks in bulk is made up for by variety. Its contents range from the Clockmaker of Sam Slick to the Imitation of Thomas a Kempis, from Little Dorrit to the Greek Lexicon. Not far from St. Augustine's Church there is a convent. It is the old Larkhill mansion transmuted, and is one of the most pleasantly situated houses in this locality. In front of it you have flowers of delicious hues, shrubs of every kind, grassy undulations, rare old shady trees, a small artificial lake, a fountain - shall we go on piling up the agony of beauty until we reach a Claude Melnotte altitude? It is unnecessary; all we need add is this - that the grounds are a lovely picture, delightfully formed, and most snugly set. The convent is a large, clean, airy establishment. The entrance hall is handsome; some of the apartments are choicely furnished, the walls being decorated with pictures, &c., made by either the nuns or their pupils. The convent includes apartments for the reception of visitors, a small chapel, with deeply-toned light, and exquisitely arranged; dining rooms, sitting rooms, two or three school rooms, lavatories, sculleries, dormitories, and a gigantic kitchen, reminding one of olden houses wherein were vast open fire-places, massive spits, and every apparatus for making meat palateable and life enjoyable. The 22 nuns before referred to live at this convent. They belong to the order of "Faithful Companions;" they lead quiet, industrious lives - have no Saurin-Starr difficulties, and appear to be contented.

At the convent there are 33 pupils - some from a distance, others belonging the town. They are taught every accomplishment; look very healthy; and, when we saw them, seemed not only comfortable but merry. Near the convent there is a commodious girls' and infants' school connected with St. Augustine's, the general average attendance being about 240. In Vauxhall-road there is another large, excellently built school belonging to the same Church, and set apart for boys. The attendance is not very numerous. At both there is room for many more scholars, and if religious bigotry did not operate in some quarters, and prevent Catholic children going to those schools recognising the principles of their own faith, the attendance at each would be much better than it is. Taking the district in its entirety, it is industriously worked by the Catholics. They deserve praise for their energy. Their object is to push on Catholicism and improve the secular position of the inhabitants, and they do this with a zeal most praiseworthy. This finishes our Augustinian mission.

VIII

QUAKERS' MEETING HOUSE.

I love Quaker ways and Quaker worship. I venerate the Quaker principles. It does me good for the rest of the day when I meet any of their people in my path. When I am ruled or disturbed by any occurrence, the sight or quiet voice of a Quaker acts upon me as a ventilator, lightening the air, and taking off a load from the bosom; but I cannot like the Quakers, as Desdemona would say, "to live with them." - Charles Lamb.

Sheep, leather, and religion were the principal things which George Fox, the founder of Quakerism, looked after. In boyhood he was a shepherd, in youth a shoemaker, in manhood an expounder of Christianity. No one could have had a series of occupations more comprehensive or practical. The history of the world proves that it is as important for men to look after their mutton as to "save their bacon;" that, after all, "there is nothing like leather;" and that there can be nothing better than religion. 219 years since the ancestors of those who now follow the "inner light" were termed Quakers. An English judge - Gervaise Bennet - gave them this name at Derby, and it is said that he did so because Fox "bid them quake at the word of the Lord." Theologically, Quakers are a peculiar people; they believe in neither rites nor ceremonies, in neither prayer-books nor hymn-books, in neither lesson reading, nor pulpit homilies, nor sacraments. They are guided by their spiritual feelings, and have a strong idea that a man has no right to open his mouth when he has got nothing to say, and that he should avoid keeping it shut when he has something worth uttering.

This is an excellent plan, and the world would be considerably benefited if it were universally observed both in religion and every-day life. Creation is killed and done for daily through an everlasting torrent of meaningless talk. Compact and quiet as it may appear, Quakerism has had its schisms and internal feuds. Early in this century, the White Quakers, who dressed themselves in light suits when outside and didn't dress at all - stripped themselves after the manner of Adamites - when within doors, created much furore in Ireland. About 30 years since, the Hicksite Quakers, who denied the divinity of Christ and the authority of the Bible, made their advent; afterwards the Beaconite Quakers put in an appearance; and then came the Wilburites. Taking all sections into account, there are at present about 130,000 Quakers in the world, and Preston contributes just seventy genuine ones to their number. In this locality they remain unchanged. Today they are neither smaller nor larger, numerically, than they were thirty years age. In the early days of local Quakerism, the country rather than the town was its favourite situation. Newton, Freckleton, Rawcliffe, and Chipping contained respectively at one time many more Quakers than Preston, but the old stations were gradually broken up, and Preston eventually got the majority of their members. A building located somewhere between Everton-gardens and Spring-gardens was first used as a meeting-house by them. In 1784 a better place was erected by the Friends, on a piece of land contiguous to and on the north side of Friargate; and in 1847 it was rebuilt. Although no one was officially engaged to map out the place, a good deal of learned architectural gas was disengaged in its design and construction. It was made three times larger than its congregational requirements - the object being to accommodate those who might assemble at the periodical district meetings. Special attention was also paid to the loftiness of the building - to the height of its ceiling. One or two of the amateur designers having a finger in the architectural pie had serious notions as to the importance of air space. They had studied the influence of oxygen and hydrogen, of nitrogen and carbonic acid gas; they had read in scientific books that every human being requires so many feet of breathing room; and after deciding upon the number of worshippers which the meeting-house should accommodate, they agreed to elevate its ceiling in the ratio of their inspiring and expiring necessities. This was a very good, salutary, Quakerly idea, and although it may have operated against the internal appearance of the building it has guaranteed purity of air to those attending it.

The meeting house is a quiet, secluded, well-made place; but it has a poor entrance, which you would fancy led to nowhere. A stranger passing along Friargate on an ordinary day, would never find the Quakers' meeting house. He might notice at a certain point on the north-eastern side of that undulating and bustling public thoroughfare a grey looking gable, having a three-light-window towards the head, with a large door below, and at its base two washing pots and a long butter mug, belonging to an industrious earthenware dealer next door; but he would never fancy that the disciples of George Fox had a front entrance there to their meeting house. Yet after passing through a dim broad passage here, and mounting half a dozen substantial steps, you see a square, neat-looking, five-windowed building, and this is the Quakers' meeting house.

Over the passage there is a pretty large room, which is used by the Friends for Sunday school purposes. The attendance at this school on ordinary occasions is about 60; at special periods it is considerably more. During the cotton famine, a few years ago, when the Quakers were manifesting their proverbial charity - giving money, food, and clothing - the attendance averaged 160; and if it was known that they were going to give something extra tomorrow it would reach that point again. Speaking of the charity of Quakers, it may not be amiss to state that they keep all their own poor - do not allow any one belonging their society ever to solicit aid from the parish, or migrate in the dark hour of poverty to the workhouse. Reverting to the meeting-house, we may observe that just within its front door particular provision has been made for umbrellas. There is a long, low stand, with a channel below it, and this will afford ample accomodation for about 160 umbrellas. Taking into account the average attendance at the meeting-house, we have come to the serious conclusion that if every member carried two umbrellas on wet Sundays, the said umbrellas could be legitimately provided for. It is not a pleasant thing for a man to carry a couple of umbrellas, and we believe it has been found very difficult for any one to put up and use two at the same time; still it is satisfactory to know that if ever the Friends of Preston decide upon such a course, there will be plenty of provision for their umbrellas at the meeting house.

The inside of the general building is severely plain. There is no decoration of any description about it, and if the gas pipes running along the side walls had not a slight Hogarthian line of beauty touch in their form, everything would look absolutely horizontal and perpendicular. The seats are plain and strong with open backs. A few of them have got green cushions running the whole length of the form. In some small cushions are dotted down here and there for individual worshippers, who can at any time easily take them up, put them under their arm, and move from one place to another if they wish for a change of location. Over the front entrance there is a gallery, but ordinarily it is empty. There is no pulpit in the house, and no description of books - neither bibles, nor hymn-books, nor prayer-books - can be seen anywhere. At the head of the place there is an elevated strongly-fronted bench, running from one side to the other, and below it an open form of similar length. The more matured Quakers and Quakeresses generally gravitate hitherwards. The males have separate places and so have the females. It is expected that the former will always direct their steps to the seats on the right-hand side; that the latter will occupy those on the left; and, generally, you find them on opposite sides in strict accordance with this idea. There is nothing to absolutely prevent an enraptured swain from sitting at the elbow of his love, and basking in the sunlight of her eyes, nor to stop an elderly man from nestling peacefully under the wing of his spouse; but it is understood that they will not do this, and will at least submit to a deed of separation during hours of worship. In addition to the 70 actual members of the society there are about 60 persons in Preston who pay a sort of nominal homage at the shrine of George Fox.

They have two meetings every Sunday, morning and evening, and one every Thursday - at half-past ten in the morning during winter months, and at seven in the evening in summer. The average attendance at each of the Sunday meetings is about 70. The character of the services is quite unsettled. Throughout Christendom the rule in religious edifices is to have a preliminary service, and then a discourse; in Quaker meeting houses there is no such defined course of action. Sometimes there is a prayer, then another, then an "exhortation" - Quakers have no sermons; at other times an exhortation without any prayer; now and then a prayer without any exhortation; and occasionally they have neither the one nor the other - they fall into a state of profound silence, keep astonishingly quiet ever so long, with their eyes shut, and then walk out. This is called silent meditation. If a pin drops whilst this is going on you can hear it and tell in which part of the house it is lying. You can feel the quietude , see the stillness; it is "tranquil and herd-like - as in the pasture - 'forty feeding like one;'" it is sadly serene, placidly mysterous, like the "uncommunicating muteness of fishes;" and you wonder how it is kept up. To those who believe in solemn reticence - in motionless communion with the "inner light," - there is nothing curious in this; it is, in fact, often a source of high spiritual ecstacy; but to an unitiated spectator the business looks seriously funny, and its continuance for any length of time causes the mind of such a one to run in all kinds of dreadfully ludicrous grooves.

Quakers don't believe in singing, and have no faith in sacred music of any kind. Neither the harp, nor the sackbut, nor the psaltery, nor the dulcimer will they have; neither organs nor bass fiddles will they countenance; neither vocalists nor instrumentalists, nor tune forks of any size or weight, will they patronise. They permit one another to enter and remain in their meeting house with the hat on or off, and with the hands either in the pockets or out of them. They have no regular ministers, and allow either men or women to speak. None, except Quakers and Ranters - the two most extreme sections of the religious community, so far as quietude and noise are concerned - permit this; and it is a good thing for the world that the system is not extended beyond their circles. If women were allowed to speak at some places of worship they would all be talking at once - all be growing eloquent, voluble, and strong minded in two minutes - and an articulative mystification, much more chaotic than that which once took place at Babel, would ensue. At the meeting house in Friargate it is taken for granted that on Sundays the morning service lasts for an hour and a half, and the evening one an hour and a quarter; but practically the time is regulated by the feelings of the worshippers - they come and go as they are "moved," and that is a liberal sort of measure harmonising well with human nature and its varied requirements.

We have paid more than one visit to this meeting house. The other Sunday evening we were there. The congregation at that time numbered just thirty-two - fifteen men, twelve women, two boys, and three girls. This was rather a small assemblage for a place which will hold between 500 and 600 persons; but it might be gratifying to the shades of its chemistry-loving, cubic-feet-of-air-admiring designers, for they would at any rate have the lively satisfaction of knowing that none of the famous 32 would suffer through want of breathing space. The members of the congregation came in at various times; four were there at half-past six; the remainder had got safely seated, in every instance, by ten minutes to seven. All the males made their appearance with their hats on; some pulled them off the moment they got seated; two or three seemed to get their convictions gradually intensified on the subject, and in about ten minutes came to the conclusion that they could do without their hats; some who had cast aside their castors at an early period reinstated them; whilst odd ones kept on their head coverings during the entire meeting. For 45 minutes, not the least effort in any lingual direction was made; no one said a word for three-quarters of an hour. There was a good deal of stirring on the forms, and creaking sounds were periodically heard; the whole indicating that the sitting posture had become uneasy, and that the paint, through warmth, had got tenacious. There was, however, neither talking nor whispering indulged in. The elderly Quakers, with their broad-brimmed, substantial hats, and white neckcloths, kept their eyes closed for a season, then opened them and looked ahead pensively, then shut them serenely again, - just

As men of inward light are wont
To turn their optics to upon 't.

The Quakeresses on the other side followed a similar programme. We saw only three of them in the olden dress - only three with narrow-barrelled high crowned bonnets, made of brown silk and garnished with white silk strings. The younger branches of Quakerdom seemed more conventional than their ancestors in general dress. There was a slight dash of antiquity in their style; but their hats and bonnets, their coats and shawls had evidently been made for ornament as well as use. Originally Quakers were peculiarly stringent in respect to the plainness of their clothes; what they wore was always good, always made out of something which could not be beaten for its excellence of quality; but it was always simple, always out of the line of shoddy and bespanglement. But Quakerism is neither immaculate nor invincible; time is changing its simplicity, its quaint old fashioned solidity of dress; "civilisation" is quietly eating away its rigidity; and the day is coming when Quakerism will don the same suit as the rest of the world. For the first ten minutes we were in the chapel silence was not to us so much of a singularity; but when the Town Hall clock struck seven, when the machinery in the dim steeple of Trinity Church, which adjoins, gave a slow confirmation of it, and when all the little clocks in the neighbouring houses - for you could hear them on account of the general silence - chirped out sharply the same thing, one began to feel dubious and mystified. But the Quakers took all quietly, and even the children present sat still. The chime of another hour quarter came in due order; still there was no sign of action. Two minutes afterwards, an elderly gentleman, whose eyes had been kept close during the greater part of the time which had passed, suddenly leaned forward; the "congregation" followed his example in a crack, and for ten minutes they prayed, the elderly gentleman leading the way in a rather high-keyed voice, which he singularly modulated. But there was not much of "the old Foxian orgasm" manifested by him; he was serene, did not shake, was not agonised. He finished as he began without any warning; the general assemblage was seated in a second; and for seven minutes there was another reign of taciturnity. When that time had elapsed the same elderly party gave an exhortation, simple in language, kindly in tone, and free from both bewilderment and fierceness. Mr. Jesper - the person to whom we have been alluding - is one of the principal speakers at this meeting house. His colleague in talking is Mrs. Abbatt, a very worthy lady, who has often the afflatus upon her, and who can hold forth with a good deal of earnestness and perspicuity. Although Mr. Jesper and Mrs. Abbatt do the greatest portion of the talking and praying, others break through the ring fence of Quakerdom's silence periodically. One little gentleman has often small outbursts; but he is not very exhilerating. All the "members" attending the meeting house are very decorous, respectable, middle-class people - substantial well-pursed folk, who can afford to be independent, and take life easily - men and women who dislike shoddy and cant as much as they condemn spangles and lackered gentility.

The aggregate of the people connected with the place are calm, steady-going beings. We have a large respect for Quakerism. Its professors are made of strong, enduring, practical metal. They never neglect business for religion, nor religion for business. They believe in paying their way and in being paid; in moral rectitude and yard wands not the millionth part of an inch too long; in yea and nay; in good trade, good purses, good clothes, and good language; in clear-headed, cool calculations; in cash, discounts, sobriety, and clean shirts; in calmness and close bargain driving; in getting as much as they can, in sticking to it a long while, and yet in behaving well to the poor. The influence of the creed they profess has made their uprightness and humanity proverbial. Their home influence has been powerful; their views in the outer world are becoming more fully realised every day. Nations have smiled contemptuously at them as they have gone forth on lonely missions of freedom and peace; but the inner beatings of the world's great heart today are in favour of liberty of thought and quietness. The Quakers have been amongst life's pioneers in the long, hard battle for human freedom and human peace. Quakerism may be a quaint, hat-loving, silence-revering concern in its meeting-houses; its Uriahs, and Abimelechs, and Deborahs, and Abigails, may look curious creatures in their collarless coats and long drawn bonnets; but they belong to a race of men and women who have kept the lamp of freedom burning; who have set a higher price upon conscience than gold; who have struggled to make everything free - the body, the religion, the bread and butter, and the trade of the nations; who are now by their doctrines slowly lifting humanity out of the red track of war, and teaching it how grand a triumph can be made all the world over by absolute Peace and Honesty.

IX

ST. PETER'S CHURCH.

Upon a high piece of enclosed land, adjoining Fylde-road, stands St. Peter's Church. Portions of its precincts are covered with gravestones; the remainder has been "considerably damaged" of late, according to the belief of one of the churchwardens, by the vicious scratching of a number of irreverent hens, whose owners will be prosecuted if they do not look better after them. The other Sunday, we saw a notice posted at the front of the church relative to the great hen-scratching question. It is said that some of these tame and reclaimed birds have penetrated a foot or two into the ground for the purpose of lying, not laying, therein; and on this account it is important that their proprietors should look more (h)energetically after them. The foundation stone of St. Peter's Church was laid by Mr. Justice Park, one of the old recorders of Preston, in 1822; Rickman, an able Birmingham architect, designed the place; and the edifice (sans steeple, which was built in 1852, out of money left by the late Thomas German, Esq.), was erected at a cost of 6,900 pounds, provided by the Commissioners for the building of new churches. St. Peter's has a lofty, commanding appearance. Learned people say it is built in the florid Gothic style of architecture, and we are not inclined to dispute their definition. It has a very churchly look, and if the steeple were at the other end, it would be equally orthodox. The world, as a rule, fixes its steeples westward; but St. Peter's, following a few others we could name, rises in the opposite direction, and, like a good Mussulman, turns to the East. There is nothing in its graveyard calling for special comment. Neither monuments nor lofty tombs relieve it. All round it has a flat dull aspect, and good arrangements have been made for walking over the tombstones and obliterating their inscriptions. There are two ways into the church at the western end; both are near each other; but one has advantages which the other does not possess. Passing through the larger you immediately face the pulpit and the congregation; entering by the other you can hang your harp on several preliminary willows - sit just sideways and hear what's going on, stay behind the screen until a point arrives when a move forward can be made without many people catching your "mould of form," or inquire who's present and who isn't, and glide out if nothing suitable is observed.

St. Peter's Church, internally, looks dirty. If cleanliness be next to godliness, a good cleaning would do it good and improve its affinities. Whitewash, paint, floor-cloths, dusters, wash leathers, and sundry other articles in the curriculum of scrubbers, renovators, and purifiers are needed. The walls want mundifying, so does the ceiling, so do the floors; the Ten Commandments need improving; the Apostles' Creed isn't plain enough; the spirit of a time worn grimness requires ostracising from the place. All is substantial; but therc is an ancient unwashed dulness about the general establishment, which needs transforming into cleanness and brightness. The pews are high, and on the average they will hold six persons each. Seven might get into them on a pinch; but if the number were much extended beyond that point, either abraison or blue places through violent pressure would be the consequence. Two or three pews at the top end will hold twelve each; but that apostolic number is not very often observed in them. The price of a single sitting in the middle aisle is 10s. per annum; the cost of a side seat is equal to three civil half-crowns. The long side seats are free; so are the galleries, excepting that portion of them in front of the organ. Often the church is not much more than half filled on a Sunday; but it is said that many sittings, calculated to accommodate nearly a full congregation, are let. Viewed from the copperhead standpoint this is right; but taking a higher ground it would be more satisfactory if even fewer pews were let and more folk attended. The church is not well arranged for people occupying side seats. In looking ahead the pillars of the nave constantly intercept their vision if they care about seeing who is reading or preaching. Wherever the pulpit were put it would blush unseen, so far as many are concerned. At present it is fixed on the south-eastern side, and only about one-fourth of those seated under the galleries can see either it or the preacher. Some of them at times complain considerably of sequestration; others feel it a little occasionally; a few think it a rather snug thing to be out of sight. A large five-light stained glass window occupies the chancel end; but there is nothing very entrancing in its appearance. The greater portion of it has a bright, amber-coloured, monotonous flashiness about it, which flares the eyes if gazed at long, and makes other things, if looked at directly afterwards, yellow-hued; and it is surmounted with a number of minor designs, reminding one of the big oddities in a mammoth keleidoscope. But the congregation have got used to the window, and will neither break it nor permit others to do so. Six spaces for tablet inscriptions occupy the base of the window. Two of them are blank; two have a great mass of letters packed into them; and two are but moderately filled in with words. At a distance nobody can see what is said upon them. It is reported that they contain the Decalogue and the Apostles' Creed; and if this be so, the incumbent, the curate, and the clerk must have been the parties for whose delight they were put up, for they are the nearest to, and can consequently best read, them. There are the full compliment of sacred enclosures and resting places at the higher end of the church - a chair for the ease of the incumbent or curate; a desk for the prayer reader; a box for the clerk; a lectern for the lesson reader; and a stout pulpit for the preacher.

The congregation of St. Peter's Church, as we have said, is small. We cannot tell whether the collections terrify folk; probably they do; for it is estimated that there are between 30 and 40 of them annually, and sometimes they come in an unbroken line for several Sundays together. A plan like this is enough to make people shy in their attendance, - is certain to make ordinarily generous beings cover what they give with their finger ends, or slip their gifts sharply into the boxes and get them instantly mixed up with the rest, so that nobody can tell whether they have contributed a simple copper, a roguish little threepenny piece, or a respectable looking shilling. There are voluntary contribution boxes at the doors, but they never get very heavy. Those attending the church are mainly working people. With the exception of about five, all have to fight briskly for a living. A greater work has been done outside than within the church. There are many schools and classes belonging, the place. In Cold Bath-street there is a large school for girls and infants, and it is very well attended. In Fylde-road there is a club for working men, open every day; and on Sundays several of the "wives and mothers of Britain" attend a class in the same building. In Brook-street there is a regular day school. On Sunday afternoons the members of an adult male class meet in it. The average attendance of these members is about 160, and their ages range from 20 to 70. The district has been well worked up; and there are many of both sexes in it prepared to either pray or fight for St. Peter's.

The music at the church is good. It costs about 30 pounds a year, and a rather strong effort is sometimes required to raise that sum. The organist immediately preceding the present one used to play for nothing; get one or two collections annually for the choir; and make up out of his own pocket any financial deficiency there might be. The gentleman who now operates upon the organ, likewise gives his services gratuitously; he also has collections for the choir; but if those said collections come short of the sum required, he is seriously impressed with the idea that the deficiency ought to come out of other people's purses, and not his. And so it does. The organist has considerable musical ability; he plays the instrument in his care with precision; but he throws too much force into its effusions - believes too much in high pressure - and the general boiler of its melody may burst some day, kill the blower instantly, and dash the choir into space. The internal service arrangements at St. Peter's are worked by an incumbent, a curate, and a clerk. The last named gentleman has been a long time at his post; he is a dry, orthodox, careful man; never mistook a three-penny for a fourpenny piece in his life; doesn't like slippery sixpences; and he gets for his general services at the church 15 pounds a year. Nobody hardly ever hears him; the responses of the choir materially swamp the music of his voice; but his lips move, and that is at least a sign of life.

The incumbent is the Rev. D. F. Chapman. He has been at the place a few years, and receives about 400 pounds a-year for his trouble. Mr. Chapman is a powerfully-constructed gentleman; is somewhat inclined to oleaginousness; has contracted a marine swing in his walk; is heavily clerical in countenance and cloth; believes in keeping his hair broad at the sides; has a strong will and an enormous opinion of the incumbent of St. Peter's; will fume if crossed; will crush if touched; can't be convinced; has his mind made up and rivetted down on everything; must have his way; thinks every antagonist mistaken; is washy, windy, ponderous; has a clear notion that each of his postulates is worth a couple of demonstrations, that all his theories are tantamount to axioms; and, finally, has quarelled more with his churchwardens than any other live parson in Preston. He once fought for weeks, day and night, with a warden as to the position of a small gas-pipe, because he couldn't get his way about it. He is well educated, but his erudition is not fairly utilised; he can read with moderate precision; but there is a lack of elocutionary finish in his tone; he can talk a long while, and now and then can say a good thing; he preaches with considerable force, makes good use of his arms, sometimes rants a little, at intervals has to pull back his sentences half an inch to get hold of the right word, talks straight out occasionally, telling the congregation what they are doing and what they ought to do; but there is much in his sermons which neither gods nor men will care about digesting, and there is a theological dogmatism in them which ordinary sinners like ourselves will never swallow. We are rather inclined to admire the gentleman who, until lately, officiated as his curate - the Rev. E. Lee, - and who, after preaching his last sermon, was next day made the recipient of that most fashionable and threadbare of all things, a presentation. Originally he indulged in odd pranks, said strange things, was laughably eccentric, and did for a period appear to be, in an ecclesiastical sense, what the kangaroo of Artemus Ward was in a zoological one - "the most amoozin little cuss ever introduced to a discriminatin public." He has still some of the "amoozin" traits about him; but during his curacy in St. Peters district he showed that he could work hard, visit often, look after the poor, be generous, get up good classes, and never tire of his duty. His salary was about 120 pounds a year, and he was benevolent with it. He has a stronger pair of lungs than any parson in Preston, and he can use them longer than most men without feeling tired. His sermons are of a practical type; he believes largely in telling people what he thinks; and never hesitates to hit rich and poor alike in his discourses. He has been transplanted to the Parish Church, and he will stir up a few of the respectable otiose souls there if he has an opportunity. There is a good deal of swagger about him; he believes in carry a stick and turning it; in admiring himself and letting other people know that he is of a cypher; there is much conceit and ever so much bombast about him; he likes giving historical lectures; thinks he is an authority on everything appertaining to Elizabeth, Mary, the Prince of Orange, &c.; is fond of attacking Bishop Goss, and getting into a groove of garrulous declamation concerning Papists; still he is a determined worker, has been a laborious curate, has troubled himself more than many people in looking after those whom parsons are so fond of calling sinners and so indifferent about visiting. He was well liked in St. Peter's district, and we hope that in the new one he has gone to he will gather friends, increase his usefulness, get married, and give fewer polemical lectures.

X

NEW JERUSALEM CHURCH.

De gustibus non est applies with as much force to religious as to secular life. People's tastes will differ; you can no more account for them in church-naming than in kissing or child-christening; and that being so, let no pious piece of perfection dispute with the New Jerusalem brethren as to their spiritual gustation. If a man were virtuously inclined to pirate in his religious nomenclature the oddities of old Carey, who coined that finely flowing word "aldeborontiphoscophornio," which is only a line ahead of that other stately polysyllable "chrononhotonthologos," why let him do so, for somebody with more madness or wisdom than yourself will some day end or mend him. Let every man have his "cogibundity of cogitation," and let people suit themselves about the names of their churches. Swedenborgians is the name commonly given to those who belong to "the New Church signified by the New Jerusalem in the Revelation." They might have cut it shorter to be sure; and they might have had a less mystical but certainly not a cleverer man for their founder than the Swedish Emanuel. No modern ever knew half so much, or knew it so oddly, as Swedenborg; and no one ever wrote so immensely on questions so varied and intractable. He knew something about everything, from toe nails to the differential and integral calculus, from iron smelting to star cycles, and in reading his works you might almost fancy, so familiar does he appear to be with spirits, that he had a quotidian nod from Michael and a daily "How are you, old boy?" from Gabriel. Emerson does well when he puts him down as the representative man of mystery; and when he calls him the mastodon and missourian of literature, he will have the concurrence of all unbiased scholars.

There are about 70 persons in Preston who care vitally for that ideal Church which St. John saw in Patmos - if New Jerusalemism, as delineated by the followers of Swedenborg, is its symbol. Only about 70 are connected as "members" with its physical temple in Avenham-road. More may be in embryo; several maybe hanging on the skirts of conviction, ready for a goodly plunge into reality; but that is the number of mortals at present associated with the "New Church signified by the New Jerusalem," in Preston. All of them are earnest, the bulk are conscientious, and on that account entitled to respect. About a quarter of a century ago, a few sincere Swedenborgians met in an office down Cannon-street, which is now used as a gilding room by a modern Revivalist. They pushed "the cause" with a fair amount of energy, and increased, though by slow degrees, the number of their members. During the period of their spiritual exercises here, the late Mr. Hugh Becconsall, a calm, benevolent-hearted man, got associated with them, and this was the means of bringing into fuller life the principles of Swedenborg in Preston. Mr. Becconsall's thoughts were quickened and changed by them; he became a devoted and sincere believer in the new Church; attended its meetings in Cannon-street; was impressed with the idea that better accomodation was required for them; and finally decided to build out of his own pocket, and endow from the same source, a new church in Avenham-road. It was estimated that the cost of the church would be 1000 pounds, which Mr. Becconsall willingly agreed to pay; but religion has no aegis against "extras" - they will creep in, are irrepressible; and, in accordance with this fatal philosophy, the church in Avenham-road cost in the end nearly 2000 pounds, which he paid without even grumbling - a privilege all Englishmen have the right to exercise freely after they have paid the piper well. The foundation stone was laid in 1843, very soon after which the Rev. James Bonwell, curate of Trinity Church, Preston, made a virulent attack upon Swedenborgianism and its followers. This gentleman, who was subsequently unrobed for immorality, charged both the ministers of the New Church party and all who listened to them, with the rebellion of Korah, Dathan, and Abiram, and uttered language implying a wish that the earth would open its mouth and swallow them up. The Rev. Augustus Clissold, M.A., formerly collegian at Oxford, who is the only profound scholar in England belonging to the New Church sect, ably answered him. There are many smart polemics but very few great scholars in the sect referred to. Twenty-five years ago New Jerusalem Church, in Avenham-road, was opened, and the believers in it increased for some time afterwards. Anything new is fashionable, and a new church always gives an impetus to the number of its worshipers. Those assembling at the church created much curiosity, and not a little cynical criticism, at first. They even do so now. Ordinarily orthodox people look down censoriously upon believers in "the New Jerusalem," and class them as a mysterious, visionary sect of religionists, given up to dreams, pious eccentricity, and self-righteousness. But they have, like other individuals, a reason for their belief; if it is madness there is method in it; and they are prepared to "argue the point," and make a respectable disturbance if their creed is assailed.

We shall not criticise their belief - neither praise nor condemn it - but just give its chief points for the benefit of unknowing ones. Here they are: they believe in a trinity, not of persons but essentials - love, wisdom, and power; they do not believe in the doctrine of faith alone, but of faith conjoined with good works; they do not believe in a vicarious atonement, but in a reconciliation of man to God; they don't believe in a resurrection of the material body, but a resuscitation of the spirit immediately after physical death; they don't believe in a physical destruction of the world by fire, but think that the world as it is now created will continue to exist - for ever; they have no faith in the Noachian deluge, and say that the sacred record of it refers to an inundation of evil and not of water; finally they believe that there will be marriages in heaven, - not wedding ring unions, not kissing, courting, and quarrelling amalgamations, but conjunctions of goodness with truth; and they have further an idea that there will be "prolifications" in heaven, not of crying children with passions for sucking bottles and sugar teats, but of truth and goodness. Swedenborg, by whom they swear, believed in three heavens and three hells; they have a similar idea, and fancy that common place sinners, who think one heaven will meet all their requirements, and that one hell will be too much for their nerves, arc wrong.

New Jerusalem Church, in Preston, has a Sunday school beneath it - a place obtained partly on the celestial and partly on the Irish principle - by heightening the roof and lowering the foundations. The school is pretty well managed; but its scholars are not numerous; they number between 60 and 70, and there is no immediate prospect of an increase. The endowment of the late Mr. Hugh Becconsall realises 100 pounds a-year for the minister - the Rev. E. D. Rendell, who has been at the church ever since its opening; and the investment of a sum of money by the late Mr. John Becconsall, of Ashton, who was a great believer in Swedenborgianism, brings in on his behalf 50 pounds more. The minister once had a "call" to Accrington, where the doctrines of the New Church obtain a very large number of admirers, and in consequence of that call, which necessarily implied a better salary, as well as a wider sphere of action, five 10 pounds notes were added to his stipend here. He was appeased by those said notes. Mr. Rendell also lives rent free in a house adjoining and belonging to the church. Its situation renders the house very convenient; but a position more distant would not have been very harrowing if freedom from rent had accompanied its tenancy.

The Church is built of stone, and has a neat appearance, but the approach to it is not very good. You have to mount a small flight of steps to get to it, and their gradient is so acute that if you should fall on them you would never proceed onward, nor lie still, but wend your way in a rolling manner to the bottom. Internally the church is one of the prettiest in Preston. It is not large; we don't suppose it will accommodate more than about 250; but it is peculiarly neat and pleasing. The walls are painted and slightly ornamented; the windows are toned a little and bordered with elegant, well-finished designs; the chancel is fronted with a gothic arch painted in marble pattern and edged with gold; beyond there is a circular window, stained in bright colours. At each end there is a gallery - one which apparently contains nothing, whilst the other is devoted to the choir. At one side of the chancel arch there is a reading desk, which looks piously at a pulpit, made just like it, on the opposite side. Few churches have windows in the roof; but this has about four - at least they are circular lights, and, in conjunction with the side windows, make the place very bright and cheerful. At the bass of the chancel, beneath the gallery, and behind the communion table, there are several paintings, some, if not all, of which were executed by the minister, who has rather vivid artistic conceptions. In the centre there is an open Bible, and on each side the Decalogue, or something to that effect, for the letters, although in gold, can't be seen very clearly at a distance. Flanking these are sacred figures, which are too small to be attractive at a greater distance than six yards. But in their aggregate the representations look well, and they give a good finish to the chancel. The seats are of various sizes; some will hold three persons, others four, and a few about six.

The church is not well attended; hardly half of it is occupied except upon special occasions. At present it appears to be a little better patronised than formerly; but even now the congregation is comparatively thin, and there will be no necessity for some time to do anything in the shape of enlarging the building. If anything is effected in this way during the present century one of two things will certainly have to happen - either three times as many as those now attending it will have to solicit admission, or those actually visiting it will have to grow three times as stout in their physiology. They are a quiet, pious-looking class of people who frequent the church. They may, like their great apostle, have seasons of inner rapture, and like him revel in the mysteries of the Arcana Coelestia, but if so they keep the thing very subdued. They never scream nor shout about anything, and would refuse to do so if you asked them. Many of them are elderly people, with decorous countenances; all of them, whether old or young, believe in good suits; very few of them are wealthy; none of them seem very poor. Calmness, with a disposition to find you a seat any time, and provide you with books, characterises them. They have fixed services, embracing prayers, lessons, psalms, hymns, and chants. They have an excellent organ, which was given to the place by Mrs. Becconsall; and their music is "ever so fair." Their services, on Sundays, are held in the morning and evening, and they can get to the latter much easier and in much better time than to the former.

Once a month there is an afternoon instead of an evening service, the minister having to officiate for a few of the followers of Swedenborg at Blackburn, who can't afford to pay, or won't get, or don't want, a regular expounder of their views. Mr. Rendell is a rather learnedly-solemn kind of gentleman. Originally he was a painter; but he had a greater passion for polemics than brushes, and was eventually recommended to, and admitted into "the Church" as a minister. He reads the scriptures and prays in black kid cloves, but he shows the natural colour of his hands when preaching. While conducting the preliminary service he wears a white surplice; in the pulpit he has a black gown. He looks very sacerdotal, coldly-clerical, singularly-sad in each place. His voice is deep toned and has a melancholy authoritative ring in it. He is fond of making critical allusions in his sermons; and is rather lengthy in his talk. Some of the old Puritans used to get to a "nineteenthly point" in their discourses, but Mr. Rendell has not reached that numeric climax. He can occasionally get to a fifth point, and then subdivide it, before giving that final "word of advice" which parsons are so enamoured of; but he never branches out beyond this stage. His style of preaching is easy; but it is very solemn. Occasionally he pushes a little Latin into his discourses and at intervals be graces them with morsels of Greek. He can be practical sometimes; can say a wise and generous thing at intervals; but he is often very mysterious, and has a large reverence for that which very few people can get at-"the spiritual sense." Mr. Rendell is an author as well as a preacher; he has dived into anti-diluvian history, and has tried to bring up mystic treasures from the post-diluvian period. Furthermore, he has written a prize essay on "The Last Judgment." And in addition to everything he is the editor of "The Juvenile Magazine;" but the salary is only poor. Still he may console himself with the thought that he gets as much for his annual services on behalf of modern juveniles as Milton did for his Paradise Lost on behalf of all posterity - a clear 5 pounds note. He has a sharp eye in his head, and there is an aristocratic reverentialness in his look. Learned he is in some things; but we are afraid he is too profound and sad. He has a good analytical faculty, and is a very fair polemical writer; but he is very solemn in tone - very serious, too wise-looking, and phlegmatic. His style of speaking has the ring of earnestness in it; and his delivery is accompanied with a tolerable amount of activity. If he were a little more buoyant, if he could put on a less learned and more cheerful look, and would not got so very grave in his style, he would be better relished. Polemically, he has done fair service for the denomination to which he belongs - done it sometimes in spite of Lily, and Linacre, and their descendants; and if he is not immaculate, he has at least the satisfaction of knowing that nobody else is, and never will be until they reach the real New Jerusalem.

XI

TRINITY CHURCH.

In a part of the town pre-eminently dim, intricate, and populous stands "The Church of the Holy Trinity." Father Time and the smoke of twice five hundred chimneys have darkened its fabric, and transmuted its chiselled stone walls into a dull pile of masonry. But it is a beautiful church for all that. If the exterior has been carbonised and begrimed, the interior has enjoyed a charmed life, and is apparently as young today as it was on "Friday, the eighth of December, in the year of our Lord one thousand eight hundred and fifteen," when "George H. Chester" consecrated the building and all thereunto belonging. The first stone of this church was laid on the 4th of June, 1814 - the natal anniversary of George III - by Sir Henry Philip Hoghton, of Hoghton, the lay rector and patron of the parish of Preston. Under that first stone there were deposited a number of coins, two scrolls, and one newspaper - the Preston Chronicle. The first minister of Trinity Church was the Rev. Edward Law, a gentleman, who, according to a local historian, "ably defended the belief of the adorable Trinity in a series of letters, assisted by the Rev. R. Baxter, of Stonyhurst, against a Unitarian minister, the Rev. T. C. Holland, which appeared in the Preston Chronicle," and were subsequently reprinted and sold for the enlightenment and mystification of all polemically-minded men. Trinity Church is built on a plot of ground once called Patten Field. Moderns know little, if anything, of that field; but Patten-street - a delicious thoroughfare proximately fronting the church - still remains as a lingering topographical reminder of olden days. There were few houses in the region of Patten Field when Trinity Church was built: pastures were its colleagues, and patches of greensward its regular companions. But things have changed since then, and a mile of houses, stretching northward, and westward, and eastward now fills up the ancient hiatus. Trinity Church cost 9,080 pounds 9s. 3d., and that sum was raised partly by subscriptions and donations and partly by the sale of pews. Who gave the ultimate threepence we cannot tell, neither are we told in what way it was expended.

The architecture of the building is Gothic. There is nothing very striking about the exterior; indeed it looks cold, and sad, and forsaken, and its associations don't improve it. The church is built upon a hill, and, therefore, can't be hid. Its approaches may have been good at one time; its environs may have been aristocratic and healthy in 1814, but they are not so now. Smoky workshops, old buildings, with the windows awfully smashed in, houses given up to "lodgings for travellers here," densely packed dingy cottages, and the tower of a wind mill, which for years nobody has been willing to either mend or pull down, are its architectural concomitants. The approaches to the church are varied and aggravatingly awkward. You can get to the church from any point of the compass, but access to it may mean anything - perhaps, a wandering up courts and passages, a turning round the corners of old narrow streets, an unsavoury acquaintance with the regions of trampery, and an uncomfortable perambulation along corn-torturing causeways and clumsily paved roads. Pigeon flyers, dog fanciers, gossipping vagrants, crying children, old iron, stray hens, women with a passion for sitting on door steps, men looking at nothing with their hands in their pockets, ancient rags pushed into broken windows, and the mirage of perhaps one policeman on duty constitute the sights in the neighbourhood. The church-yard, which contains several substantial tombs and monuments, is in a decent state of preservation. It looks grave as all such places must do; but it is kept in order, and men of the Hervey type of mind might meditate very beneficially amongst its tombs. Trinity may not be the longest, but it is certainly about the widest, church in the town. It is neither a high nor a low, but an absolutely broad church.

Internally it is excellent. On entering the place you are perfectly surprised at its capaciousness. Nothing cramped, nothing showy, nothing dim, grim, nor shabby-genteel enters into its proportions. It is finely expansive, airy, light, and well made. Goodness of build without gaudiness, sanctity without sadness, and evenness of finish without new-fangled intricacy, pervade it. It is fit for either beggars or plutocrats. There is not a better, not a plainer, neater, nor more respectable looking church in the town. And there is not a cleaner. Some of our churches have for years been cultivating a close and irreligious acquaintance with dirt - with dust, cobwebs, mould, and other ancient kinds of mild nastiness; but Trinity Church is a model of cleanliness. Everything in it seems clean - the windows, pews, cushions, mats, floors, &c., are all clean; there is even an air of cleanliness about the sweeping brushes and the venerable dust bin. The church has accomodation for about 1,400 persons of ordinary proportions. The seats are constructed on comfortable principles , and that very traditional article - green baize - plays an important and goodly part in them. At the top and bottom of the middle range, on the ground floor, the seats are of various shapes - some narrow, some broad, a few oblong, and others inclining to the orthodox square. The central ones are regular, and so are those at the sides. In the galleries there is a slight irregularity of shape in the seats; but they are all substantial, and the bulk easy. There are 46 free pews or benches in the church. They run along the sides on the ground floor, and will accommodate nearly 280 persons. All the other seats, excepting about two, were sold to various parties at the time the church was opened-not for any fixed price all round, but for just as much as the trustees could get. Many were bought by high-class local families, and the names of several of the original and present proprietors - inscribed on small brass plates - may now be seen on the front sides. Fifty of the pews have ground rents, amounting respectively to 1 pounds a year, attached to them. Several of the pews are let, the owners caring little for them, or having removed to other towns; many have been re-sold at intervals; and three have been forfeited through their proprietors having neglected to pay certain trifling rates laid upon them. The pews have deteriorated much in price. Once upon a time, when nearly all the fashionable families of Preston went to Trinity Church, neither Platonic love nor current coin could secure a pew. It was a la mode in its most respectable sense, it was Sabbatical ton in its genteelest form, to have and to hold a pew at Holy Trinity when George the Third was king. And for a considerable period afterwards this continued to be the case. The "exact thing" on a Sunday in Preston, 40 nay 20 years ago, was to own a pew at Trinity Church, to walk up to it, and to sit therein: it was superior to every modern process, and beat "Walking in the Zoo" and all that species of delightful work hollow. Pews were then worth something; they are now worth little. Only the other week a pew, originally bought for about 70 pounds, was sold by auction for 8 pounds! And it is said that some proprietors would not be very unwilling to give a pew or two now, if nicely asked, just to get out of the ratepaying clauses.

Trinity Church has a plain, yet pleasing, chancel. It is neat and good, simple yet well-proportioned and elegant. The chancel window is but sparingly stained; still it has a tasteful and rather stately appearance. Amber is the most prominent colour in it, and loyalty the principal virtue represented on it. There are a few small emblematic-looking characters towards the base, which few can make out; but everybody can see and understand the rather large English outburst of loyalty surmounting the window. The display consists of the Royal arms, well and broadly defined, with a crown above them, and a lion above all. This speaks well for the lion, which ought to be satisfied. Plain Gothic-bordered tablets, with a central monogram, occupy the wall below the window. They have a good effect, and give a somewhat artistic richness to the chancel. Within and at each end of the communion rails there is a fine old oak chair. Both are beautifully carved and are valuable. The reading-desk and the pulpit are placed opposite each other, and at the sides of the chancel. They are very tall, but altitude rather improves than diminishes their appearance. They are well made, are fashioned of dark oak, and have carved Gothic canopies. We have seen nothing so tall nor so respectable-looking in the arena of virtuous rostrumdom for a long period. On each side of the pulpit-desk there is a small circular hole, and those said holes have a history. "What are they used for?" said we one day, whilst in the pulpit, to a friend near us. "For?" said the sagacious party, "they are for nothing;" and then followed a history which we thus summarise for the benefit of parsons in general:- A few years ago a gentleman with a red-hot dash of Hibernian blood in his veins was the curate here. When he came, the stands of two gas lights were fixed in the holes named; but one Sunday, when wilder than usual, he gave the bottom of the right-hand stand a vehement beating, smashed his ring in the encounter, and frightened the incumbent, who, being apprehensive as to the fate of the two stands and their globes, had them shifted further back and more out of the curate's reach. They were in imminent peril every minute, and a change was really necessary.

Not many years ago - plenty of people can remember it - the congregation of Trinity Church was both large and influential. The elements of influence and the representatives of wealth may still be seen in it; but few and far between are the worshippers. Pews may be owned, seats may be taken, few sittings may be to let, but where are the worshippers? What a pity it is, that a church of proportions so goodly, an edifice with accomodation so capacious, a building with arrangements so substantial and excellent should be deserted in a manner so absolute? A screw of large dimensions is loose somewhere. The population of the district seems great - dense; many of the people round about the church stand singularly in need of entire acres of virtue, some of them are thorough-going heathens, and think heathenism a rather jolly thing at times. And yet this most excellent church is comparatively empty - desolate - reminding one painfully of Ossian's picture of Balclutha's walls. The congregation of Trinity Church is better than it was a few years ago, but it is still lamentably, small. There is often "a beggarly account of empty boxes" - a great deal of nothing in the church, and how to remedy this defect is a problem. The present congregation consists of a very moderate number of middle class people, a few elderly well-to-do individuals, a thin scattering of poor folk, and a small body of Sunday school scholars. The Recorder of Preston, who has been connected with the management of the church since the time it was opened, attends regularly when health permits: Trinity Church is, of course, in the hands of trustees, and as people of an inquiring turn of mind sometimes wonder who they are we will give their names. Here are the trustees: Mr. T. B. Addison, Mr. John Cooper, Mr. Thos. Walmsley, Mr. John Swainson, Mr. John Bickerstaffe, Mr. Thomas Houlker, and Mr. Isaac Gate. The present churchwardens are Mr. W. Fort and Mr. W. H. Smith, and they have discharged their duties - looked after the church, kept it clean, preserved its order - in thoroughly commendable style. Testimonials are due for their services.

The music at Trinity Church has for a considerable period been a troublesome, irregular, unsatisfactory thing. Years ago it was fine; there was full cathedral service in the church then; and the orchestral performances were attractive. But dullness and poorness are now their characteristics. The organ is one of the best in the town; its tones are fine and musical; it could perhaps be improved in one or two particulars; but everything in it is good as far as it goes. The tunes, however, which come from it are of a very ordinary character. Some of them may be tasteful;

but the bulk seem weak and wearisome - lack fine-flowing harmony, and can neither be joined in nor appreciated by many parties. The members of the choir are not a very lustrous class of vocalists; but they do their best, and appear to fight through the musical fog surrounding them very patiently. We believe the tunes are selected by the incumbent. If so, let us hope that he will see the propriety of recognising something a little brisker and more classical - something rather livelier and more popularly relishable. Many clergymen simply select the hymns and leave the music to the choir: the incumbent might try this plan as an experiment. Squabbling about music, carping, and fighting, and biting about it, have in the past done much harm to Trinity Church. There is more peace now than there used to be amongst the singers; but there will never be very much contentment, and never much harmony of music, until they are permitted to moderately follow the custom of other places - to swim with the tide - and have a reasonable share of their own way. Singers can, as a rule, quarrel enough among themselves when in the enjoyment of the fullest privileges; and interference with their services, if they are really worth anything, only makes them more ill-natured, angular, and combative. They are awkward people to deal with, and have strange likings for "hot water."

The minister of Trinity Church is the Rev. J. T. Brown, and his salary amounts to about 300 pounds a year. He was christened at the place; was in after years curate of it; and is now its incumbent. About two years ago, when he came to the church in the last-named capacity, the congregation was wretchedly thin - awfully scarce, and just on the borders of invisibility. It has since improved a little; but working up a forsaken place into real activity is a difficult task, which at times staggers the ablest of men. Mr. Brown is a scholar, and a thoroughly upright man. He believes not in fighting down other people's creeds; never rails against religious antagonists; has a natural dislike to platform bigotry and pulpit wrathfulness; is generously inclined; will give but not lend; objects to everything in the shape of loud clerical display; is strongly evangelical in his tastes; is exact, and calm, and orderly, even to the cut of his whiskers; won't be brought out and exhibited; doesn't care about seeing other people make exhibitions; and thinks every minister should mind his own business, and leave other people alone. But he is far too good for a parson. A gentle melancholy seems to have got hold of him. He always preaches sincerely; a quiet spirit of simple unadorned, piety pervades his remarks - but he depresses you too much; and is rather predisposed to a calm mournful consideration of the great sulphur question. He never gets into a lurid passion, never horrifies, but calmly saddens you, in his discourses. He is fond of quoting good old Richard Baxter and John Banyan, and he might have worse authorities. But he is very serious, and his words sometimes chill like a condensation of Young's "Night Thoughts." If he had more dash and blithesomeness in him, if he could fling a little more of this world's logic into his sermons, if he would periodically blow his own trumpet very audibly, and make a smart "spread" now and then, he would gather force. The best of things will sink if there be not some noise and show made about them. If Mr. Brown knew the "Holloway's Pills and Ointment" theory better than he does, he would have a fuller congregation; but he is too honest and too good for superficial emblazonry, and he believes in quietness.

Trinity Church has some excellent schools for boys, girls, and infants. The attendance is only poor; but it is better than it was. The boys' school is improving; that of the girls is also recruiting the strength it lost last Whitsuntide but one, when a number of its attendants left in a body because Mr. Brown objected to a display of orange and blue ribbons which they were senselessly enamoured of; and with respect to the infants they are regularly growing in size if not in numbers. Mrs. Brown, wife of the incumbent, not only industriously visits the district, like a genuine Christian lady as she is, but teaches in the girls school, and at intervals when at church - here is an example for parsons' wives - looks after a number of the scholars personally, whilst her own servants are quietly occupying the family pew. We could like to see both the church and the schools of Mr. Brown full; he has our best wishes in this respect; and we hope he may find some talisman by which the difficulty will be satisfactorily solved.

XII

LANCASTER-ROAD CONGREGATIONAL CHAPEL

Preston Congregationalism is a very good, a very respectable, and a very quarrelsome creature. It is liberal but gingerly; has a large regard for freedom, but will quarrel if crossed; can achieve commendable triumphs in the regions of peace, but likes a conscientious disturbance at intervals; believes in the power of union, but acts as if a split were occasionally essential; will nurse its own children well when they are quiet, but recognises the virtues of a shake if uneasiness supervenes; respects its ministers much, but will order them to move on if they fret its epidermis too acutely; can pray well, work well, fight well; and from its antagonisms can distil benefits. About nine years since, a sacred stirring of heads, a sharp moving of tongues, and a lively up-heaving of bristles took place at Cannon-street Congregational Chapel, in this town. The result of the dispute involved, amongst other things, a separation - a clear marching from the place of several parties who, whether rightly or wrongly, matters not now, felt themselves aggrieved. They did not leave the chapel in processional order, neither did they throw stones and then run, when they took their departure. The process of evaporation was quiet and orderly. For 12 months the seceders worshipped on their own account, in accordance with the principles of Congregationalism, at the Institution, Avenham, and whilst there they gathered strength. In the meantime they negotiated for land upon which to build a new chapel and schools; and finally they purchased a site on the higher side of the Orchard, contiguous to the old Vicarage - a rare piece of antique, rubbishy ruin in these days - and very near, if not actually upon, ground which once formed the garden of the famous Isaac Ambrose, who was Vicar of Preston in 1650, and afterwards ejected; with many more in the land, on account of his religious opinions. Thinking it good to harmonise with that ancient wisdom which recommends people to carry the calf before beginning with the cow, the new band of Congregationalists under notice, commenced operations on the site named by erecting a large school room in which for about a year they worshipped. In due time they got the chapel built, and for about seven years it has been open.

Its position is prominent; but its associations, like those of the generality of sacred edifices, has a special bearing upon the world we live in. Above it there is a portion of the old vicarage buildings, graced in front with various articles, the most prominent being a string of delapidated red jackets; right facing it we have the sable Smithsonian Institute, flanked with that gay and festive lion which is for ever running and never stirring; below there are classic establishments for rifle-shooting, likeness taking, and hot pea revelling; and ahead there is the police station. The chapel stands well, occupies high and commanding ground, and looks rather stately. Its exterior design is good; and if the stone of its façade had been of a better quality - had contained fewer flaws and been more closely jointed - it would have merited one of our best architectural bows. The chapel and school, and the land upon which they are erected, cost 7,000 pounds, and about 1,000 pounds of that sum remains to be paid. This is not bad. Considering the brevity of their existence and the severe times they have had to pass through, the Lancaster-road Congregationalists must have worked hard and put a very vigorous Christian screw into operation to reduce their debt so rapidly.

The inside of the chapel is plain, very neat, and quite genteel. We have seen no Congregational place of worship in this part equal to it in ease and elegance of design. It is amphi-theatrical, is galleried three quarters round, and derives the bulk of its beauty - not from ornament, not from rich artistic hues, nor rare mouldings, nor exquisite carvings, but from its quiet harmony of arrangement, its simple gracefulness of form, its close adherence in outline and detail to the laws of symmetry and proportion. The circular style prevails most in it, and how to make everything round or half-round seems to have been the supreme job of the designer. The gallery above, the seats below, the platform, the pulpit on which it stands, the chairs behind, the orchestra and its canopy, the window-heads, the surmountings of the entrance screen, the gas pendants, and scores of other things, have all a strong fondness for circularity; and the same predilection is manifested outside; the large lamps there being quite round and fixed upon circular columns. The pews in the chapel are very strong, have receding backs, and make sitting in them rather a pleasing, easy, contented affair. The highest price for a single seat is 3s. 6d. per quarter; the lowest 1s. There are a few free sittings in the place, and although they may seem a long way back - being at the rear of the gallery - their position is not to be despised. They are not so far distant as to render hearing difficult; and they obviate that unseemly publicity which is given to poor people in some places of worship. How to give the poorest and hungriest folk a very good seat in a very prominent place - how to herd them together and piously pen them up in some particular place where everybody can see them - appears to be an object in many religious edifices. But that is a piece of benevolent shabbiness which must come to grief some day. In the meantime, and until the period arrives when honest poverty will be considered no crime, and when a seat next to a poor man will be thought nothing vulgar, or contaminating, whilst worshipping before Him who cares for souls not lucre, hearts not wealth, let the poor be put in some place where they can hear fairly without being unduly exhibited. The chapel we are noticing has a spacious appearance within, and has none of that depressing dulness which makes some people very sad long before they have been ministerially operated upon. From side windows there comes a good light; and from the roof, which has a central transparency, additional clearness is obtained. The light from the ceiling would be improved if the glass it were kept a little cleaner.

The congregation is neither a very large nor a particularly small one. It is fairly medium - might be worse, and would in no way be hurt if it were enlarged. The "members" number about 120, and they are just about as good as the rest of mortals, who have "made their calling and election sure." The congregation consists almost entirely of middle and working class people. There is not so much of that high, gassy pride , that fine mezzotinto , isolated hauteur and self-righteousness in the place which may be seen in some chapels. Of course, particles of vanity, morsels of straight-lacedness, lively little bits of cantankerousness, and odd manifestations of first person pronoun worship periodically crop up; but altogether the congregation has a quiet, unassuming, friendly disposition. Nobody in it appears to be very much better or worse than yourself; there is an evenness of tone and a sociality of feeling in the spot; and a stranger can enter it without being violently stared at, and can sit down without feeling that his room is nearly if not quite as good as his company. The music is fairly congregational; individuals in various parts of the chapel have sufficient courage to sing; and the choir is moderately harmonious; but the melody one hears in the place is rather flat and meagre; it lacks instrumental relief; and it will never be really up to the mark until an organ is obtained.

The first regular minister of this chapel was the Rev. G. W. Clapham; he was connected with it for some years; then had a "difficulty" with certain parties - deacons amongst the rest, of course; and afterwards left the place, uttering, in a quiet Shaksperian tone, as he departed, "Now mark how I will undo myself:" He threw to the winds his Congregationalism, and a few months ago joined, in due clerical order, the Church of England. The present pastor of Lancaster-road Congregational Chapel is the Rev. E. Bolton. The "church" tried the merits of about 30 ministers before making a selection. The height, depth, weight, tone of voice, matter, manner, theology, brains, and spirit of that band of 30 were duly weighed, and finally, Mr. Bolton was picked out. A salary of 300 pounds was offered him. He might have got other places, and if he had followed the clerical wisdom of his generation he would have tried to secure one of them; for they all, more or less, implied a better salary than that which the Preston people offered him. But he fixed upon Preston just because he fancied more good might be done therein than elsewhere. A trick like this - a generosity so distinct as this - is a real oasis in the ecclesiastical desert. Few parsons would imitate it. How to get the biggest salary, and lug in the "will of the Lord" as an excuse for changing to some locality where it could be snugly got, is the question which many pious men seem desirous of solving. Mr. Bolton has different ideas, and finds some compensation in goodness achieved as well as in money pocketed. He has been at Lancaster-road Chapel three months, and, unlike many new parsons, he had more sense than preach his best sermons first - than make a grand pyrotechnic dash at the onset and settle down into a round of prating mediocrity afterwards. When tried he gave the people a fair average specimen of what he could do - did not say his best nor his commonest things; began with a fire which he could keep up; and the result is not disappointment, but an increasing relish.

Mr. Bolton is a plain, dark-complexioned, clear-headed man - rather clerical in look; well-built; married; about 38 years of age; fond of a billycock; teetotal, but averse to drowning other people with water; doesn't think it sinful to smoke just one pipe of tobacco after he has done a day's work; had rather visit poor than rich people; dislikes namby-pambying and making a greater fuss over high than low class members of his church; thinks that those in poverty need most looking after, and that those with good homes and decent purses should try to look a little after themselves; believes in working hard; cares precious little for deacons - we rather like that, for deacons are queer birds to encounter; is original in thought, fairly up in theology, and straightforward in language. It is rather a treat to see him preach. He does not, like the bulk of parsons, solemnly work out all his divinity in the pulpit: preaching is not a sad, up and down, air-sawing, monotonous thing with him; he steps out of the sacred box when his feelings begin to warm up, moves to one side of it, then round the back of it, and then to the other side of it; talks to you and not at you; is quite conversational in style, and ignores everything conventional and stereotyped in manner. He exercises his lungs with considerable force at times; but he never tears nor disturbs the circumambient air with religious agony. It is as pleasant to hear as to see him. Good sound sense, neatly adjusted argument, newness of thought, and clear illustration characterise his expressions. He is liberal and independent in tone; speaks easily, and if he now and then wanders a little he always returns to the question with vigour, and freshness. He has no written sermons; a few notes are sufficient for him; he does not believe in long discourses; he has an idea that it is better to say a little and let it be well understood than float into immensity, let off fireworks there, and dumfounder everybody. But he has his faults. He has quite as much confidence in himself as is requisite for the present. He is rather too impervious and too oracular; but then who would not be if they had the chance? We like him well on the whole, and as he is new amongst us, it is but right that we should deliver him with charity. Adjoining the chapel there are many class-rooms, and a fine school. Boys, girls, and infants are accommodated in them. The average Sunday attendance is about 200. We believe Mr. Bolton will add numeric strength to both the chapel and schools. And if he does, let no one make the least conceivable noise, for there is room enough for all in Preston. The town isn't a quarter as virtuous as it should be; the bulk of us are scarcely half as good as we ought to be; and if anybody can do any good in any way let it be done without a single whimper.

XIII

SAUL-STREET PRIMITIVE METHODIST CHAPEL

There is nothing very time-worn about Methodism; it is only 140 years old; but during that period its admirers have contrived to split numerous hairs, and have extended very fairly what is known as "the dissidence of dissent." The ring of Methodism includes many sections: it embraces, amongst others, ordinary Wesleyans, Bryanites, New Connectionists, Primitives, United Free Church men, and Independent Methodists. They can't all be right; but they think they are; and that is enough. They have as yet requested nobody to be responsible for them; and weighing that over well, the fairest plan is to let the creed of each alone - to condemn none, to give all legitimate chance, and permit them to "go on." Antique simplicity seems to be the virtue of those whom we have now to describe. And yet there is nothing very ancient about them. There is more in the sound than in the name of primitive Methodists. They are a comparatively young people with a somewhat venerable name. It was not until 1810 that they were formed into a society. Originally they werc connected with the Wesleyan Methodists; but they disagreed with them in the course of time, and left them eventually. The immediate cause of separation was, we are informed, a dispute as to the propriety of camp meetings, and the utility of female preaching. The Wesleyans couldn't see the wisdom of such meetings nor the fun of such preaching: probably they thought that people could get as much good as they would reasonably digest in regular chapel gatherings, and that it was quite enough to hear women talk at home without extending the business to pulpits. The Primitives believed otherwise - fancied that camp meetings would be productive of much Christian blissfulness, and thought that females had as much right to give pulpit as caudle lectures. With a chivalry nearly knightly they came to the rescue, and gave woman a free pass into the regions of language and theology. A third point of difference had reference to the representative character of Wesleyan conferences; but into that question we need not enter.

The first regular quarters of Preston Primitive Methodism were in Friargate, in a yard facing Lune-street - in a small building there, where a few men with strong lungs and earnest minds had many seasons of rejoicing. The thermometer afterwards rose; and for some time a building which they erected in Lawson-street, and which is now used as the Weavers' Institute, was occupied by them. Often did they get far up the dreamy ladder of religious joy, and many a time did they revel with a rich and deafening delightfulness in the regions of zeal there. They were determined to "keep the thing warm," and to let outsiders know that if they were not a large, they were a lively, body. Primitive Methodism does not profess to be a fine, but an earnest, thing - not a trimmed-up, lackadaisical arrangement, but a strong, sincere, simple, enthusiastic species of religion. It has largely to do with the heart and the feelings; is warm-natured, full of strong, straightforward, devotional vigour; combines homeliness of soul with intensity of imagination; links a great dash of honest turbulence with an infinitude of deep earnestness; tells a man that if he is happy he may shout, that if under a shower of grace he may fly off at a tangent and sing; makes a sinner wince awfully when under the pang of repentance, and orders him to jump right out of his skin for joy the moment he finds peace; gives him a fierce cathartic during conversion, and a rapturous cataplasm in his "reconciliation." Primitive Methodism occupies the same place in religion as the ballad does in poetry. It has an untamed, blithesome, healthy ring with it; harmonises well with the common instincts and the broad, common intuitions of common life; can't hurt a prince, and will improve a peasant; won't teach a king wrong things; is sure to infuse happiness amongst men of humbler mould. Its exuberance is necessary on account of the materials it has to deal with; its spiritual ebullitions and esctacies are required so that they may accord with, and set all a-blaze, the strong, vehement spirits who bend the knee under its aegis. Primitive Methodism has reached deeper depths than many other creeds - has touched harder, wilder, ruder souls than nearly "all the isms" put together. It may not have made much numeric progress, may not have grown big in figures nor loud in facts, but it has done good - has gone down in the diving bell of hope to the low levels of sin, and brought up to the clear rippling surface of life and light many a pearl which would have been lost without it. Primitive Methodism is just the religion for a certain class of beings just the exact article for thousands who can't see far ahead, and who wouldn't be able to make much out if they could. There are people adoring it who would be stupid , reticent , and recalcitrant under any other banner , who would "wonder what it all meant" if they were in a calmer, clearer atmosphere - who would be muddy-mottled and careless in a more classical and ambrosial arena. After this learned morsel of theorising, we shall return to the subject.

In 1836 the Primitive Methodists left their Lawson-street seminary and pitched their tent eastwards - on a piece of land facing Saul-street and flanking Lamb-street. Its situation is pretty good, and as it stands right opposite, only about eight yards from, the Baths and Washhouses, we would suggest to the Saul-street brethren the propriety of putting up some sign, or getting some inscription made in front of their chapel, to the effect that "cleanliness is next to godliness," and that both can be obtained on easy terms. The chapel is a very ordinary looking building, having a plain brick front, with sides of similar material, and a roof of Welsh slate, which would look monotonous if it were not relieved on the western side by 19 bricks and two stones, and on the eastern by four stones, one brick, and a piece of rod-iron tacked on to keep a contiguous chimney straight. The chapel has a somewhat spacious interior; and has a large gallery fixed on six rather slender iron pillars. The pews have at some time had one or more coats of light delicate green paint - the worst colour which could be chosen for endurance - put upon them, and many are now curiously black at the rear, through people leaning back against them. A glance round shows the various sombre places, and their relative darkness gives a fair clue as to the extent of their use.

At one end there is a small gallery for the choir and the organ, and in front of it the pulpit, a plain moderately-subtantial affair, is located. The organ is a very poor one. It has a tolerably good appearance; but it is a serious sinner with reference to its internal arrangements. We quietly examined it very recently, and should have gone away with a determination not to be comforted if an intimation had not been made to the effect that "the organist was organising a plan for a new organ," and that there was some probability of a better instrument being fit up before very long. The members of the choir are of a brisk, warbling turn of mind, and can push through their work blithely. The singing is thoroughly congregational - permeates the whole place, is shot out in a quick, cheerful strain, is always strong and merry, is periodically excellent, is often jolly and funny, has sometimes a sort of chorus to it, and altogether is a strong, virtuously-jocund, free and easy piece of ecstacy which the people enjoy much. It would stagger a man fond of "linked sweetness long drawn out," it might superinduce a mortal ague in one too enamoured of Handel and Mozart; but to those who regularly attend the place, who have got fairly upon the lines of Primitive action, it is a simple process of pious refreshment and exhileration.

The chapel will hold between 700 and 800 persons; if hydraulicised 1000 might be got into it; but such a number is rarely seen in the place; and the average attendance may be set down at about 600. There are about 400 members in connection with the place, and they respectively contribute 1d. per week towards the expenses. We may here remark that in Preston there are two Primitive Methodist chapels, that in Saul-street being the principal one. The "circuit" runs mainly westward, its utmost limit in that direction being Fleetwood. Formerly three ministers were stationed at Saul-street chapel; but two are now considered sufficient; and they are, as a rule, married men, the circuit being considered sufficiently large to keep parties in the "olive branch" category. In the whole circuit there are between 700 and 800 "members." The congregation of Saul-street chapel is almost entirely of a working-class character. In the front and on each side of the body of the building there are a few free seats, which are mainly used by very poor humble-looking people.

The ministers are the Rev. J. Judson, who is the superintendent, and the Rev. W. Graham. They are paid on a systematic and considerate plan. Money is given to them to accordance with the number of their family. They get so much per head - the more numerous the family and the larger the pay becomes. But it is not very extraordinary at the best of times; and if even a preacher happened to have a complete houseful of children, if his quiver were absolutely full of them, he would not be pecuniarly rich. The bulk of Primitive Methodist preachers are taken from the working classes, and the pay they receive is not more than they could earn if they kept out of the ministry altogether. They become parsons for the love of "the cause," and not for loaves and fishes. Reverting to Mr. Judson, it may be said that he is a quiet, earnest, elderly, close-shaven, clerical looking gentleman - has a well-defined, keen solemnity on his countenance, looks rather like a Catholic priest in facial and habilimental cut, is one of the old school of Primitive preachers, is devout but not luminous, good but not erudite, is slow and long-drawn in his utterances, but he can effervesce on a high key at intervals, and can occasionally "draw out" the brethren to a hot pitch of exuberance. His general style is sincere; he means well; but his words, like cold-drawn castor oil, don't go down with overmuch gusto.

The junior preacher - Mr. Graham - is more modernised in manner and matter. He is an earnest, thoughtful, plodding man, can preach a fair sermon tears a little sometimes, and can "bring down the house" in tolerably good style. Both of them are hard workers, both are doing good, and neither must be despised on account of humility of position. Primitive, like Wesleyan, preachers are changed periodically; superintendents can, under certain conditions, stay at one place for three years, but no longer; junior men have to cut their straps every two years. Since this description was first published both the ministers named have gone; the Rev. Thomas Doody having succeeded as superintendent, and the Rev. John Hall as junior. Mr. Doody is a middle-aged gentleman, is a pretty good preacher, has considerable zeal in him, and fires up more energetically than his predecessor. Mr. Hall is a young man with a rather elderly look. His style is discursive, his lucid intervals not as electrical as those of some Primitive parsons, but he is a good fellow, and if he had more physical force and more mental condensation be would "go down" better.

There are numerous collections, some fixed, and some incidental, at Saul-street, and on special occasions they can raise sums of money which would put to the blush the bulk of loftier and more "respectable" congregations. Not much time is lost by the Saul-street Primitives: every Monday evening they have preaching at the place; on Tuesday evening three or four class meetings, in which singing, praying, and talking are carried on; on Wednesday ditto; on Thursday evening the singers work up their exercises; on Friday evening there is a meeting of leaders, or committee men; on Saturday evening a band of hope meeting; and on Sundays they are throng from morning till night. Their prayer meetings are pious and gleeful affairs. Throughout the whole of such gatherings, and in fact generally when prayer is being gone on with, the steam is kept well up, and the safety valve often lifts to let off the extra pressure. Sharp shouts, breezy "Amens," tenderly-attenuated groans, deep sighs, sudden "Hallelujahs," and vivacious cries of "Just now," "Aye," "Glory," "Yes," "Praise the Lord," &c. - all well meant - characterise them. But prayer meetings are not half so stormy as they used to be; twenty or thirty years since they were tremendously boisterous; now, whilst a fair amount of ejaculatory talk is done at them, they are becoming comparatively quiet, and on Sundays only a few of the old-fashioned and more passionately devoted members make noises. Love feasts are held occasionally at Saul-street as at all other Primitive Methodist chapels. The "members" give their "experience" at these gatherings - tell with a bitter sorrow how sinful they once were, mention with a fervid minuteness the exact moment of their conversion, allude to the temptations they meet and overcome, the quantity of grace bestowed upon them, the sorrows they pass through, and the bliss they participate in. We have heard men romance most terribly at some of these love feasts; but we are not prepared to say that anybody does so at Saul-street Chapel.

Immediately adjoining the chapel there is a large and well made building, which has only been erected about two years. The lower portion of it is used for class rooms; the upper part is appropriated for Sunday school purposes. The average attendance of scholars is 350. Belonging the school there is a good library. The building cost about 1,000 pounds and is entirely free from debt. Considering everything the Saul-street

Primitives are doing a praiseworthy work; they may lack the spiciness and finish of more fashionable bodies; they may have little of that wealthiness about them which gives power and position to many; but they are a class of earnest, useful, humble souls, drawing to them from the lowly walks of life men and women who would be repelled by the processes of a more aesthetic and learned creed. We have a considerable regard for Primitive Methodism; in some respects we admire its operations; and for the good it does we are quite willing to tolerate all the erratic earnestness, musical effervescence, and prayerful boisterousness it is so enamoured of.

XIV

ST. IGNATIUS'S CATHOLIC CHURCH.

Catholicism owes much to the Jesuits; and, casuistically speaking, the Jesuits owe their existence to a broken leg. Ignatius of Loyola was their founder. He was at first a page, then a soldier, then got one of his legs broken in battle, was captured and confined as an invalid, had his immortal leg set and re-set, whiled away his time whilst it was mending in reading romances, got through all within his reach, could at last find nothing but the Lives of the Saints, had his latent religious feelings stirred during their perusal, travelled to different places afterwards, and at last established the order of Jesuits - an order which has more learning within its circle than perhaps any other section of men, which has sent out its missionaries to every clime, has been subjected to every kind of vicissitude, has been suppressed by kings and emperors, ostracised by at least one Pope, and shouted down often by excited peoples in the heated moments of revolution; but which has somehow managed to live through it all and progress. The men fighting under the standard of Ignatius have a tenacity, a mysterious irrepressibleness about them which dumfounds the orthodox and staggers the processes of ordinary calculators. In Preston we have three churches, besides an auxiliary chapel, wherein priests of the Jesuit order labour. By far the largest number of Preston Catholics are in charge of those priests, and the generality of them don't seem to suffer anything from the "tyranny" - that is the phrase some of us Protestants delight to honour - of their supervision. They can breathe, and walk about, laugh, and grow fat without any difficulty, and they are sanguine of being landed in ultimate ecstacy if they conduct themselves fairly.

In a former article we referred to one of the Catholic churches in this town - St Wilfrid's - which is looked after by Jesuit priests - on this occasion we purposely alluding to another - St. Ignatius's. The Catholics in the district of this church are very strong; they number about 6,000; are mainly of a working-class complexion; and are conveniently and compactly located for educational and religious purposes. Catholics are so numerous in the neighbourhood - are so woven and interwoven amongst the denizens of it - that it is a good and a safe plan never to begin running down the Pope in any part of it. Murphyites and patent Christians fond of immolating Rome, &c., would have a very poor chance of success in this district. The church of St. Ignatius stands in the square which bears its name. The first stone of the edifice was laid on the 27th of May, 1833: to 1858 the church was enlarged, and in the course of the re-opening services the famous Dr. Manning (now Archbishop of Westminster) preached a sermon. The building is erected in the "perpendicular English" style of architecture - literally, a very general thing, the horizontal style being yet unworkable; is railed round; and has a dim, quiet elegance about its exterior. At the southern end there is a tower, with a spire, (surmounted by a cross) above it; the total height being 120 feet, It may be information to some people when we state that the first spire attached to any place of worship in Preston, was that we now see at St. Ignatius's. Indeed, up to 1836, it was the only spire which could be found between the Ribble and the Lune. Spires have since sprang up pretty numerously in Preston; but there was a time, and not very long since either, when the line in the well known doggrel verse "High church and LOW STEEPLE" was descriptively correct. The original cost of St. Ignatius's church, with the adjoining priests' house, was about 8,000 pounds and of that sum upwards of 1,000 pounds was raised by small weekly offerings from the poor. The church has got an outside clock with three faces, and they would sustain no injury whatever if they were either washed or re-gilt. We don't think the clock would "strike" against such a thing. The enlargement of the church, which was at the chancel end, cost about 3,000 pounds, and the money was quite ready when the job was finished.

The building is cruciform in shape, and has a fine interior - is lofty, capacious, and cathedral-like. The high altar is very choice and beautiful; and the contiguous decorations are profuse and exquisite. The painting is rich and elaborate, and the most frigid soul, if blessed with even a morsel of artistic taste, would be inclined to admire it. There is a large window behind the altar, and it is a very handsome affair; but it is rather too bright - flashes and crystalises a little too strongly; and needs a deeper tone somewhere to make it properly effective. Not very far from the pulpit, which is massive, elegant, and calculated to hold the stoutest priest in the country, there are two large statues, standing on tall stone columns - opposite each other - at the sides of the nave. One of them represents St. Joseph, and the other, we believe, St. Ignatius. Not very far from this part of the building there used to be a statue of St. Patrick; but it was removed to one side, awhile since, either to make room for some other ornament, or to edify those belonging "ould Ireland" who may happen to sit near its present position. Towards the higher end, and on each side of the church, there is an opening, projecting back several yards. A gallery occupies each of these spaces, and beneath there are seats. The roof of the nave, which is finely decorated, depends upon parallel stone columns; but they are rather heavy - are massive and numerous enough to support another church, if ever one should be erected above the present edifice. The seats are of plain stained wood, and the doors are gradually disappearing. Open seats are desiderated and whenever the opportunity occurs, the doors are attacked. Some of the pews have doors to them, and so long as the present occupiers hold their sittings in them they will not, unless it is requested, be disturbed; but as soon as they leave, the doors will be quietly taken off and either sold, or judiciously split up, or quietly buried.

Adjoining the chancel there are four of those mystic places called confessionals. The other evening we were in every one of them, viewed them round from head to foot, asked a priest who was with us the meaning of everything visible, and left without noticing in any of them anything to particularly fret at. "Confession is good for the soul," we are told; and by all means let those who honestly believe in it "go the entire figure" without molestation or insult. Every morning, on week days, there is mass in the church at seven, half-past seven, and eight o'clock; every Friday evening there is benediction; and on Sundays a great business is done - at eight, nine, ten, and eleven, in the forenoon, at three in the afternoon, and at half-past six in the evening, there are masses, combined more or less with other ceremonies. The "proper services" are understood to be at eleven and half-past six. The nine and ten o'clock masses are by far the best attended; partly because they appear to be more convenient than the others, and partly because the work is cut comparatively short at them. Human nature, as a rule, can't stand a very long fire of anything, doesn't like to have even too much goodness pushed upon it for too long a time, believes in a very short and very sweet thing. It may have to pay more for it, as it has at the ten o'clock mass on a Sunday, at St. Ignatius's - for the price of seats at that time is just double what it is at any other; only the work is got through sharply, and that is something to be thankful for. School children have the best seats allotted to them at the mass just named, and the wealthiest man in the place occupying the most convenient seat in it has to beat a mild retreat and take his hat with him when they appear. The more fashionable, and solemnly-balanced Catholics attend the services at eleven and half-past six. They are made of respectable metal which will stand a good deal of calm hammering, and absorb a considerable quantity of virtuous moisture. At this, as at all other Catholic chapels, the usual aqueous and genuflecting movements are made; and they are all done very devotedly. More water, we think, is spilled at the entrance, than is necessary; and we would recommend the observance of a quiet, even, calm dip - not too long as if the hand were going into molasses, nor too fleetingly as if it had got hold of a piece of hot iron by mistake.

At ten and three on Sundays the music is sung by a number of girls, occupying one of the small galleries, wherein there is an organ which is played by a nun. The singing is sweet, and the nun gets through her work pleasantly. The Catholic soldiers stationed at Fulwood Barracks make St. Ignatius's their place of devotional resort. They attend the nine o'clock Sunday morning mass, and muster sometimes as many as 200. One of the finest sights in the church is that which the guilds of the place periodically make. On the first Sunday in every month the girls' and women's guilds, numbering about 600 members, attend one of the morning masses; on the third Sunday in each month the members of the boys' and men's guilds, numbering between 400 and 500, do like-wise. Fine order prevails amongst them; numerous captains are in command; special dresses are worn by many of the members; some of the girls are in white; all the members wear sashes, crosses, &c.; and, after entering, their bright golden-hued banners, are planted in lines at the ends of the seats, giving a rare and imposing beauty to the general scene. The church will hold about 1,000 persons; and the complete attendance on a Sunday is about 3,500. The congregation is principally made up of working-class people, and they have got a spirit of devotion and generosity within them which many a richer and more rose-watered assembly would do well to cultivate.

There are four priests at St. Ignatius's, and in addition to the duties discharged by them in the church, they have special departments of labour to look after outside it. Father J. Walker, the principal priest, superintends the female guilds, and visits the soldiers at the Barracks; Father R. Brindle attends to the male guilds; Father Boardman hangs out an educational banner, and has the management of the various schools; the fourth priest officiates as auxiliary. Wonders used to be worked in this district by the Rev. Father Cooper - an indefatigable, far-seeing, mild-moving man, in very plain clothes, who could any time get more money for religious and educational purposes than half a score of other priests. He was always planning something for the improvement of the district; was always looking after the vital end - the money; and was always bringing in substantial specimens of the current coin. He included Protestants among his supporters; people who in nine cases out of ten would give to nobody else - were always calmly tickled and trotted into a generous mood by him. St. Ignatius's district was stirred into full and active life by Father Cooper; he extended and elaborated the church; improved the schools greatly; touched with the wand of progress everything belonging the mission; and the Catholics of the neighbourhood may thank all their stars in one lot for his 15 years residence amongst them. A man like Father Cooper was bad to follow; it was no easy matter putting his shoes on and walking in them regularly through the district; but his successor - Father Walker, who has seen something of the world, has done service in the West Indies, has fought with mosquitoes, confronted black and yellow fever, preached to dark men and soldiers, and made himself moderately acquainted with the hues and habits of butterflies, centipedes, and snakes, if the museum at Stonyhurst College is anything to go by, was not the priest to be either disheartened or ignored.

Father Walker is a locomotive, wiry, fibrous man - full of energy, wide awake, - tenacious, keenly perceptive; could pass his sharp eye round you in a second and tell your age, weight, and habits; could nearly look round a corner and say how many people were in the next street; has a touch of shrewd, sudden-working humour to him; can stand a joke but won't be played with; has a strong sense of straightforwardness; is tall, dark complexioned, weird-looking, wears bushy hair, which is becoming iron grey, and uses a thin penetrating pair of spectacles. He has been at St. Ignatius's for two-and-a-half years; the decorations in the church are mainly due to him; and he has earned the respect and affection of the people. His style of preaching is clear, sonorously-sounding, and vigorous - is not rhetorically flashy, but strong, impetuous, and full of energy. The ardour of his nature makes his utterances rapid; but they are always distinct, and there is nothing extravagant or tragic in his action. He is a clear-headed, determined, sagacious man, and would be formidable, if put to it, with either his logic or fists.

Father Brindle, who has been at the church about ten years, is a quiet, mildly-flowing, gently-breathing man; has nothing vituperative or declamatory in his nature; works hard and regularly; has an easy, gentle, subdued style of preaching; but knows what common sense means, and can infuse it into his discourses. If he had a little more force he would be able to knock down sinners better. The oracle can't always be worked with tranquillity; delinquents need bruising and smashing sometimes. Father Boardman - an active, unassuming sort of gentleman - has been at the church for about a year. He is quick in the regions of education and literature; knows much about old and new books; has a lively regard for ancient classical and religions works; is perhaps better acquainted with the 26,000 volumes in Stonyhurst College library than anybody else; likes to preach on tuitional questions; has a mortal dislike of secular education. He is plodding, intelligent, up to the mark in his business, and if 50 changes were made it is quite probable no improvement would be made upon him.

Father Baron comes next. When we visited St. Ignatius's he had only been there a few weeks, and since then he has gone to some place near London. For a long time Father Baron was at Wakefield, and during his stay there he officiated as Catholic chaplain of the gaol. He was the first priest in the kingdom who made application, under the Prison Ministers Act, for permission to hold regular gaol services. In Wakefield he earned the respect of all classes; and there was general regret expressed when it became known he had to leave. Protestants as well as Catholics liked him, and, if he had stayed in Preston, the very same feeling would have been created. He is just about the most fatherly and genial man we have seen; has a venerated, rubicund, cozy look; seems like the descendant of some festive abbot or blithesome friar; makes religion agree with him - some people are never happy unless they are being tortured by it; has hit upon the golden mean - is neither too ascetical nor too jocund; is simply good and jolly; has ever so much vivacity, sprightliness, and poetic warmth in his constitution; can preach a lively, earnest, sermon; has a strong imitative faculty; is brisk in action; can tell a good tale; is fine company; would'nt hurt anybody; would step over a fly rather than kill it unkindly; and is just such a man as we should like for a confessor if we were a believer in his Church. He has been succeeded by Father Pope, who is no relative of the old gentleman at Rome, but is we believe, a nephew of the celebrated Archbishop Whately.

All the priests at St. Ignatius's avoid in their discourses that which is now-a-days very fashionable - attacking other people's creeds. A person who has regularly attended the church for twenty years, said to us the other day that he had never heard one sermon wherein a single word against other folks creeds had been uttered. The great object of the priests is to teach those who listen to them to mind their own business; and that isn't a bad thing at any time. The music at St. Ignatius's is of a high order. It is not nice and easy, but rich and vigorous - fine and fierce, comes out warm, and has with it a strong compact harmony indicative of both ability and earnestness. The conductor is energetic and efficient, wields his baton in a lively manner, but hits nobody with it. There is a very fair organ in the church, and it is pleasantly played. The blowers also do their duty commendably.

Adjoining the church there is the priests' house - a rather labrynthal, commodious place with plain, ancient furniture. Beyond, is a very excellent school for girls as well as infants of the gentler sex. It is supervised by nuns, some of whom are wonderfully clever. They are "Sisters of the Holy Child;" are most painstaking, sincere, and useful; never dream about sweethearts; devote their whole time to religion and education. All of them are well educated; two or three of them are smart. The school, which has an average attendance of 550, is in a high state of efficiency; is, in fact, one of the best to the country. The sceptical can refer to Government reports if they wish for absolute proof. Still further on there is another school, set apart for the instruction of middle class boys, and in charge of three Xavierian brothers. About 90 boys attend it, and they are well disciplined. At the rear of the school there is a fine playground for the boys - it is about the largest in Preston; and close to it we have the old graveyard of the church, which is in a tolerably fair state of order. Brothers of the Xavierian type have been in charge of the school for about nine years. The three now at it are mild, obliging, quiet-looking men.

They live in a house hard by, and do all the household work themselves, Well done, Xavierians! you will never be aggravated with the great difficulty of domestic life - servant-maidism; will never have to solve the solemn question as to when it is "Susan's Sunday out;" will never be crossed by a ribbon-wearing Jemima, nor harrowed up in absent moments by pictures of hungry "followers" fond of cold joints and pastry. In addition to looking after the school, the Xavierians in question give religious instruction at nights, and on Sundays, to the children attending St. Ignatius's school in Walker-street. The Sunday after we visited the church, about fifty whom they had been training, received their "first communion," and in addition, got a medal and their breakfast given, - two things which nobody despises as a rule, whether on the borders of religious bliss or several miles therefrom. The school in Walker-street is attended, every day, by about 400 boys and infants, and is in an improving condition. The Sunday schools are in a very flourishing state; the girls attending them numbering about 650, and the boys about 500. Taking all into account, a great educational work is being carried on in the district of St. Ignatius. The importance of secular and religious instruction is fully appreciated by the priests; they know that such instruction moulds the character, and tells its tale in after life; they are active and alive to the exigences of the hour; are on the move daily and nightly for the sake of the mind and the soul; and they, like the rest of their brethren, set many of our Protestant parsons an example of tireless industry, which it would be well for them to imitate, if they wish to maintain their own, and spread the principles they believe in.

XV

VAUXHALL-ROAD PARTICULAR BAPTIST CHAPEL.

"Don't be so particular" is a particularly popular phrase. It comes up constantly from the rough quarry of human nature - is a part of life's untamed protest against punctilliousness and mathematical virtue. Particular people are never very popular people, just because they are particular. The world isn't sufficiently ripe for niceties; it likes a lot, and pouts at eclectical squeamishness; it believes in a big, vigorous, rough-hewn medley, is choice in some of its items, but free and easy in the bulk; and it can't masticate anything too severely didactic, too purely logical, too strongly distinct, or too acutely exact. But it does not follow, etymologically, that a man is right because he is particular. He may be very good or very bad, and yet be only such because he is particularly so. Singularity, eccentricity, speciality, isolation, oddity, and hundreds of other things which might be mentioned, all involve particularity. But we do not intend, to "grammar-out" the question, nor to disengage and waste our gas in definitions. The particular enters into all sorts of things, and it has even a local habitation and a name in religion. What could be more particular than Particular Baptism? Certain followers of a man belonging the great Smith family constituted the first congregation of

English Baptists. These were of the General type. The Particular Baptists trace their origin to a coterie of men and women who had an idea that their grace was of a special type, and who met in London as far back as 1616. The doctrines of the Particular Baptists are of the Calvinistic hue. They believe in eternal election, free justification, ultimate glorification; they have a firm notion that they are a special people, known before all time; that not one of them will be lost; and they differ from the General Baptists, so far as discipline is concerned, in this - they reject "open communion," will allow no membership prior to dipping; or, - to quote the exact words of one of them, who wrote to us the other day on the subject, and who paled our ineffectual fire very considerably with his definition - "All who enter our pail must be baptised." If there is any water in the "pail" they will; if not, it will be a simple question of dryness.

The chapel used by the Particular-Baptists, in Vauxhall-road, Preston, has a curious history. It beats Plato's theory of transmigration; and is a modern edition of Ovid's Metamorphoses. The building was erected by Mr. George Smith (father of the late Alderman G. Smith, of this town), and he preached to it for a short time. Afterwards it was occupied by a section of Methodists connected with the "Round Preachers." Then it was purchased by a gentleman of the General Baptist persuasion, who let it to the late Mr. Moses Holden - a pious, astronomical person, who held forth in it for a season with characteristic force. Subsequently it was taken possession of by the Episcopalians, the Rev. Mr. Pearson, late of Tockholes, being the minister. He, along with some of his flock, was in the habit of holding prayer meetings, &c., in different parts of the town; the Vauxhall-road building being their central depot. But when the Rev. Carus Wilson was appointed Vicar of Preston an end was put to both their praying and preaching. When the Episcopalians made their exit, a section of religious people called the Fieldingites obtained the building. They drove a moderately thriving business at the place until permission was unwittingly given for a Mormon preacher to occupy the pulpit just once - a circumstance which resulted in a thorough break-up; many of the body liking neither Joe Smith nor his polygamising followers. After the Mormon fiasco and the evaporation of the Fieldingites, another denomination took it. The Particular Baptists - some people call them Gadsbyites - were at this period working the virtues of their creed in a small room towards the bottom of Cannon-street; and on hearing that Vauxhall-road Chapel was on sale, they smiled, made a bid at it, and bought it. Their first minister, after the removal, was a certain Mr. Mc.Kenzie, who stimulated the elect with many good things, and eventually died. The question as to who should be his successor next presented itself; "supplies" were tried; various men from various parts were invited into the pulpit, looked at, and listened to; the object being to get "the right man in the right place."

There was considerable difference of opinion as to that said "right man;" one portion of "the church" wanting a smart, well-starched, polished individual, and the other desiring a plain, straightforward "gospel preacher" - a man of the Gadsby kidney, capable of hitting people hard, and telling the truth without any fear. This was in 1848, and about this time a plain, homely, broad-hearted "Lancashire chap," named Thomas Haworth, a block printer by trade, and living inthe neighbourhood of Accrington, who had taken to preaching in his spare time, was "invited" to supply the Vauxhall-road pulpit. "Tommy" - that's his recognized name, and he'll not be offended at us for using it - came, saw, and conquered. He made his appearance in a plain coat, a plain waistcoat, and a pair of plain blue-coloured corduroy trousers; and as he went up the steps of the pulpit, people not only wondered where he came from, but who his tailor was. And if they had seen his hat, they would have been solicitous as to its manufacturer. The more elaborate portion of the "church" pulled uncongenial features at the young block-printer's appearance, thought him too rough, too unreclaimed, too outspoken, and too vehement; the plain people, the humble, hard-working, unfashionable folk liked him, and said he was "just the man" for them. Time kept moving, Tommy was asked to officiate in the pulpit for 52 Sundays; he consented; kept up his fire well and in a good Gadsbyfied style; and when settling day came a majority of the members decided that he should remain with them. The "non-contents" moved off, said that it would not do; was too much of a good thing; escaped to Zoar; and, in the course of this retreat, somebody took - what! - not the pulpit, nor its Bible, nor the hymn books, nor the collecting boxes, nor the unpaid bills belonging the chapel, but - the title deeds of the old place! and to this day they have not been returned. This was indeed a sharp thing. How Shylock - how the old Jew with his inexorable pound of flesh-worship, creeps up in every section of human society! Vauxhall-road Chapel, which has passed through more denominational agony than any twenty modern places of worship put together, is situated in a poor locality - in a district where pure air, and less drink, and more of "the Christ that is to be," as Tennyson would say, are needed than the majority of places in the town.

Architecturally the chapel is nothing; and if it were not for a few tall front rails, painted green, a good gable end pointed up, and a fairly cut inscription thereon, it would, ecclesiastically speaking, seem less than nothing. It has just been re-painted internally, and necessarily looks somewhat smart on that account; but there is no pretension to architecture in the general building. Between 500 and 600 persons might be accomodation in it; but the average attendance is below 200. People are not "particular" about what church or chapel they belong to in its locality; and some of them who belong to no place seem most wickedly comfortable. There is a great deal of heathenish contentment in Vauxhall-road district, and how to make the people living there feel properly miserable until they get into a Christian groove of thought is a mystery which we leave for the solution of parsons. The interior of Vauxhall-road Particular Baptist Chapel is specially plain and quiet looking, has nothing ornamental in it and at present having been newly cleaned, it smells more of paint than of anything else. The pews are of various dimensions - some long, some square, all high - and, whilst grained without, they are all green within. This is not intended as a reflection upon the occupants, but is done as a simple matter of taste. The "members" of the chapel at present are neither increasing nor decreasing - are stationary; and they wilt number altogether between 50 and 60. Either the chapel is too near the street, or the street too near the chapel, or the children in the neighbourhood too numerous and noisy; for on Sundays, mainly during the latter part of the day, there is an incessant, half-shouting, half-singing din, from troops of youngsters adjoining, who play all sorts of chorusing games, which must seriously annoy the worshippers.

The music at the chapel is strong, lively, and congregational. Sometimes there is more cry than wool in it; but taken altogether, and considering the place, it is creditable. There is neither an organ, nor a fiddle, nor a musical instrument of any sort that we have been able to notice, in the place. All is done directly and without equivocation from the mouth. The members of the choir sit downstairs, in a square place fronting the pulpit; the young men - in their quiet moments - looking very pleasantly at the young women, the older members maintaining a mild equillibrium at the same time, and all going off stiffly when singing periods arrive. The hymn books used contain, principally, pieces selected by the celebrated William Gadsby, and nobody in the chapel need ever be harassed for either length or variety of spiritual verse. They have above 1,100 hymns to choose from, and in length these hymns range from three to twenty-three verses. Whilst inspecting one of the books recently we came to a hymn of thirteen verses , and thought that wasn't so bad - was partly long enough for anybody; but we grew suddenly pale on directly afterwards finding one nearly twice the size - one with twenty-three mortal verses in it. It is to be hoped the choir and the congregation will never he called upon to sing right through any hymn extending to that disheartening and elastic length. We have heard a chapel choir sing a hymn of twelve verses, and felt ready for a stimulant afterwards to revive our exhausted energies; if twenty-three verses had to be fought through at one standing, in our hearing, we should smile with a musical ghastliness and perish.

At the back of the chapel there is a Sunday-school. It was built in 1849. The number of scholars "on the books" is 120, and the average attendance will be about 90. In connection with the school there is a nice little library, and if the children read the books in it, and legitimately digest their contents, they will be brighter than some of their parents. There are two Sunday services at the chapel - one in the morning, and the other in the evening. No religious meetings are held in it during weekdays; the minister couldn't stand them; he is getting old and rotund; and, constitutionally, finds it quite hard enough to preach on Sundays. "He would be killed," said one of the deacons to us the other day, in a very earnest and sympathetic manner, "if he had to preach on week days - he's so stout, you know, and weighs so heavy." We hardly think he would be killed by it. Standing in a narrow pulpit for a length of time must necessarily be fatiguing to him; but why can't things be made easy? If a high seat-a tall, broad, easy, elastic-bottomed chair - were procured and fixed in the pulpit, he could sit and preach comfortably; or a swing might be procured for him. Such a contrivance would save his feet, check his perspiration, and console his dorsal vertebra. We suggest the propriety of securing a chair or a swing. It would be grand preaching and swinging.

The congregation at Vauxhall-road Chapel is pre-eminently of a working-class character. Nearly the whole of the pew holders are factory people; not above six or seven of them find employment outside of mills. They are a plain, honest, enthusiastic, home-spun class of folk. A few there may be amongst the lot who are authoritative, or saucy, or ill-naturedly solemn; but the generality are simple-dealing, quaintly-exhuberant, oddly-straightforward, and primitively-pious people - distinctly sincere, periodically eccentric, and fond of a good religious outburst, a shining spiritual fandango now, and then.

As we have before intimated the minister of the Chapel is Mr. Thomas Haworth. During the first 18 years of his ministry he received 20s. a week for his services; for three years afterwards he got 25s.; during the last two he has had 30s. per week; and his temporal consolation is involved in a sovereign and a half at present. Be is 54 years of age, has had very little education, believes in telling the truth as far as he knows it, and cares for nobody. He has a strongly intuitive mind; is full of human nature; is broad-faced, very fat and thoroughly English in look: has a chin which is neither of the nutmeg nor the cucumber order, but simply double; weighs heavier than any other parson in Preston; couldn't run; gets out of breath and pants when he goes up the pulpit stairs; has his own ideas, and likes sticking to them, about everything; has neither cunning nor deception in him; is rough but honest; is without polish but full of common sense; would have been a good companion for Tim Bobbin in his better moments, and for Sam Slick in his unctuous periods; cares more for thoughts than grammar; likes to rush out in a buster when the spell is upon him; can either shout you into fits or whisper you to sleep - is, in a word, a virtuous and venerable "caution." He is the right kind of man for humble, queer-thinking; determined, sincerely-singular Christians; is just the sort of person you should hear when the "blues" are on you; has much pathos, much fire, much uncurbed virtue in him; is a sort of theological Bailey's Dictionary - rough, ready, outspoken, unconventional, and funny; is a second Gadsby in oddness, and force, and sincerity, but lacks Gadsby's learning. Unlike the bulk of parsons, Mr. Haworth does his own marketing. You may see him almost any Saturday in the market, with a huge orthodox basket in his hand - a basket bulky, and made not for show, but for holding things.

He has no pride in him, and thinks that a man shouldn't be ashamed of buying what he has to eat, and needn't blush if he has to carry home what he wants to digest. His sermons in both manner and matter are essentially Haworthian. There is no gilt, no mock modesty in his stylc; there is to vapid sentimentalism in the ideas he expounds. A broad, unshaven, every-day Lancashire vigour pervades both; and what he can't make out he guesses at. In the pulpit he seems earnest but uneasy - honest, but fidgetty about his eyes, and legs. Watch him: he preaches extemporaneously, but often peers up and winks, and often looks down at his bible and squeezes his eyes. He has a great predilection for turning to the left - that he apparently thinks is the right side for small appeals of a special character; and when he gets back again, for the purpose of either looking at his book or sending out a new idea, he makes a short oscillating waddle - a sharp, whimsical, wavy motion, as if he either wanted to get his feet out of something or stir forward about half an inch. He pitches his hands about with considerable activity, and often flings himself suddenly into a white-heat, tantrum of virtue, and the brethren like him when be does this. He is original when stormy; is refreshing when his temper is up. His style is natural - is a reflection of himself - is warm with life, is odd, and at times fierce through the power of his sincerity. His illustrations are all homely; his theories most original; his expressions most honest and quaint. He has a fondness for the Old Testament - likes to get into the company of Isaiah, Jeremiah, &c.; sometimes touches the hem of Habakkuk's garment; and nods at a distance occasionally at Joel and the other minor prophets. We should like to see a Biblical Commentary from his pen; it, would be immortal on account of its straightforwardnsss and oddity. Adam Clarke and Matthew Henry must sometimes turn over in their graves when he expounds the more mysterious passages of sacred writ. To no one does Mr. Haworth hold the candle; he is candid to all, and pitches into the entire confraternity of his hearers sometimes. He said one Sunday "None of you are ower much to be trusted - none of us are ower good, are we? A, bless ya, I sometimes think if I were to lay my head on a deacon's breast - one of our own lot - may be there would be a nettle in't or summut at sooart." He is partial to long "Oh's," and "Ah's" and solemn breathings; and sometimes tells you more by a look or a subdued, calmly-moulded groan than by dozens of sentences. He spices his sermons considerably with the Lancashire dialect; isn't at all nice about aspirates, inflection, or pronunciation; thinks that if you have got hold of a good thing the best plan is to out with it, and to out with it any way, rough or smooth, so that it is understood. He never stood at philological trifles in his life, and never will do. Those who listen to him regularly think nothing of his singularities of gesture and expression; but strangers are bothered with him. Occasionally the ordinary worshippers look in different directions and smile rather slyly when he is budding and blossoming in his own peculiar style; but they never make much ado about the business, and swallow all that comes very quietly and good-naturedly. Strangers prick their ears directly, and would laugh right out sometimes if they durst. There are not many collections at the chapel, but those which are made are out of the ordinary run. Two were made on the Sunday we were there, and they realised what? - not 5 pounds, nor 10 pounds, nor 12 pounds, as is the custom at some of our fashionable places of worship, - no, they just brought in 63 pounds 3s. 9d. At the request of the minister, who announced the sum, the congregation set to and sung over it for a short time.

Simplicity and liberality, mingled with much earnestness and a fair amount of self-righteousness, are the leading traits of the "elect" at Vauxhall-road chapel; whilst their minister is a curious compilation of eccentricity, sagacity, waddlement, winking, straightforwardness, and thorough honesty.

XVI

CHRIST CHURCH.

About 33 years since there was a conquest somewhat Norman in Preston and the neighbourhood; and the "William" of it was an industrious ex-joiner. In 1836, and during the next two years, four churches - three in Preston and one in Ashton - were erected through the exertions of the Rev. Carus Wilson, who was vicar here at that time; each of them was built in the Norman style; and the general of them was a plodding man who had burst through the bonds of joinerdom and winged his way into the purer and more lucrative atmosphere of architectural constructiveness. One of the sacred edifices whose form passed through his alembic was Christ Church and to this complexion of a building we have now come. There is so much and so little to be said about Christ Church that we neither know where to begin nor how to end. Nobody has yet said that Christ Church, architecturally, is a very nice place; and we are not going to say so. It is a piece of calm sanctity in-buckram, is a stout mass of undiluted lime stone, has been made ornate with pepper castors, looks sweetly-clean after a summer shower, is devoid of a steeple, will never be blown over, couldn't be lifted in one piece, and will nearly stand forever. It is as strong as a fortress; has walls thick enough for a castle; is severely plain but full of weft; has no sympathy with elaboration, and is a standing protest against masonic gingerbread. It rests on the northern side of Fishergate-hill; between Bow-lane and Jordan-street, is surrounded with houses, has two entrances with gateposts which might, owing to their solidity, have descended lineally from the pillars of Hercules; is entirely out of sight on the eastern side; and from the other points of the compass can be seen better a mile off with a magnifying glass than 20 yards off without one. There is something venerable and monastic, something substantial and coldly powerful about the front; but the general building lacks beauty of outline and gracefulness of detail. Christ Church is the only place of worship in Preston built of limestone; and if it has not the prettiest, it has the cleanest exterior. There is no "matter in its wrong place" (Palmerston's definition of dirt) about it. If you had to run your hand all round the building - climbing the rails at the end to do so - you might get scratched, but wouldn't get dirtied. The foundation stone of Christ Church was laid in 1836, and in the following year the place was opened. Adjoining the church there is a graveyard, which is kept in excellent condition. Some burial grounds are graced with old hats, broken pots, ancient cans, and dead cats; but this has no such ornaments; it is clean and neat, properly levelled, nicely green-swarded, and well-cared for. The first person interred in the ground was the wife of the first incumbent - the Rev. T. Clark. Outside and in front of the building there is a large blue-featured clock with a cast-iron inside. It was fixed in 1857, and there was considerable newspaper discussion at the time as to what it would do. Time has proved how well it can keep time. It is looked after by a gentleman learned in the deep mysteries of horology, who won't allow its fingers to get wrong one single second, who used to make his own solar calculations in his own observatory, on the other side of Jordan (street), who gets his time now from Greenwich, who has drilled the clock into a groove of action the most perfect, and who would have just cause to find fault with the sun if antagonising with its indications. He his thoroughly master of the clock, and could almost make it stop or go by simply shouting or putting up his finger at it. It is a good clock, however blue it may look; it has gone well constantly; and, if we may credit the words of one of the clock manager's sanguine brethren, "is likely to do so." At the entrance doors there are two curious pieces of wood exactly like spout heads. Some people say they are for money; but we hardly think so, for during our visits to the church we have seen no one go too near them with their hands.

The interior of Christ Church is plain, and rather heavy-looking. But it is very clean and orderly. The chancel of the building is circular, tastefully painted, with a calm subdued light, and looks rich. The ceiling of the church is lofty, and very woody - is crossed by four or five unpoetical-looking beams which deprive the building of that airiness and capaciousness it would otherwise possess. Contiguous to the chancel there is a galleried transept; a large gallery also runs along the sides and at the front end of the general building. The seats below are substantial and high; very small people when they sit down in them go right out of sight - if you are sitting behind you can't see them at all; people less diminutive show their occiput moderately; ordinarily-sized folk keep their heads and a portion of their shoulders just fairly in sight. About 560 people can be accommodated below and 440 in the galleries. There are several free sittings in front of the pulpit - good seats for hearing, but rather too conspicuous; just within each entrance on the ground floor there are more free sittings; and all the pews in the galleries except the two bottom rows - let at a low figure - are, we believe, also free. Altogether there are about 400 seats free and tolerably easy in the building. There are many pretty stained glass memorial windows in the church; indeed, if it were not for these the building would have a very cold and unpleasantly Normanised look. They tone down its severity of style, and cast gently into it a mellowed light akin to that of the "dim religious" order. They are narrow, circular-headed; and occupy the front, the sides, the transept, and the chancel. All the lower windows in the building, except two or three, are filled in with stained glass. The windows were put in by the following parties:- Four by Mr. Edward Gorst (afterwards Lowndes), one in memory of his wife and two children, another in memory of Mr. Septimus Gorst, his wife and only child, and two in commemoration of the 20 years services of the late Rev T. Clark at the church; five by the late Mr. J. Bairstow - two of them being in memory of his sisters, Miss Bairstow and Mrs. Levy; two in memory of the late Mr. J. Horrocks, sen., and Mrs. Horrocks his wife, by their children; one in memory of the late Mr. John Horrocks, jun., by his widow and two sisters; one to the memory of Mr. Lowndes by his son; two by the late Mrs. Clark, one, we believe, being in memory of her mother, whilst the other does not appear to have any personal reference; one by the Rev. Raywood Firth, the present incumbent, in memory of Miss Buck, who remembered him kindly in her will; and one by the Rev. Mr. Firth and his wife, which was put up when the Rev. T. Clark relinquished the incumbency, and gave way for his son-in-law. This "in memoriam" act was done out of affection and not because the incumbency was changing hands. The pulpit in the Church is tall and somewhat handsome. It occupies a central position, in front of the chancel, and is flanked by two reading desks, one being used for prayers and the other for lessons. There is no clerk at this church; and there were never but two connected with the place; one being the late Mr. Stephen Wilson, of the firm of Wilson and Lawson; and the other the late Mr. John Brewer, of the firm of Bannister and Brewer of this town. The responses are now said by the choir; and everything appertaining to the serious problems of surplice and gown arranging, pulpit door opening and shutting, is solved by black rod in waiting - the beadle.

The first incumbent of Christ Church was the Rev. T. Clark - a kindly-exact, sincere, quiet-moving gentleman, who did much good in his district, visited poor people regularly, wasn't afraid of going down on his knees in their houses, gave away much of that which parsons and other sinners generally like to keep - money, and was greatly respected. We shall always remember him - remember him for his quaint, virtuous preciseness, his humble, kindly plodding ways, his love of writing with quill pens and spelling words in the old-fashioned style, his generosity and mild, maidenly fidgetiness, his veneration for everything evangelical, his dislike of having e put after his name, and his courteous, accomplished, affable manners. For 27 years - having previously been curate at the Parish Church in this town - Mr. Clark was incumbent of Christ Church.

He was succeeded by his son-in-law, the Rev. Raywood Firth, who has worked through Longfellow's excelsior gamut rapidly and successfully. The father of Mr. Firth was a Wesleyan Methedist minister, and, singular to say, was at one time - in some Yorkshire circuit we believe - the superintendent of a gentlemen who is now, and has been for some years, the incumbent of a Preston church. A few years ago Mr. Firth visited Preston as secretary of a society in connection with the Church of England; then got married to the daughter of the Rev. T. Clark; subsequently became curate of that gentlemen's church; and in 1864 was made its incumbent. Well done! The ascent is good. We like the transition. Mr. Firth is a minute, russet-featured gentleman; is precise in dress, neat in taste; gets over the ground quietly and quickly; has a full, clear, dark eye; has a youthful clerical countenance; has given way a little to facial sadness; is sharp and serious; has a healthy biliary duct, and has carried dark hair on his head ever since we knew him; is clear-sighted, shy unless spoken to, and cautious; is free and generous in expression if trotted out a little; is no bigot; dislikes fierce judgments and creed-reviling; likes visiting folk who are well off; wouldn't object to tea, crumpet, and conversation with the better end of his flock any day; visits fairly in his district, and says many a good word to folk in poverty, but would look at a floor before going down upon it like his predecessor; thinks that flags and boards should be either very clean or carpeted before good trousers touch them; minds his own business; is moderately benevolent, but doesn't phlebotomise himself too painfully; never sets his district on fire with either phrensied lectures or polemical tomahawking; takes things easily and respectably; believes in his own views rather strongly at times; loves putting the sacred kibosh upon things occasionally; is well educated, can think out his own divinity; need never buy sermons; has a clear, quiet-working, fairly-developed brain; is inclined to thoughtfulness and taciturnity; might advantageously mix up with the poor of his district a little more; needn't care over much for the nods of rich folk, or the green tea and toast of antique Spinsters; might be a little heartier, and less reserved; is a sincere man; believes in what he teaches; and is thoroughly evangelical; is more enlightened than three-fourths of our Preston Church of England parsons, and doesn't brag over his ability. His salary is about 400 pounds a year, and that is a sum which the generality of people would not object to. He is a good reader, is clear and energetic, but shakes his head a little too much. In the pulpit he never gets either fast asleep or hysterical. He can preach good original sermons - carefully worked out, well-balanced, neatly arranged; and he can give birth to some which are rather dull and mediocre. His action is easy, yet earnest - his style quiet yet dignified; his matter often scholarly, and never stolen. He is not a, "gatherer and disposer of other men's stuff," like some clerical greengrocers: what he says is his own, and he sticks to it.

There are two full services, morning and evening, and prayers in an afternoon, on Sundays, at the church; and on a Tuesday evening there is another service, - attended only slenderly, and patronised principally, we are afraid, by elderly females, whose sands have run down, and who couldn't do much harm now if they were very solicitous on the subject. The attendance on Sundays is pretty large - particularly in a morning. The adult congregation used to be very select and high in the instep - was a kind of second edition of St. George's, in three volumes. It is still numerous, but not so choice; still proud but not so well bred; still stiff, serene, lofty-minded, and elanish, but not so wealthy as is formerly was. The superior members of the congregation, as a rule, gravitate downwards, have seats on the ground floor, - it is vulgar to sit in the galleries. They are all excellently attired; the "latest thing" may be seen in hair, and bonnets, and dresses; the best of coats and the cleanest of waistcoats are also observable. A cold tone of gentle-blooded, high-middle-class respectability prevails. Much special adhesiveness exists amongst them. Small charmed circles, little isolated coteries, fond of exclusive devotional dealing, and "keeping themselves to themselves," are rather numerous. Many good and some very inquisitive and gossipy people attend - individuals who know all your concerns, can tell how many glasses you had last week and where you had them at, and like to make quiet hints on the subject to others. The congregation is substantial in look, and possesses many excellent qualities; but there is a great amount of what Dr. Johnson would call "immiscibility" in it. Nearly every part of it has a very strong notion that it is better than any other part. As in the grocer's shop pictured by one of our best wits, so is it here - the tenpenny nail looks upon the tin tack and calmly snubs it; the long sixes eye the farthing dips and say they are poor lights; the bigger articles seem cross and potent in the face of the smaller; the little look big in the face of the less; and the infinitessimal clap their wings when they make a comparison with nothing. The congregation at Christ Church won't mix itself up; is fond of "distance"; says, in a genteely pious tone, "keep off"; can't be approached beyond a certain point; isn't sociable; won't stand any hand-shaking except is its own peculiar circles. We know a person who has gone for above 20 years to one of our Methodist chapels, and yet nobody has ever said, on either entering or leaving the place, "How are you?" The very same thing would have happened if that same person had gone to Christ Church, unless there had been some connection with a special circle. In all our churches and chapels there is sadly too much of this rigid isolation, this frigid "Don't know you" business. Clanishness and cleanliness occupy front ranks at Christ Church, and if the Scotch tartans were worn in it, the theory of distinction would be consummated. We would advise Mr. Firth to write northward - beyond the Firth of Forth (oh!) - for samples of plaids. The congregation on the whole is pretty liberal; can subscribe fair sums of money; but the collections are not now what they once were; the main reason being that there is not the same wealth in the place as there used to be.

The music at Christ Church was, until lately, very good; it now seems to be degenerating a little. There is a splendid organ in the building. It cost about 1,000 pounds, and, with the exception of that at St. George's, is about the best in the town. The late Mr. J. Horrocks, jun., contributed handsomely towards the organ; played it gratuitously; gave liberally towards the choir expenses; and Christ Church is under a lasting debt of gratitude to him for his excellent services. The organ is blown by two small engines, driven by water; so that its music literally resolves itself into a question of wind and water. The tones of the instrument are good, and they are very fairly brought out by the present organist. The services are well got through, and whilst Puritanism is on the one hand avoided in them, Ritualism is on the other distinctly discarded. A medium course, which is the best, is observed in the church, and so long as Mr. Firth remains at the place there will be nothing bedizened or foolish in its ceremonies. A small memorial place of worship, which will operate as a "chapel of ease" for Christ Church, has been built in Bird-street. Belonging to Christ Church there are some good day and Sunday schools. They are numerously attended, and well supervised. Adults have a room to themselves on a Sunday, and they go through the processes of instruction patiently, benignly, and without thrashing. At one time there was a school connected with the church in Wellfield-road; but when St. Mark's was erected the building and the scholars were transferred to its care. Viewing everything right round, it may be said that Christ Church is a good substantial building, but is rather too plain and weighs too much for its size; that its minister is a mildly-toned, well-educated, devout gentleman, with no cant in him, with a tender bias to the side of gentility, and born to be luckier than three-fourths of the sons of Wesleyan parsons; that its congregation is influential, rose-coloured, good-looking, numerous, thinks that everybody is not composed exactly of the same materials, believes that familiarity is a flower which must be cautiously cultivated; that its religious and educational operations are extensive; and that if all who are influenced by them would only carry out what they are taught - none of us do this over well - they would be models from which plaster casts might be taken either for artistic purposes or the edification of heathens generally.

XVII

WESLEY AND MOOR PARK METHODIST CHAPELS

These two places of worship must constitute one dose. They are in the same circuit, are looked after by the same ministers, and if we gave a separate description of each we should only be guilty of that unpleasant "iteration" which Shakspere names so forcibly in one of his plays. Wesley Chapel is the older of the two, and, therefore, must be first mentioned. It is situated in North-road, at the corner of Upper Walker-street, and we dare say that those who christened it thought they were doing a very hand-some thing - charming the building with a name, and graciously currying favour with the Wesley family. People have a particular liking for whoever or whatever may be called after them, and good old John may sometimes look down approvingly upon the place and tell Charles that he likes it. The chapel, which was built in 1838, enjoys the usual society of all pious buildings: it has two public houses and a beershop within thirty yards of its entrance, and they often seem to be doing a brisker business than it can drive, except during portions of the Sunday when they are shut up, and, consequently, have not a fair chance of competing with it. The chapel is square in form, has more brick than stone in its composition, and has a pretty respectable front, approached by steps, and duly guarded by iron railings. Neither inside nor outside the building is there anything architecturally fine. A decent mediocrity generally pervades it. The entrances are narrow, and there is often a good deal of pushing and patient squeezing at the neck of them. But nobody is ever hurt, and not much bad temper is manifested when even the collateral pew doors mix themselves up with the crowd, and prevent people from getting in or out too suddenly. The chapel, although simple in style, is clean, lofty, and light. A gallery of the horse shoe pattern runs round the greater portion of it. Thin iron pillars support the gallery and the "chancel" end, which is arched and recessed for orchestral accomodation, is flanked by fluted imitation columns.

There is accomodation in the place for between 800 and 900 persons; but it is not often that all the seats are filled. The average attendance will be about 800; and nearly every one making up that number belongs to the working-class section of life. Amongst the body are many genial good-hearted folk-people who believe is doing right without telling everybody about it, in obliging you without pulling a face over it; and there are also individuals in the rank and file of worshippers who are very Pecksniffian and dismal, cranky, windy, authoritative, who would look sour if eating sugar, would call a "church meeting" if you wore a lively suit of clothes, and would tell you that they were entitled to more grace than anybody else, and had got more. The better washed and more respectably dressed portion of the congregation sit at the back of the central range of seats on the ground floor, also along portions of the sides, and in front of the gallery. Towards the front of the central seats there is a confraternity of humble earnest-looking beings, including several aged persons, who are true types in form, manner, and dress, of unsophisticated Methodists. Here, as elsewhere, there are very few people in the chapel ten minutes "before the train starts." Those present at that time are mainly middle-aged, unpretentious, and very seriously inclined; others of a higher type follow; and then comes the rush, which lasts for about five minutes. Worship is conducted in the chapel with considerable quietness. You may hear the long-drawn gelatinous sigh, the subdued, quiet, unctuous "amen," and if the thing gets hot a few lively half-innate exclamations are thrown into the proceedings. But there is nothing in any of them of a turbulent or riotous character. The parsons can draw out none of the worshippers into a very ungovernable frame of mind; and we believe none of the people have for some time been very violent in either their verbal expressions or physical contortions. They are beginning to take things quietly, and to work inwardly during periods of bliss. There are about 400 "members" in connection with Wesley Chapel, and we hope they are nearly half as good as such like people usually profess to be. The rule in life is for people to be about one-third as virtuous as they say they are; and if they can be got a trifle beyond that point by any legitimate process, it is something to be thankful for.

There is a very fair organ at Wesley Chapel, and the person who plays it does the requisite manipulative business with good ordinary skill. The choir is a sort of family compact; the members of one household preponderate in it; but its arrangements are well worked, and the music, taking everything into account, is pretty fair. It is far from being classical; but it will do. The singing in the galleries and below is full, if not very sweet; is spirited and generously expressed if not so melodious. Quite the old style of vocalising prevails in some quarters of the place, and it is mainly patronised by old people; they swing backwards and forwards gently and they sing, get into all kinds of keys, experimentally, put their hands on the pew sides or fronts, beating time with the music as the business proceeds, and like singing hymn ends over again. There is a school beneath the chapel. On week-days its average attendance is about 115; and on Sundays 450.

We must now for a moment pass on to Moor Park Chapel. This is a new, and somewhat genteel-looking building - has a rather "taking" outside, and is inclined to be smart within. It was opened on the 26th of June, 1862. A style of architecture closely resembling that of Lancaster-road Congregational Chapel has been followed in its construction. There is much circular work in its ornamental details; its general arrangements are neat, and well finished; nothing cold or sulkily Puritanical presents itself; a degree of even taste and polish has been observed in its make. This is a more "respectable" chapel than its companion at the top of Walker-street; its patrons are supposed to be a somewhat richer class. It will accommodate about 900 people; but, as at Wesley Chapel, so here - there are more sittings than sitters. "It has been known to hold 1,300, on an excursion," said a quiet-minded young man to us when we were at the chapel; but we didn't understand the young man, couldn't fathom his "excursion" sentiments, and afterwards threw ourselves into the arms of one of the ministers for numeric protection. There is a good gallery in the building, and the pillars which support it prop up a sort of arched canopy, like an oblong umbrella, which is too low, too near the head, and must consequently both confine the air, and develope sweating when the place is filled. There is a neat pulpit in the chapel, and it is ornamented with what seem to be panels of opaque glass. We were rather distressed on first seeing them, being apprehensive that one of the preachers might, some very fine Sunday, when in a mood more rapturous than usual, send the points of his shoes right through them; but our mind was eased when an explanation was made to the effect: that the "glass" was ornamental zinc, and that the feet of the preachers couldn't get near it. Behind the pulpit there is a circular niche for the members of the choir, who, aided and abetted in musical matters by a pretty good harmonium, acquit themselves respectably.

The congregation, as hinted, is more "fashionable" than that at Wesley Chapel: it is more select, has more pride in it, sighs more gently, moans less audibly, turns up its eyes more delicately, hardly ever gets into a "religious spree," and is inclined to think that piety should be genteel as well as vital. The members here number 280. Immediately adjoining the chapel there is good school accomodation; and the attendance appears to be very creditable. On week days the average is two hundred; and on Sundays it reaches about four hundred. At both Wesley and Moor Park Chapels there are week-night services and class meetings. The former are rather dull and badly attended; and a special effort on the part of both those who talk and those who listen is required to get up the proceedings into a state of pleasant activity ; the latter are fairly managed, and are somewhat like "experiences meetings;" talking, singing, and praying are done at them; there is a constant fluctuation , whilst they are going on, between bliss and contrition; and you are sometimes puzzled to find out - taking the sounds made as a criterion - whether the attendants are preparing to fight, or fling themselves into a fit of crying, or hug and pet each other.

The circuit embraces the two chapels named, also Kirkham, Freckleton, Bamber Bridge, Longridge, Moon's Mill, Wrea Green, and Ashton; it has now about 795 members; and all of them, with the exception of 115, as figures previously given show, are in Preston. The circuit, so far as members go, is slightly decreasing in power; but it may recruit its forces by and bye; There has been a species of duality in it during the past three years; its energies have been a little divided; faction has reigned in it; there have been too many Raynerites and Adamites and sadly too few Christians in it; pious snarling and godly backbiting have been too industriously exercised; and one consequence has been weakened power and a declension of progress. But the brethren are getting more cheerful, much old spleen has subsided, and, we hope, they will all kiss and get kind again soon.

When this sketch was first printed the Rev. T. A. Rayner was the superintendent minister; the Rev. J. Adams being second in command; and they worked the different sections alternately. Mr. Rayner is an elderly gentleman, with a strong osseous frame, which is well covered with muscle and adipose matter; he has been about 34 years in the ministry, and should, therefore, be either very smart or very dull by this time; he has a portly, grave, reverential look; carries with him both spectacles and an eye-glass; is slow and coldly-keen in his mental processes; thinks that he can speak with authority; and that all minor dogs must cease barking when he mounts the oracular tripod; he is sincere; works well, for his years, and in his own way does his best; he is a man of much experience, and has fair intellectual powers; but his temperament is very icy and flatulent; his humours heavy and watery, and a phlegmagog purge would do him good. He is a rigid methodical man; believes in original rules and ancient prerogatives; is a Wesleyan of the antique type, but is devoid of force and enthusiasm; he never sets you on fire with declamation, nor melts you with pathos; he had rather freeze than burn sinners; he thinks the harrier principle of catching a hare is the surest, and that travelling on a theological canal is the safest plan in the long run. He is more cut out for a country rectory, where the main duties are nodding at the squire and stunning the bucolic mind with platitudes, than for a large circuit of active Methodists; he would be more at home at a rural deanery, surrounded by rookeries and placid fish ponds, than in a town mission environed by smoke and made up of screaming children and thin-skinned Christians. Mr. Rayner has many good properties; but short sermon preaching is not one of them. Some of the descendants of that man who, according to "Drunken Barnaby," slaughtered his cat on a Monday, because it killed a mouse on the Sunday, were in the bait of preaching for three hours at one stretch. Mr. Rayner never yet preached that length of time, and we hope he never will do; but he can, like the east wind, blow a long while in one direction. One Sunday evening; when we heard him, be preached just one hour, and at the conclusion intimated that he had been requested to give a short sermon, but had drifted into a rather prolix one. We should like to know what length he would have run out his rhetoric if be had been requested to give a long discourse. By the powers! it would have "tickled the catastrophe" of each listener finely - doctors would have had to be called in, a vast amount of physic would have been required, and it would never have got paid for in these hard times so that bad debts would have been added to the general calamity. We could never see any good in long sermons and nobody else ever could except those giving them. Neither could we ever see much fun in a parson saying - "And now lastly" more than once. In the 60 minutes discourse to which we have alluded, the preacher got into the lastly part of the business five times. If that other conclusive phrase - "And now, finally brethren" - had been taken advantage of, and similarly worked, we might never have got home till morning. Summarising Mr. Rayner, it may be stated that he is calm, phlegmatic, earnest but too prolix, likes to wield the rod of authority and occupy one of the uppermost seats in the synagogue, is an industrious minister but adheres to a programme antique and chilling, is a real Wesleyan in his conceptions, but behind the times in spirit and mental brilliance, is in a word good, grim, imperial, cold as ice, steady, and soundly orthodox.

Mr. Adams, the junior minister, is quite of a different mould; he is sprightly, gamey, wide awake, full of courage, with a smack of Yankee audacity in his manner, and a fair share of conceit in his general make up. There is much determination in him, much of the lively bantam element about him. He has a sharp round face which has not been spoiled by sanctimoniousness. He is sanguine, combative, go ahead, and would like a good fight if he got fairly into one. He cares little for forms and ceremonies; is a good mower; wears a billycock which has passed through much tribulation - we believe it was once the subject of a church meeting; can play cricket pretty well, and enjoys the game; is frank, candid, and speaks straight out; can say a good thing and knows when he has said it; has an above-board, clear, decisive style; is not a great scholar, and would be puzzled, like the generality of parsons, if asked how many teeth he had in his head, or who was the grandfather of his mother's first uncle; knows little of Latin and less of Greek, but understands human nature, and that, says the Clockmaker, beats scholarship; has been in America, which accounts for the nasal ring in his talk; is active, sanguine, free, and easy, and would enjoy either a ridotto or a fast; can utter lively, merry things in his sermons, and does not object sometimes to recognise the wisdom of Shakspere. Mr. Adams is a good platform speaker, and he can give straight shots as a preacher. Sometimes his discourses are only common-place, wordy, and featherless; but in the general run he is much above the average of sermonisers. He has good action, can put out considerable canvas when very warm, smacks the pulpit sides with his hands when, particularly earnest, and occasionally makes a direct aim at the Bible before him, and hits it. We rather like his style; it is free, but not coarse; spirited, but not crazy; determined, but not bigoted; and it is in no way spice with either cant or hallowed humbug. Mr. Adams was five years in America, and he is now completing the tenth year of his career as a regular Wesleyan minister. He has a large veneration for his own powers and thinks there are few sons of Adam like him in the Methodist world; still he is a hard-working, shrewd, clear-headed little man, a good preacher, with a deal of every day fun and sunshine in his heart, and calculated to take a considerably higher post than that which he now occupies.

XVIII

PRESBYTERIAN AND FREE GOSPEL CHAPELS.

"Who are the Presbyterians?" we can imagine many curious, quietly-inquisitive people asking; and we can further imagine numbers of the same class coming to various solemn and inaccurate conclusions as to what the belief of the Presbyterians is. Shortly and sweetly, we may say that they believe in Calvinism, and profess to be the last sound link in the chain of olden Puritanism. They do not believe in knocking down May poles, nor in breaking off the finger and nose ends of sacred statues, nor in condemning as wicked the eating of mince pies, nor in having their hair cropped so that no man can get hold of it, like the ancient members of the Roundhead family; but in spiritual matters they have a distinct regard for the plain, unceremonious tenets of ancient Puritanism - for the simplicity, definitiveness, and absolutism of Calvinism. Some persons fond of spiritual christenings and mystic gossip have supposed that the Presbyterians who, during the past few years, have endeavoured to obtain a local habitation and a name in Preston, were connected with the Unitarians; others have classed them as a species of Independents; and many have come to the conclusion that their creed has much Scotch blood in it - has some affinity to the U.P. style of theology, and has a moderate amount of the "Holy

Fair" business to it. The most ignorant are generally the most critically audacious; and men knowing no more about the peculiarities of creeds than of the capillary action of woolly horses are often the first to run the gauntlet of opinionism concerning them. The fact of the matter is, the Preston Presbyterians are no more and no less, in doctrine, than Calvinists. In discipline and doctrine they are on a par with the members of the Free Church of Scotland; but they are not connected with that church, and don't want to be, unless they can get something worth looking at and taking home.

Historically, the Presbyterians worshipping in Preston don't pretend to date as far back as some religious sects, but they do start ancestrally from the first epoch of British Presbyterianism. Their spiritual forefathers had a stern beginning in this country; they were cradled in fierce tomes, said their prayers often amid the smoke of cannons and the tumult of armies; and maintained their vitality through one of the sternest and most revolutionary periods of modern history. In the 17th century they were, for a few moments, paramount in England; in 1648 nearly all the parishes in the land were declared to be under their form of church government; but the tide of fortune eventually set in against them; at the Restoration Episcopacy superseded their faith; and since then they have had to fight up their way through a long, a circuitous, and an uneven track. Their creed, as before intimated, is Calvinistic, and that is a sufficient definition of it. They believe in a sort of universal suffrage, so far as the election of their pastors is concerned; and if they have grievances on hand they nurse them for a short time, then appeal to "the presbytery." and in case they can't get consolation from that body they go to "the synod." We could give the history of this sect, but in doing so we should have to quote many "figures" and numerous "facts" - things which, according to one British statesman, can never be relied upon - and on that account we shall avoid the dilemma into which we might be drifted. It will be sufficient for our purpose to state that in 1866 a few persons in Preston with a predilection for the ancient form of Presbyterianism held a consultation, and decided to start a "church." They had a sprinkling of serious blood in their arteries - a tincture of well-balanced, modernised Puritanism in their veins - and they honestly thought that if any balm had to come out of Gilead, it would first have to pass through Presbyterianism, and that if any physician had to appear he would have to be a Calvinistic preacher.

They, at first, met privately, and then engaged the theatre of Avenham Institution - a place which had previously been the nursery of Fishergate Baptism and Lancaster-road Congregationalism. From the early part of January, 1866, till September, 1867, they were regaled with "supplies" from different parts of the kingdom. When they met on the second Sunday - it would be unfair to criticise the first Curtian plunge they made - 14 persons, including the preacher, put in an appearance; but the number gradually extended; courage slowly accumulated, and eventually - in September, 1867 - the Rev. A. Bell, a gentleman young in years, and fresh from the green isle, who pleased the Preston Presbyterians considerably, was requested to stop with them and endeavour to make them comfortable. Mr. Bell thought out the question briefly, got a knowledge of the duties required, &c., and then consented to stay with the brethren. And he is still with them; hoping that they may multiply and replenish the earth, and spread Presbyterianism muchly. From the period of their denominational birth up to now the Preston Presbyterians have worshipped in the theatre of the Institution, Avenham - a place which everybody knows and which we need not describe. There is nothing ecclesiastical about it; the place is fit for the operations of either lecturers, or preachers, or conjurors; and it will do for the inculcation of Presbyterianism as well as for anything else. The leaders of the Presbyterian body are looking out for a site upon which a new chapel may be erected, but they have not yet found one. By-and-bye we hope they will see a site which will suit their vision, will come up to their ideal, and, in the words of Butler, be "Presbyterian true blue."

The members of "the church" number at present about 112; and the average congregation will be about 200. It includes Scotchmen, Irish Presbyterians, people who have turned over from Baptism, Independency, Catholicism, and several other creeds, and all of them seem to be theologically satisfied. There ought to be elders at the place; but the denomination seems too young for them; as it progresses and gets older it will get into the elder stage. There is no pulpit in the building, and the preacher gets on very well is the absence of one. If he has no pulpit he has at least this consolation that he can never fall over such a contrivance, as the South Staffordshire Methodist once did, when in a fit of fury, and nearly killed some of the singers below. The congregation consists principally of middle and working class people. Their demeanour is calm, their music moderate, and in neither mind nor body do they appear to be much agitated, like some people, during their moments of devotion.

The preacher, who has been about six years in the ministry, and gets 250 pounds a year for his duties here, is a dark-complexioned sharp-featured man - slender, serious-looking, energetic, earnest, with a sanguine-bilious temperament. He is a ready and rather eloquent preacher; is fervid, emphatic, determined; has moderate action; never damages his coat near the armpits by holding his arms too high; has a touch of the "ould Ireland" brogue in his talk; never loudly blows his own trumpet, but sometimes rings his own bell a little; means what he says; is pretty liberal towards other creeds, but is certain that his own views are by far the best; is a steady thinker, a sincere minister, a tolerably good scholar, and a warm-hearted man, who wouldn't torture an enemy if he could avoid it, but would struggle hard if "put to it." Like the rest of preachers he has his admirers as well as those who do not think him altogether immaculate; but taking him in toto - mind, body, and clothes - he is a fervent, candid, medium-sized, respectable-looking man, worth listening to as a speaker of the serious school, and calculated, if regularly heard, to distinctly inoculate you with Presbyterianism. It is as "clear as a bell" that he is advancing considerably the cause he is connected with, and that his "church" is making satisfactory progress. There is a Sabbath school attached to the denomination. The scholars meet every Sunday afternoon in the Institution; and their average attendance is about 90. As a denomination the Presbyterians are pushing onwards vigorously, though quietly, and their prospects are good.

To the Free Gospel people we next come. They don't occupy very fashionable quarters; Ashmoor-street, a long way down Adelphi-street, is the thoroughfare wherein their spiritual refuge is situated. If they were in a better locality, the probability is they would be denominationally stronger. In religion, as in everything else, "respectability" is the charm. We have heard many a laugh at the expense of these "Free Gospel" folk, but there is more in their creed, although it may have only Ashmoor-street for its blossoming ground, than the multitude of people think of. They were brought into existence through a dispute with a Primitive Methodist preacher at Saul-street chapel; although previously, men holding opinions somewhat similar to theirs, were in the town, and built, but through adverse circumstances had to give up, Vauxhall-road chapel. In the early stages of their existence the Free Gospellers were called Quaker Methodists, because they dressed somewhat like Quakers, and had ways of thinking rather like the followers of George Fox. In some places they are known as Christian Brethren; in other parts they are recognised as a kind of independent Ranters.

About ten years ago, the Preston Free Gospel people got Mr. James Toulmin to build a chapel for them in Ashmoor-street; they having worshipped up to that time, first at a place on Snow-Hill and then in Gorst-street. He did not give them the chapel; never said that he would; couldn't afford to be guilty of an act so curious; but he erected a place of worship for their pleasure, and they have paid him something in the shape of rent for it ever since. The chapel is a plain, small, humble-looking building - a rather respectably developed cottage, with only one apartment - and we should think that those who attend it must be in earnest. The place seems to have been arranged to hold 95 persons - a rather strange number; but upon a pinch, and by the aid of a few forms planted near the foot of the pulpit, perhaps 120 could be accommodated in it.

There are just fourteen pews in the chapel, and they run up backwards to the end of the building, the highest altitude obtained being perhaps four yards. A good view can be obtained from the pulpit. Not only can the preacher eye instantaneously every member of his congregation, but he can get serene glimpses through the windows of eight chimney pots, five house roofs, and portions of two backyards. In a season of doubt and difficulty a scene like this must relieve him.

There are about 30 "members" of the chapel. The average attendance on a Sunday, including all ranks, will be about 50. The worshippers are humble people - artisans, operatives, small shopkeepers, &c. A few of the hottest original partisans were the first to leave the chapel after its opening. There is a Sunday school connected with the body, and between 40 and 50 children and youths attend it on the average. Voluntaryism in its most absolute form, is the predominant principle of the denomination. The sect is, in reality, a "free community." Their standard is the bible; they believe in both faith and good works, but place more reliance upon the latter than the former; they recognise a progressive Christianity, "harmonising," as we have been told, "with science and common sense;" they object to the Trinitarian dogma, as commonly accepted by the various churches, maintaining that both the Bible and reason teach the existence of but one God; they have no eucharistic sacrament, believing that as often as they eat and drink they should be imbued with a spirit of Christian remembrance and thankfulness; they argue that ministers should not be paid; they dispense with pew-rents; repudiate all money tests of membership - class-pence, &c.; make voluntary weekly contributions towards the general expenses, each giving according to his means; and all have a voice in the regulation of affairs, but direct executive work is done by a president and a committee. The independent volition of Quakerism is one of their prime peculiarities. If they have even a tea-party, no fixed charge for admission is made; the price paid for demolishing the tea and currant bread, and crackers being left to the individual ability and feelings of the participants.

Service is held in the chapel morning and evening every Sunday, and the business of religious edification is very peacefully conducted. There is a moderate choir in the chapel, and a small harmonium: The singing is conducted on the tonic sol fa principle, and it seems to suit Mr. William Toulmin, brother of the owner of the chapel, preaches every Sunday, and has done so, more or less, from its opening. He gets nothing for the job, contributes his share towards the church expenses as well, and is satisfied. Others going to the place might preach if they could, but they can't, so the lot constantly falls upon Jonah, who gives homely practical sermons, and is well thought of by his hearers. He is a quaint, cold, generous man; is original, humble, honest; cares little for appearances; wears neither white bands nor morocco shoes; looks sad, rough and ready, and unapproachable; works regularly as a shopkeeper on week days, and earnestly as a preacher on Sundays; passes his life away in a mild struggle with eggs, bacon, butter, and theology; isn't learned, nor classical, nor rhetorical, but possesses common sense; expresses himself so as to be understood - a thing which some regular parsons have a difficulty in doing; and has laboured Sunday after Sunday for years all for nothing - a thing which no regular parson ever did or ever will do. We somewhat respect a man who can preach for years without pocketing a single dime, and contribute regularly towards a church which gives him no salary, and never intends doing. The homilies of the preacher at Ashmoor-street Chapel may neither be luminous nor eloquent, neither pythonic in utterance nor refined in diction, but they are at least worth as much as he gets for them. Any man able to sermonise better, or rhapsodise more cheaply, or beat the bush of divinity more energetically, can occupy the pulpit tomorrow. It is open to all England, and possession of it can be obtained without a struggle. Who bids?

XIX

ST. JAMES'S CHURCH.

There is a touch of smooth piety and elegance in the name of St. James. It sounds refined, serious, precise. Two of the quietest and most devoted pioneers of Christianity were christened James; the most fashionable quarters in London are St. James's; the Spaniards have for ages recognised St. James as their patron saint; and on the whole whether referring to the "elder" or the "less" James, the name has a very good and Jamesly bearing. An old English poet says that "Saint James gives oysters" just as St. Swithin attends to the rain; but we are afraid that in these days he doesn't look very minutely after the bivalve part of creation: if he does he is determined to charge us enough for ingurgitation, and that isn't a very saintly thing. He may be an ichthyofagic benefactors only - we don't see the oysters as often as we could like. Not many churches are called after St. James, and very few people swear by him. We have a church in Preston dedicated to the saint; but it got the name whilst it was a kind of chapel. St. James's church is situated between Knowsley and Berry-streets, and directly faces the National school in Avenham-lane. "Who erected the building?" said we one day to a churchman, and the curt reply, with a neatly curled lip, was, "A parcel of Dissenters."

Very few people seem to have a really correct knowledge of the history of the place, and, for the satisfaction of all and the singular, we will give an account of it, in the exact words of the gentleman who had most to do with the building originally. Mr. James Fielding deposeth:- St. James's was erected by the Rev. James Fielding and his friends. The occasion of its erection was this - Vauxhall-road Chapel, in which Mr. Fielding had been preaching four or five years, had become too small for the accomodation of the congregation worshipping there, and it was thought advisable to open a subscription for a new and larger building. The first stone of St. James's was laid by Mr. Fielding, May 24th, 1837, and the place was opened for divine worship in January, 1838, under the denomination of "The Primitive Episcopal Church," [that beats the "Reformed Church," - eh?] by the Rev. J. R. Matthews, of Bedford, who was a clergyman of the Established Church. The building was computed to seat about 1,300 people. The cost of the place was about 1,500 pounds. After the opening, Mr. Fielding commenced his ministry in the new church - the congregation removing from Vauxhall Chapel into that place of worship. Not long afterwards Mr. Fielding had a severe attack of illness, and was laid aside from his work. From this, together with the urgency of the contractors for the payment of their bills, it was thought advisable to sell the premises. The late vicar of Preston, Rev. Carus Wilson, in conjunction with his friends, offered 1,000 pounds for the building. This was believed to be considerably under its real value, being 500 pounds below the cost amount. However, under the circumstances it was decided to accept the offer. The transfer of the premises took place in April, 1838. Mr. Fielding continued his ministry in Preston in several other places for thirteen years after the erection of St. James's.

The late John Addison, Esq., of this town, says, in a document written by himself, which we have before us, and which is entitled "Some account of St. James's Church, in the parish of Preston" - "A body of Dissenters having erected a large building, capable of holding 1,100 persons, and having opened it for public worship under the name of St. James's Church, but, being unable to pay the expenses, offered it for sale. The building being situated directly opposite the Central National School, and in the immediate neighbourhood of the infant school and Church Sunday schools , a few of the committee of the National school thought it desirable that the building should be purchased and made into a church for the accomodation of the children of the schools and of the neighbourhood." And the result was the purchase of the Rev. James Fielding's "Primitive Episcopal Church."

The building is made mainly of brick, and looks very like a Dissenting place of worship. It is a tame, moderately tall, quadrangular edifice, flanked with stone buttresses, heavy enough to crush in its sides, fronted with a plain gable, pierced with a few prosaic windows, and surmounted with collateral turrets and a small bell fit for a school-house, and calculated to swivel whilst being worked quite as much as any other piece of sacred bell-metal in the Hundred of Amounderness. There is a small graveyard in front of the church containing a few flat tombstones and six young trees which have rather a struggling time of it in windy weather. The ground spaces at the sides of the church are decorated with ivy, thistles, chickweed, and a few venerable docks, The internal architecture of the building is as dull and modest as that of the exterior. The seats are stiff, between 30 and 40 inches high, and homely. Just at present they have a scraped care-worn look, as if they had been getting parish relief; but in time, when cash is more plentiful, their appearance will be improved. A considerable sum of money was once spent upon the cleaning and renovation of the church; but the paint which was put on during the work never suited; it was either brushed on too thickly or varnished too coarsely; it persisted in sticking to people rather too keenly at times; would hardly give way if struggled with; and taking into account its tenacity and ill-looks - it was finally decided to rub it off, make things easy with pumice stone, and agitate for fresh paint and varnish when the opportunity presented itself.

There is a large gallery in the church; but, like everything else, it is plain, The only striking ornament in the building is a sixteen-spoked circular window (at the chancel end), and until made to turn round it will never be popularly attractive. In 1846 the chancel, which isn't anything very prepossessing, was added to the church. The pulpit is high and rather elegant in design; the reading desk is a gothicised fabric, and, with its open sides, reminds one more of a genteel open gangway on which everything can be seen, than of a snug high box, like those in which old-fashioned clerks used to sup gin and go to sleep during the intervals. Until recently there were two wooden gas stands at the sides of the reading desk. They looked like candlesticks, and short-sighted people, with thin theological cuticles, and a horror of Puseyism, disliked them. Eventually the wood was gilded, and, seeing this, as well as knowing that candles were never gilded, and that, therefore, the stands couldn't be candles, the dissatisfied ones were appeased. There are about 400 free sittings in the church; but few people appear to care much for them. These seats are situated on each side of the building, at the rear, and in the gallery; and they will be dying of inanition by and bye if somebody doesn't come to the rescue. People don't seem to care about having a thing for nothing in the region of St. James's church. They would probably flock in greater numbers to the edifice if there were an abundance of those oysters which it is said "Saint James gives;" but they appear to have a sacred dread of free seats. Very recently we were at the church, and on the side we noticed seventeen free pews. How many people do you think there were in them? Just one delicious old woman, who wore a brightly-coloured old shawl, and a finely-spreading old bonnet, which in its weight and amplitude of trimmings seemed to frown into evanescence the sprightly half-ounce head gearing of today. Paying for what they get and giving a good price for it when they have a chance is evidently an axiom with the believers in St. James's. There is at present a demand for seats worth from 7s. to 10s. each; but those which can be obtained for 1s. are not much thought of, and nobody will look on one side at the pews which are offered for nothing. That which is not charged for is never cared for; and further, in respect to free pews, patronage of them is an indication of poverty, and people, as a rule, don't like to show the white feather in that department.

The congregation is thin, but select - is constituted of substantial burgeois people, and a few individuals who are comparatively wealthy. There is a smart elegance about the bonnets and toilettes of some of the females, and a studied precision in respect to the linen, vests, and gloves of several of the males. Nothing gloomy, nor acetose, nor piously-angular can be observed in them; nothing pre-eminently lustrous is seen in the halo of the respective worshippers; yet there is a finish about them which indicates that they have no connection with the canaillc, and that they are in some instances approaching, and in others directly associated with, the "higher middle class." There are only two services a week - morning and evening, on a Sunday - at St. James's. Formerly there were more - one on a Sunday afternoon, and another on a Thursday evening; but as the former was only attended by about 30, and the latter by eight or ten, and as the fund for maintaining a curate who had the management of them was withdrawn, it was decided some time ago to drop the services. The Sunday congregation, although it does not on many occasions half fill the church, is gradually increasing, and it is hoped that during the next twenty-years it will swell into pretty large proportions.

The choral performances form the main item of attraction in the services. Without them, the business would be tame and flavourless. They give a warmth and charm to the proceedings. The members of the choir sit in collateral rows in the chancel; they are all surpliced; all very virtuous and clerical in look; seldom put their hands into their pockets whilst singing; and, whatever quantity of "linen" may be got out by them they invariably endeavour to obviate violence of expression. Their appearance reminds one of cathedral choristers. In precision and harmony they are good; and, as a body, they manage all their work - responses, psalm-singing, &c. - in a very satisfactory style. For their services they receive nothing, except, perhaps, an annual treat in the shape of a country trip or social supper. They wouldn't have money if it were offered to them. St. James's is the only Preston church in which surpliced choristers sing, and we believe they have tended materially to increase the congregation. The choral system now followed at St. James's was inaugurated in 1865, Originally, the choir consisted of 12 boys and 10 men, but, if anything, parties who are under the painful necessity of shaving now preponderate. In one corner at the chancel end there is a moderately well-made organ; but it is not an A1 affair, although it is played with ability by a gentleman who is perhaps second to none hereabouts in his knowledge of ecclesiastical music. Like the singers, the organist resolves his services into what may be termed a "labour of love." In other ways much may be fish which cometh to his net; but he is, ORGANICALLY, of a philanthropic turn of mind. The necessary expenses of the choir amount to about 25 pounds a-year, and they are met by private subscriptions from the congregation.

The lessons are read in the church by Mr. Gardner, who comes up to the lectern undismayed, with a calm, military cast of countenance, and goes through his articulative duties in a clear, distinct style, saying nothing to anybody near him which is not contained in the book before him, and making neither incidental comment nor studied criticism upon any of the verses be reads. The Rev. John Wilson, son-in-law of the present vicar of Preston, is the incumbent of St. James's. He is the seventh minister who has been at the place since its transference from the Primitive Episcopalians. The first of the seven was the Rev. W. Harrison; the next was the Rev. P. W. Copeman; afterwards came the Rev. W. Wailing, who was succeeded by the Rev. Mr. Betts, whose mantle fell upon the Rev. J. Cousins. Then came the Rev A. T.

Armstrong, and he was followed by the present incumbent. During the reign of Mr. Cousins there was a rupture at the place, and many combative letters were written with reference to it. Up to and for some time after his appointment the Sunday schools of the Parish and St. James's Churches were amalgamated - were considered as one lot; but through some misunderstanding a separation ensued. Mr. Cousins, who had no locus standi as to the possession of the schools, took with him some scholars, drilled them after his own fashion for a time, and eventually the present day and Sunday schools in Knowsley-street were built and opened on behalf of St. James's. The day school is at present in excellent condition, and has an average attendance, boys and girls included, of 400; the Sunday school has an average attendance of something like 200, the generality of the children being of a respectable, well-dressed character, although no more disposed, at times, than other juveniles, to be docile and peaceful.

The Rev. J. Wilson has been at St. James's upwards of 15 years. He was curate of the Parish Church from 1847 to 1850. In the latter year he left in order to take the sole charge of a parish in Norfolk. In 1854 he gravitated to Preston again, and in the course of a year was made incumbent of St. James's. For some time he had much to contend with in the district; and he has had up-hill work all along. He was one of the original agitators for an alteration of the Parish Church, and in one sense it may be said that the move he primarily made in the matter eventuated in the restoration of that building. The creation of St. Saviour's Church is also largely due to him, and owing to the building being in St. James's district, which is a "Blandsford parish," and the only one of the kind in Preston we may remark, he has the right of presentation to it. Mr. Wilson is a calm, middle-sized, rather eccentric looking gentleman, tasteful in big hirsute arrangements, and biased towards a small curl in the front of his forehead. He is light on his feet, has a forward bend in his walk, as if trying to find something but never able to get at it; has a passion for an umbrella, which he carries both in fine and wet weather; likes a dark, thin, closely-buttoned overcoat, and used to love a down-easter wide-awake hat. He is a frank, independent, educated man; has no sham in him; is liberal is far as his means will allow; works hard; has an odd, go-ahead way with him; cares little about bowing and scraping to people; often passes folk (unintentionally) without nodding; and has nothing of a polemically virulent character in his disposition. There is something genuine, honest, gentlemanly, and unreadable in him. He almost reminds one of Elia's inexplicable cousin. He has a special fondness for architecture; plans, specifications, &c., have a charm for him; he is a sort of clerical Inigo Jones; and ought to have been an architect. He is a rather polished reader; but he holds his teeth too tightly together, and there is a tremulousness in his voice which makes the utterances thereof rather too unctuous. As a preacher he is clear, calm, and methodical. His sermons, all written, are scholarly in style cool in tone, short, and, in the orthodox sense, practical. In their delivery he does not make much stir, he goes on evenly and rapidly, looking little to either the right hand or the left, broiling none, and foaming never. Occasionally, but it is quite an exception, he forgets his sermons - leaves them at home - and this is somewhat awkward when the mistake is only found out just before the preaching should be gone on with. But the company are kept serene by a little extra singing, or something of that kind, and in the meantime a rapid rush is made to the parsonage, and the missing manuscript is secured, conveyed to the church either in a basket or a pocket, taken into the pulpit, looked at rather fiercely, shook a little, and then read through. How would it be if the manuscript could not be found? Long official life appears to be the rule at St. James's. Mr. Wm. Relph, who died last year, was a churchwarden at the place for 21 years; Mr. Bannister has been in office as churchwarden for nearly as long; the person who was beadle up to last year had officiated in that capacity for nearly eleven years; the organist has been at the church above 15 years; the mistress of the school belonging the church has been at her post about as long; and the schoolmaster has been in office 13 or 14 years. If long service speaks well for a place, the facts we have given are creditable alike to the church and the officials. Mr. Wilson, who gets about 300 pounds a year, is well-respected by all; he manages to keep down unpleasant feuds; regulates the district peacefully, if slowly, deserves a handsomer church, and would be quite willing, we believe, to be its architect if one were ordered.

XX

THE MORMONS.

There are about 1,100 different religious creeds in the world, and amongst them all there is not one more energetic, more mysterious, or more wit-shaken than Mormonism. It is a mass of earnest "abysmal nonsense," an olla-podrida of theological whimsicalities, a saintly jumble of pious staff made up - if we may borrow an idea - of Hebraism, Persian Dualism, Brahminism, Buddhistic apotheosis, heterodox and orthodox Christianity, Mohammedanism, Drusism, Freemasonry, Methodism, Swedenborgianism, Mesmerism, and Spirit-rapping. We might go on in our elucidation; but what we have said will probably be sufficient for present purposes. There are some deep-swimming fish in the "waters of Mormon;" but the piscatorial shoal is sincere enough, though mortally odd-brained and dreamy. On the 22nd of September, 1827, a rough-spun American, named Joseph Smith, belonging to a family reputed to be fond of laziness, drink, and untruthfulness, and suspected of being somewhat disposed to sheep-stealing, had a visit from "the angel of the Lord." He had previously been told that his sins were forgiven; that he was a "chosen instrument," &c., and on the day named Joseph found, somewhere in Ontario, a number of gold plates, eight inches long and seven wide, nearly as thick as tin, fastened together by three rings, and bearing inscriptions, in "Reformed Egyptian," relative to the history of America "from its first settlement by a colony that came from the Tower of Babel at the confusion of tongues, to the beginning of the 5th century of the Christian era." These inscriptions were originally got up by a prophet named Mormon were, as before stated, found by Joseph Smith, were read off by him to a man rejoicing in the name of Oliver Cowdery, and they constitute the contents of what is now known as the Book of Mormon. Smith did not translate the "Reformed Egyptian" openly - if he had been asked to do so, he would have said, "not for Joe;" he got behind a blanket in order to do the job, considering that the plates would be defiled if seen by profane eyes; and deciphered them by two odd lapidistic transparencies, called "Urim and Thummin," which he found at the same time as he met with the records. Report hath it that Joe's "translation" of the sacred plates is substantially a paraphrase of a romance written by one Solomon Spalding; but the Mormons, or rather the members of "The Church of Jesus Christ of Latter Day Saints," deny this, and say that at least eleven persons saw the original plates after transcription. They may have seen them; but nobody else has, and Heaven only knows where they are now.

Did you ever, gentle reader, see the "Book of Mormon?" We have one before us, purchased from a real live Salt Lake missionary; but it is so dreadfully dry and intricate, and seems to be such a dodged-up paraphrase of our own Scriptures, that we are afraid it will never do us any good. It professes to be a "record of the people of Nephi, and also of the Lumanites their brethren, and also of the people of Jared, who came from the tower." The Mormons think it equal in divine authority to, and a positive corollary of, the Old and New Testaments. It consists of several books, and many chapters; the books being those of Nephi, Jacob, Enos, Jarom, Mosiah, Alma, Helaman, Nephi, Mormon, Ether, and Moroni. The language is quaint and simple in syllabic construction; but the book altogether is a mass of dreamy, puzzling history - is either a sacred fiction plagiarised, or a useless and senile jumble of Christian and Red Indian tradition. Smith, the founder of Mormonism, had only a rough time of it. His Church was first organised in 1830, in the State of New York. Afterwards the Mormons went into Ohio, then established themselves in Missouri, were next driven into Clay County, subsequently look refuge in Illinois, and finally planted themselves in the valley of the great Salt Lake, where they may now be found. Smith came to grief in 1844, by a pistol shot, administered to him in Illinois by a number of roughs; and Brigham Young, a man said to be "very much married," and who will now be the father of perhaps 150 children, was appointed his successor. Mormonism is disliked by the bulk of people mainly on account of its fondness for wives. The generality of civilised folk think that one fairly matured creature, with a ring on one of her left-hand fingers, is sufficient for a single household - quite sufficient for all the fair purposes of existence, "lecturing" included; but the Latter-day Saints, who were originally monogamists, and whose "Book of Mormon" condemns polygamy, believe in a plurality of housekeepers. They contend that since the finding of the sacred record by Smith there has been a "divine" revelation on the subject, and that their dignity in heaven will be "in proportion to the number of their wives and children" in this.

Leaving the polygamic part of the business, we may

observe that the Mormons believe that God was once a man, but is now perfect; that any man may rise into a species of deity if he is good enough; that mortals will not be punished for what Adam did, but for what they have done themselves; that there can be no salvation without repentance, faith, and baptism; that the sacrament - bread and water-must be taken every week; that ministerial action must be preceded by inspiration; that Miraculous gifts have not ceased; that the soul of man "co-existed equal with God;" that the word of God is recorded in all good books; that there will be an actual gathering of Israel, including the Red Indians, whom they regard with much interest as being the descendants of an ancient tribe whose skins were coloured on account of disobedience in some part of America about 2,400 years ago; that the "New Zion" will be established in America; and that there will be a final resurrection of the flesh and bones - without the blood - of men. Some of their moral articles of belief are good, and if carried out, ought to make the Salt Lake Valley a decent, peaceable place, notwithstanding all the wives therein. In one of the said articles they express their belief in being "honest, true, chaste, temperate, benevolent, virtuous, and upright," and further on they come down with a crash upon idle and lazy persons, by saying that they can be neither Christians nor enjoy salvation.

In 1837, certain elders of the Mormon church, including Orson Hyde and Heber C. Kimball, were sent over to England as missionaries; the first town they commenced operations in, after their arrival, was - PRESTON; and the first shot they fired in Preston was from the pulpit of a building in Vauxhall-road, now occupied by the Particular Baptists. Things got hot in a few minutes here; it became speedily known that

Hyde, Kimball, and Co. were of a sect fond of a multiplicity of wives; and the "missionaries" had to forthwith look out for fresh quarters. They secured the old Cock Pit, drove a great business in it, and at length actually got about 500 "members." Whilst this movement was going on in the town, the missionaries were pushing Mormonism in some of the surrounding country places. At Longton, nearly everybody went into raptures over the "new doctrine;" Mormonism fairly took the place by storm; it caught up and entranced old and young, married and single, pious and godless; it even spread like a sacred rinderpest amongst the Wesleyans, who at that time were very strong in Longton - captivating leaders, members, and some of the scholars in fine style; and the chapel of this body was so emptied by the Mormon crusade, that it was found expedient to reduce it internally and set apart some of it for school purposes. To this day the village has not entirely recovered the shock which Mormonism gave it 30 years ago. During the heat of the conflict many Longtonians went to the region of Mormondom in America, and several of them soon wished they were back again. In Preston, too, whilst the Cock Pit fever was raging numbers "went out." After the work of "conversion," &c., had been carried on for a period in the sacred Pit mentioned, the Mormons migrated to a building, which had been used as a joiners shop, in Park-road; subsequently they took for their tabernacle an old sizing house in Friargate; then they went to a building in Lawson-street now used as the Weavers' Institute, and originally occupied by the Ranters; and at a later date they made another move - transferred themselves to a room in the Temperance Hotel , Lime-street, which they continue to occupy , and in which, every Sunday morning and evening , they ideally drink of Mormondom's salt-water, and clap their hands gleefully over Joe Smith's impending millenium.

There are only about 70 members of the Mormon Church in Preston and the immediate neighbourhood at present; but they are all hopeful, and fancy that beatification is in store for them. We had recently a half-solemn, half-comic desire to see the very latest development of Preston Mormonism in its Lune-street home; but having an idea that strangers might be objected to whilst the "holding forth" was going on, that, in fact, the members had resolved themselves, through diminished numbers, into a species of secret conclave, we were rather puzzled to know how the business of seeing and hearing could be accomplished. Nevertheless we went to the Temperance Hotel, and after some conversation with a person there - not a Mormon - we decided to go right into the meeting-room, the idea being that, under any circumstances, we could only be pitched into, and then pitched out. And with this notion we entered the place, put our hat upon a table deliberately, took a seat upon a form quietly, and then looked round coolly in anticipation of a round of sauce or a trifle of fighting. But peace was preserved. There were just six living beings in the room - three well-dressed moustached young men, a thinly-fierce-looking woman, a very red-headed youth, and a quiet little girl. For about 30 seconds absolute silence prevailed. The thin woman then looked forward at the red-haired youth and in a clear voice said "Bin round there yet - eh?" which elicited the answer "Yea, and comed whoam." "Things are flat there as well as here aren't they - eh?" And the red-haired youth said "Yea." "Factories arn't doing much now, are they?" said she next, and the rejoinder was "They arn't; bin round by Bowton, and its aw alike." This slightly refreshing prelude was supplemented by sapient remarks as to the weather &c.; and we were beginning to wonder whether the general service was simply going to amount to this kind of conversation or be pushed on "properly" when in stepped a strong-built dark-complexioned man, who marched forward with the dignity of an elder, until he got to a small table surmounted by a desk, whence he drew a brown paper parcel, which he handed to one of the moustached young men, who undid it cautiously and carefully, "What is it going to be?" said we, mentally; when, lo! there appeared a white table cloth, which was duly spread. The strong built man then dived deeply into one of his coat pockets, and fetched out of it a small paper parcel, flung it upon a form close by, seized a soup plate into which he crumbled a slice of bread, then got a double-handled pewter pot, into which he poured some water, and afterwards sat down as generalissimo of the business. The individual who manipulated with the table cloth afterwards made a prayer, universal in several of its sentiments; but stiffened up tightly with Mormon notions towards the close.

Two elderly men and a lad entered the room when the orison was finished, and a discussion followed between the "general" and the young man who had been praying as to some hymn they should sing. "Can't find the first hymn," said the young man; and we thought that a pretty smart thing for a beginning. "Oh, never mind - go farther on - any - long meter," uttered his interlocutor, and he forthwith made a sanguine dash into the centre of the book, and gave out a hymn. The company got into a "peculiar metre" tune at once, and the singing was about the most comically wretched we ever heard. The lad who came in with the elderly men tried every range of voice in every verse, and thought that he had a right to do just as he liked with the music; the elderly men near him hammed out something in a weak and time-worn key; the woman got into a high strain and flourished considerably at the line ends; the little girl said nothing; the three young men seemed quite unable to get above a monotonous groan, and the general looked forward, then down, and then smiled a little, but uttered never a word, and seemed immensely relieved when the singing was over. The bread which had been broken into the soup plate was next handed round, and it was succeeded by the pewter pot measure of water. This was the sacrament, and it was partaken of by all - the young as well as the old. During the enactment of this part of the programme a gaily-dressed young female, sporting a Paisley shawl, ear-rings, a chignon, a small bonnet, and the other accoutrements of modern fashion, dropped in, and also took the sacrament. Another hymn was here given out, and the young woman with the Paisley shawl, &c., rushed straight into the work of singing without a moment's warning. She carried the others with her, and enabled them to get through the verses easily. Just when the singing was ended, a rubicund-featured and bosky female, who had, perhaps, seen five-and-forty summers, landed in the room, took a seat, and then took the sacrament. She was the last of the Mohicans, and after her appearance the door was closed, and the latch dropped.

Speaking succeeded, and the talkers got upon their feet in accordance with certain nods and memoes from the chairman. They all eulogised in a joyous strain the glories of Mormonism, but never a syllable was expressed about wives. A young moustached man led the way. He told the meeting that he had long been of a religious turn of mind; that he was a Wesleyan until 17 years of age; that afterwards he found peace in the Smithsonian church; that the only true creed was that of Mormonism; that it didn't matter what people said in condemnation of such creed; and that he should always stick to it. The thin woman, who seemed to have an awful tongue in her head, was the second speaker. She panegyrised "the church" in a phrensied, fierce-tempered, piping strain, talked rapidly about the "new dispensation," declared that she had accepted it voluntarily, hadn't been deceived by any one - we hope she never will be - and that she was happy. Her conclusion was sudden, and she appeared to break off just before reaching an agony-point. The third talker was one of the old men, and he commenced with things from "before the foundations of the world," and brought them down to the present day. His speech was earnest, florid, and rather argumentative in tone. After stating that he had a pious spell upon him before visiting the room, and that the afflatus was still upon him, he entered into a labyrinthal defence of "the church." "Mormonism," he said, "is more purer than any other doctrine that is," and "this here faith," he continued, "has to go on and win." He talked mystically about things being "resurrectioned," contended that the Solomon Spalding theory had been exploded, and quoting one of the elders, said that Mormonism began in a hamlet and got to a village, from a village to a town, thence to a city, thence to a territory, and that if it got "just another kick it would as sure as fate be kicked into a great and mighty nation." This "old man eloquent" seemed over head and ears in Mormonism, and almost shook with joy at certain points of his discourse.

The fourth, and the last, speaker was the chairman. He

raised his brawny frame slowly, held a Bible in one hand, and started in this fashion - "Well I s'pose I've to say something; but I can't tell what it'll be." This declaration was followed up by a long, wandering mass of talk, full of repetition and hypothetical theology - a mixture of Judaism, Christianity, and Mormonism, and from the whole he endeavoured to distil this "fact" that both Isaiah and St. John had made certain prophetic statements as to the Book of Mormon and its transcription by Joe Smith. It did not, however, appear from what he said that either Isaiah or the seer of Patmos had named anything about the blanket trick which had to be adopted by Joe is translating "the Book." But that was perhaps unnecessary; and we shall not throw a "wet blanket" upon the matter by further alluding to it. When the chairman had done his speech, the doxology was sung, and this was supplemented by benediction, pronounced by a young man who shut his eyes, stretched his hands a quarter of a yard out of his coat sleeves, and in a most inspired and bishoply style, delivered the requisite blessing. Hand-shaking, in which we found it necessary to join, supervened, and then there was a general disappearance. The whole of the speakers at this meeting - which may be taken as a fair sample of the gatherings - were illiterate people, individuals with much zeal and little education; and the manner in which they crucified sentences, and maltreated the general principles of logic and common-sense, was really disheartening. They are very earnest folk; we also believe they are honest; but, after all, they are "gone coons," beyond the reach of both physic and argument. We knew none of the Mormons who attended the meeting described, and singular to say the proprietor of the establishment wherein they assembled had no knowledge of either their names or places of abode. They pay him his rent regularly, and he deems that enough. All that we really know of the sect is, that their chairman is either a mechanic or a blacksmith somewhere, is plain, muscular, solemn looking, bass-voiced, and dreamy; and that his flock are a small, earnest, and preciously-fashioned parcel of sincere, yet deluded, enthusiasts.

XXI

ST. WALBURGE'S CATHOLIC CHURCH.

This is a church in charge of the Jesuits, and by them and it we are reminded of what may fairly be termed the great leg question. The order of Jesuits, as we lately remarked, was originated by a damaged leg; and St. Walburge's church, Preston, owes its existence to the cure of one. Excellent, O legs! Tradition hath it that once upon a time - about 1160 years ago - a certain West Saxon King had a daughter born unto him, whose name was Walburge; that she went into Germany with two of her brothers, became abbess of a convent there, did marvellous things, was a wonder in her way, couldn't be bitten by dogs - they, used to snatch half a yard off and then run, that she died on the 25th February, 778, that her relics were transferred, on the 12th October following, to Eichstadt, at which place a convent was built to her memory, that the said relics were put into a bronze shrine, which was placed upon a table of marble, in the convent chapel; that every year since then, between the 12th of October and the 25th of February, the marble upon which the shrine is placed has "perspired" a liquid which is collected below in a vase of silver; and that this liquid, which is called "St. Walburge's oil," will cure, by its application, all manner of physical ailments. This is the end of our first lesson concerning St. Walburge and the wonderful oil.

The second lesson runneth thus:- About five and twenty years ago there lived, as housemaid at St. Wilfrid's presbytery, in this town, one Alice Holderness. She was a comely woman and pious; but she fell one day on some steps leading to the presbytery, hurt one of her legs - broke the knee cap of it, we believe - and had to be carried straight to bed. Medical aid was obtained; but the injured knee was obstinate, wouldn't be mended, and when physic and hope alike had been abandoned, so far as the leg of Alice was concerned, the Rev. Father Norris, who, in conjunction with the Rev. Father Weston, was at that time stationed at St. Wilfrid's, was struck with a somewhat bright thought as to the potency of St. Walburge's oil. A little of that oil was procured, and this is what a sister of the injured woman says, in a letter which we have seen on the subject, viz.: - That Father Norris dipped a pen into the oil and dropped a morsel of it upon her knee, whereupon "the bones immediately snapped together and she was perfectly cured, having no longer the slightest weakness in the broken limb."

This is a strange tale, which people can either believe or disbelieve at their own pleasure. All Protestants - ourselves included - will necessarily be dubious; and if any polemical lecturer should happen to see the story he will go wild with delight, and consider that there is material enough in it for at least six good declamatory and paying discourses. Well, whether correct or false, the priests at St. Wilfrid's believed in the "miraculous cure," and decided forthwith to agitate for a church in honour of St. Walburge. That church is the one we now see on Maudlands - a vast and magnificent pile, larger in its proportions than any other Preston place of worship, and with a spire which can only be equalled for altitude by two others in the whole country. What a potent architectural charm was secreted in that mystic oil with which Father Norris touched the knee of Alice! In the "Walpurgis dance of globule and oblate spheroid," there may be something wonderful, but through this drop of oil from the Walpurgian shrine an obstreperous knee snapped up into compact health instantly, and then a large church, ornamental to Preston and creditable to the entire Catholic population, arose. There used to be a hospital, dedicated to Mary Magdalen, either actually upon or very near the site occupied by St. Walburge's Church; but that building disappeared long ago, and no one can tell the exact character of it. Prior to, and until the completion of, the erection of St. Walburge's Church, schools intended for it, and built mainly at the expense of the late Mr. W. Talbot, were raised on some adjoining land. Service in accordance with the Catholic ritual was held therein until the completion of the Church. Father Weston was the leading spirit in the construction of St. Walburge's, and to him - although well assisted by Father Williams - may be attributed the main honour of its development into reality. Father Cobb, of St. Wilfrid's, laid the foundation stone of St. Walburge's Church, on Whit-Monday, 1850; and on the 3rd of August, 1854, the building was opened, the ceremony being of a very grand and imposing description. The spire of the church was not completed until 1887. The entire cost of the place has been about 15,000 pounds.

St. Walburge's is built in the early decorated Gothic style of architecture, and it is beyond all controversy, a splendid looking building. At the eastern end there is a remarkably fine seven-light stained glass window. This is flanked by a couple of two-light windows; and the general effect is most imposing. The central window is 35 feet high. At the western end there is a beautifully-coloured circular window, 22 feet in diameter, which was given by Miss Roper; and beneath it there are small coloured lights, put in by Father Weston out of money left him by Miss Green. Nearly all the side windows in the church are coloured, and four of them are of the "presentation" stamp. The most prominent thing about the church is the spire, which, as well as the tower, is built of limestone, and surmounted by a cross, the distance from its apex to the ground being about 301 feet. We saw the weather vane fixed upon this spire, and how the man who did the job managed to keep his head from spinning right round, and then right off, was at the time an exciting mystery to us which we have not yet been able to properly solve. A little before the actual completion of the spire, we had a chance of ascending it, but we remained below. The man in charge wanted half-a-crown for the trip; and as we fancied that something like 5 pounds ought to be given to us for undertaking a journey so perilous, it was mutually decided that we should keep down. Why, it would be a sort of agony to ascend the spire under the most favourable circumstances; and as one might only tumble down if ascension were achieved, the safest plan is to keep down altogether. We have often philosophised on the question of punishment, and, locally speaking, we have come to this conclusion, that agony would be sufficiently piled in any case of crime, if the delinquent were just hoisted to the top of St. Walburge's spire and left there. From the summit of the tower, which is quite as high as safe-sided human beings need desire to get, there is a magnificent view: Preston lurches beneath like a hazy amphitheatre of houses and chimneys; to the east you have Pendle, Longridge, and the dark hills of Bowland; northwards, in the far distance, the undulating Lake hills; westward, the fertile Fylde, flanked by the Ribble, winding its way like a silver thread to the ocean; and southwards Rivington Pyke and Hoghton's wooded summit with a dim valley to the left thereof, in which Blackburn works and dreams out its vigorous existence. The general scenery from the tower is panoramic and charming. The view from the spire head must be immense and exquisite, but few people of this generation, unless a very safe plan of ascension is found out, will be able to enjoy it. In the tower there is a large bell, weighing 31 cwt.; and it can make a very considerable sound, drowning all the smaller ringing arrangements in the neighbourhood. Some time, but not yet, there will probably be a peal of twelve bells in the tower, for it has accomodation for that number.

Internally the church is very high and spacious; is decorated artistically in many places; and a sense of mingled solemnity and immensity comes over you on entering it. The roof is a tremendous affair; it is open, and supported by eleven huge Gothic-fashioned principals, each of which cost 100 pounds, and it is panelled above with stained timber. But we don't care very much for the roof. No doubt it is fine; but the whole of the wood work seems too, heavy and much too dark. There is a cimmerian massiveness about it; and on a dull day it looks quite bewildering. If it were stained in a lighter colour its proportions would come out better, and much of that gigantic gloom which now shadows it would be removed. There are canopied stands for two and twenty statues towards the base of the principals; but the whole of them, except about five, are empty. Saints, &c., will be looked after for these stands when money is more abundant, and when more essential work has been executed. What seems to be proximately wanted in the church is a good sanctuary - something in keeping with the general design of the building and really worthy of the place. It is intended, we believe, to have a magnificent sanctuary; but a proper design for one can't be exactly hit on; when it is, the past liberality of the congregation is a sufficient guarantee that the needful article - money - will be soon forthcoming. Notwithstanding the greatness of the church, it will not seat as many as some smaller places of worship. This is accounted for through its having no galleries. There is a small elevation in the shape of a gallery at the western end, which is seldom used; but the sides of the church are open, the windows running along them rendering this necessary. The church will comfortably seat about 1,000 persons; 1,700 have been seen in it; but there had to be much crushing, and all the aisles, &c., had to be filled with standing people to admit such a number. The seats are all well made and all open.

On a Sunday masses are said at eight, nine, ten, and eleven, and there is an afternoon service at three. The aggregate average attendance on a Sunday is about 3,000. There are three confessionals in the church, towards the south-eastern-corner; they stand out like small square boxes, and although made for everybody seem specially adapted for thin and Cassius-like people. Falstaff's theory was - more flesh more frailty. If this be so, then, there are either very few "great" sinners at St. Walburge's or the large ones confess somewhere else. The worshippers at this church are, in nine cases out of ten, working people. The better class of people sit at the higher end of the central benches; and if one had never seen them there no difficulty would be experienced in finding out their seats. You may always ascertain the character of worshippers by what they sit upon. Working-class people rest upon bare boards; middle-class individuals develop the cushion scheme to a moderate pitch; the upper species push it towards consummation-like ease, and therefore are the owners of good cushions. Very few cushions can be seen in St. Walburge's; those noticeable are at the higher end; and the logical inference, therefore, is that not many superb people attend the place, and that those who do go sit just in the quarter mentioned. At the doors of this church, as at those of other Catholic places of worship in the town, you may see men standing with boxes, asking for alms. These are brothers of the Society of St. Vincent de Paul. The object of this society is to visit and relieve the sick and the poor. The brothers are excellent auxiliaries of the clergy; and, further, do the work of the mendicity societies, like those now being established in London, by examing applications for relief, and so disappointing impostors. The conference of St. Vincent attached to St. Walburge's Church numbers 16 active members, who collected and distributed in food and clothing during last year 112 pounds. The brothers are deserving of all praise for spending their evenings in visiting the sick and distressed, in courts and alleys, after their day's work.

The singers at this church occupy a small balcony on the south side. They are a pretty musical body - got through their business ever so creditably; but they are rather short of that which most choirs are deficient in - tenor power. They would be heard far better if placed at the western end but a good deal of expense would have to be incurred in making orchestral arrangements for them there; so that for some time, at least, they will have to be content with their grated and curtained musical hoist on the southern side, singing right out as hard as they can at the pulpit, which exactly faces them, and at the preacher, if they like, when he gets into it. The organ, which is placed above the singers, and would crush them into irrecoverable atoms if it fell, is a fine instrument; but it is pushed too far into the wall, into the tower which backs it, and if there are any holes above, much of its music must necessarily escape up the steeple. The organ is played with taste and precision. The members of the choir sing gratuitously.

Since the opening of St. Walburge's there have been twelve different priests at it. Three are in charge of it now. Father Weston was the first priest, and, as already stated, was the mainspring of the church. He died on the 14th of November, 1867, and to his memory a stained glass window will by and bye be fixed in the church. This window is in Preston now; we have seen it - it is a most beautiful piece of workmanship; and as soon as the requisite money is "resubscribed," the original contributions having, through unfortunate financial circumstances, been more than half sacrificed, it will be fixed. Father Henry, late rector of Stonyhurst College, was for some time at St. Walburge's, and during his stay the work begun by Father Weston, and pushed on considerably by successive priests, was elaborated and finished. The three priests now at St. Walburge's are Fathers J. Johnson (principal), Payne, and Papall. Father Johnson, who has been at the church about fourteen months, is a spare, long-headed, warm-hearted, unostentatious man. He is between 50 and 60 years of age; has a practical, weather-beaten, shrewd look; would be bad to "take in;" has much latent force; is a kindly, fatherly preacher; is dry in humour till drawn out, and then can be very genial; is a sharp man, mentally and executively; has been provincial of the Jesuits and rector of Stonyhurst College; knows what's what, and knows that he knows it; is determined, but can be melted down; seems cold and sly, but has a kind spirit and an honest tongue in his bead; and is the right man for his position.

Father Payne has been at St. Walburge's about four years. He has passed 40 summers in single blessedness, and says he intends to "last it out." His preaching is serious and earnest in style. His eloquence may not be so captivating as that of some men; but it comes up freely, and involves utterances of import. Father Payne has not much action, but he has a good voice; he lifts his arms slowly and regularly, leans forward somewhat, occasionally seizes both his hands and shakes them a little; but beyond this there is not much motion observable in him. He has a keen, discreet sense of things, and, like the rest of his order, can see a long way. In private life - that is to say when he is out of the pulpit and off general duty - he is an affable, clear, merry, brisk-talking little gentleman, fond of a good joke, a blithe chat, and a hearty laugh. He is a pleasant Payne when in company, and if you knew him you would say so. The last Daniel who cometh up to judgment is Father Papall - the very embodiment of vivaciousness, linguistic activity, and dignity in a nut shell. Dark-haired, sharp-eyed, spectacled; diminutive, warm-blooded, he is about the most animated priest we know of. He has English and Italian blood in his veins, and that vascular mixture works him up beautifully. No man could stand such an amalgam without being determined, volatile, practical, and at times dreamy; and you have all these qualities developed in Father Papall. He is 40 years of age, and has seen more foreign life than many priests. He has been in Italy, where he resided for years, in Holland, Belgium, Germany, France, America, &c.; and he has been at St. Walburge's in this town, for 14 months. He is all animation when conversing with you; and in the pulpit he talks from head to foot - stirs all over, fights much with his sleeves, moves his arms, and hands, and fingers as if under some hot spell of galvanism, and fairly gets his "four feet" into the general subject, and revels with a delicious activity in it at intervals. He is an earnest preacher, has good intellectual constructive-ness, and if he had not to battle so much with our English idioms and curious modes of pronunciation he would be a very potent speaker, and a racy homilist. He has a sweeping powerful voice; you could almost hear him if you were asleep, and this fact may account for the peculiarly contented movements of several parties we observed recently at the church whilst Father Papall was preaching. At least 20 near us went to sleep in about five minutes after he began talking, slept very well during the whole sermon, and at its conclusion woke up very refreshed, made brisk crosses, listened awhile to the succeeding music, &c., and then walked out quite cool and cheerful.

Most excellent schools are situated near and on the northern side of the church. The average daily attendance of boys is 200; that of the girls 260; that of the infants, 350. The boys seem well trained; the girls, who are in charge of nuns - called "Companions of the Holy Child Jesus" - are likewise industriously cared for; and the infants are a show in themselves. We saw these 350 babies, for many of them are nothing more, the other day, and the manner in which they conducted themselves was simply surprising. The utmost order prevailed amongst them, and how this was brought about we could not tell. One little pleasant-looking nun had charge of the whole confraternity, and she could say them at a word - make them as mute as mice with the mere lifting of her finger, and turn them into all sorts of merry moods by a similar motion, in a second. If this little nun could by some means convey her secret of managing children to about nineteen-twentieths of the mothers of the kingdom, who find it a dreadful business to regulate one or two, saying nothing of 350, babes and sucklings, she would confer a lasting benefit upon the householders of Britain. Night and Sunday schools - the latter being attended by about 700 boys and girls - are held in the same buildings. There are five nuns at St. Walburge's; they live in a convent hard by; and like the rest of their class they work hard every day, and sacrifice much of their own pleasure for the sake of that of other people - a thing which the generality of us have yet to take first lessons in.

XXII

UNITARIAN CHAPEL.

There is something so severely mental, and so theologically daring in Unitarianism that many can't, whilst others won't, hold communion with it. Unbiased thinkers, willing to give all men freedom of conscience, admit the force of its logic in some things, the sincerity of its intentions in all, but deem it too dry and much too intellectual for popular digestion. The orthodox brand it as intolerably heretical and terribly unscriptural; the multitude of human beings; - like "Oyster Nan" who couldn't live without "running her vulgar rig" - consider it downright infidelity, the companion of rationalism, and the "stepping Stone to atheism." Still there are many good people who are Unitarians; many magnificent scholars who recognise its principles; and if "respectability" is any proof of correctness - this age, in the obliquity of its vision, and in the depth of its respect for simple "appearances," says it is - then Unitarianism ought to be a very proper article, for its congregations, though comparatively small, are highly seasoned with persons who wear capital clothes, take their time from the best of watches, and have ever so much of what lawyers call "real and personal" property. Men termed "Monarchians" were the first special professors of Unitarianism. They made their appearance between the second and third centuries, and, if Tertullian tells the truth, they consisted of "the simple and the unlearned." Directly after the Reformation Unitarianism spread considerably on the continent, and Transylvania, which now contains about 56,000 of its followers, became its great stronghold. Unitarianism got into England about the middle of the 16th century; and many of the Presbyterian divines who were ejected during the century which followed - in 1662 - gradually became believers in it. In England the Unitarians have now about 314 chapels and emission stations; in Scotland there are only five congregations recognising Unitarianism; in Ireland about 40; in our colonies there are a few; in the United States of America the body has 256 societies; in France, Germany, Holland, &c., the principles of Unitarianism are pretty extensively believed in. Some of our greatest thinkers and writers have been Unitarians: Milton was one, so was John Locke, and so was Newton. In different ages there have been different classes of Unitarians; in these days there are at least two - the conservative and the progressive; but in the past the following points were generally believed, and in the present there is no diversity of opinion regarding them, viz., that the Godhead is single and absolute, not triune; that Christ was not God, but a perfect being inspired with divine wisdom; that there is no efficacy in His vicarious atonement, in the sense popularly recognised; and that original sin and eternal damnation are in accordance with neither the Scriptures nor common sense.

The origin of Unitarianism in Preston, as elsewhere, is mixed up with the early strivings and operations of emancipated Nonconformity. We can find no record of Nonconformists in Preston until the early part of the 18th century. At that period a chapel was erected at

Walton-le-Dale, mainly, if not entirely, by Sir Henry de Hoghton - fifth baronet, and formerly member of parliament for Preston - who was one of the principal patrons of Nonconformity in this district. Very shortly afterwards, and under the same patronage, a Nonconformist congregation was established to Preston - meetings having previously been held in private houses - and the Rev. John Pilkington, great uncle of W. O. Pilkington, Esq., of the Willows, near this town, who is a Unitarian, was the minister of it, as well as of that in Walton. In 1718, a little building was erected for the Nonconformists of Preston on a piece of land near the bottom and on the north side of Church-street. This was the first Dissenting chapel raised in Preston, and in it the old Nonconformists - Presbyterians we ought to say - spent many a free and spiritually-happy hour. Eventually the generality of the congregation got into a "Monarchian" frame of mind, and from that time till this the chapel has been held by those whom we term Unitarians. The "parsonage house" of the Unitarian minister used to be in Church-street, near the chapel; but it has since been transmuted into a shop. One of the ministers at this place of worship towards the end of the last century, was a certain Mr. Walker, but he couldn't masticate the Unitarian theory which was being actively developed in it, so he walked away, and for him a building in Grimshaw-street - the predecessor of the present Independent Chapel there - was subsequently erected.

The edifice wherein our Unitarian friends assemble every Sunday, is an old-fashioned, homely-looking, little building - a tiny, Quakerised piece of architecture, simple to a degree, prosaic, diminutive, snug, dull. It is just such a place as you could imagine old primitive Non-conformists, fonder of strong principles and inherent virtue than of external embellishment and masonic finery, would build. It can be approached by two ways, but it is of no use trying to take advantage of both at once. You would never get to the place if you made such an effort. There is a road to it from Percy-street - this is the better entrance, but not much delight can be found in it; and there is another way to the chapel from Church-street - up a delicious little passage, edged on the right with a house-side, and on the left with a wall made fierce with broken glass, which will be sure to cut the sharpest of the worshippers if they ever attempt to get over it. What there really is behind that glass-topped wall we are at a loss to define; but it is evidently something which the occupier of the premises apprehends the Unitarians may have an illicit liking for? If they want to get to it we would recommend the use of some heavy, blunt instrument, by which they could easily break the glass, after which they might quietly lift each other over. Recently, a small sign has been fixed at the end of the passage, and from the letters upon it an inference may be safely drawn that the Unitarian Chapel is somewhere beyond it. To strangers this will be useful, for, prior to its exhibition, none except those familiar with the place, or gifted with an instinct for threading the mazes of mystery, could find out, with anything like comfort, the location of the chapel. Whether the people have or have not "sought for a sign," one has at any rate been given to them here. A small, and somewhat neat, graveyard is attached to the chapel; there are several tomb-stones laid flat upon the ground; and in the centre of it there is a rather elaborate one, substantially railed round, and surmounting the vault of the Ainsworth family. The remains of the late W. Ainsworth, Esq., a well-known and respected Preston gentleman, are interred here.

At the northern side of, and directly adjoining, the chapel there is a small Sunday school, It was erected about 15 years ago; the scholars previous to that time having met in a little building in Lord's-walk. The average attendance of scholars at present is about 60. The chapel, internally, is small, clean, plain, and ancient-looking. A central aisle runs directly up to the pulpit, and it is flanked with a range of high old-fashioned pews, some being plain, a few lined with a red-coloured material, and several with faded green baize, occasionally tacked back and elaborated with good old-fashioned brass nails. The seats vary in size, and include both the moderately narrow and the full square for family use. There are nine variously shaped windows in the building: through three of them you can see sundry things, ranging from the spire of the Parish Church to the before-mentioned wall with the broken glass top; through some of the others faint outlines of chimneys may be traced. The chapel is light and comfortable-looking. There seems to be nothing in the place having the least relationship to ornament except four small gas brackets, which are trimmed up a little, and surmounted with small crosses of the Greek pattern. At the west end, supported by two pillars, there is a small gallery, in which a few elderly people, the scholars, and the choir are deposited. The body of the chapel will accommodate about 200 persons. The average attendance, excluding the scholars, will be perhaps 60. When we visited the place there were 50 present - 45 downstairs and five in the gallery; and of these, upwards of 30 were females.

The congregation is quite of a genteel and superior character. There are a few rather poor people embraced in it; but nine out of ten of the regular worshippers belong to either independent or prosperous middle class families. The congregation, although still "highly respectable," is not so influential in tone as it used to be. A few years ago, six or seven county magistrates might have been seen in the chapel on a Sunday, and they were all actual "members" of the body; but death and other causes have reduced the number of this class very considerably, and now not more than two are constant worshippers. There is neither sham, shoddy, nor rant amongst them. From one year end to another you will never hear any of them during any of the services rush into a florid yell or reduce their spiritual emotions to a dull groan. They abstain from everything in the contortional and ejaculative line; quiet contemplative intellectualism appears to reign amongst them; a dry, tranquil thoughtfulness, pervades the body. They are eclectical, optimic, cool; believe in taking things comfortably; never conjure up during their devotions the olden pictures of orthodoxy; never allow their nerves to be shattered with notions about the "devil," or the "burning lake" in which sinners have to be tortured for ever and ever; never hear of such things from the pulpit, wouldn't tolerate them if they did; think that they can get on well enough without them. They may be right or they may be very wrong; but, like all sections of Christians, they believe their own denominational child the best.

There are two services every Sunday in the Unitarian chapel - morning and evening - and both are very good in one sense because both are very short. There have been many ministers at the chapel since its transformation into a Unitarian place of worship; but we need not unearth musty records and name them all. Within modern memory there have been just a trinity of ministers at the chapel - the Rev. Joseph Ashton, an exceedingly quiet, unassuming, well learned man, who would have taken a higher stand in the town than he did if he had made more fuss about himself; the Rev. W. Croke Squier, who made too much fuss, who had too big a passion for Easter-due martyrdoms and the like, for Corn Exchange speeches, patriotic agony points , and virtuous fighting, but who was nevertheless a sharp-headed, quick-sighted, energetic little gentleman ; and the Rev. R. J. Orr - the present minister - who came to Preston about a year and a half since. Mr. Orr is an Irishman, young in years, tall, cold, timid, quiet, yet excellently educated. He is critical, seems slightly cynical, and moves along as if he either knew nobody or didn't want to look at anybody. There is somewhat of the student, and somewhat of the college professor in his appearance. But he is a very sincere man; has neither show nor fussiness in him; and practices his duties with a strict, quiet regularity. He may have moods of mirth and high moments of sparkling glee, but he looks as if he had never only laughed right out about once in his life, and had repented of it directly afterwards. If he had more dash and less shyness in him, less learned coolness and much more humour in his composition, he would reap a better harvest in both pulpit and general life. Mr. Orr is no roaring will o' the wisp minister; what he says he means; and what he means he reads. His prayers and sermons are all read. He is not eloquent, but his language is scholarly, and if he had a freer and more genial expression he would be better appreciated. If he were livelier and smiled more he would be fatter and happier. His style is his own; is too Orrible, needs a little more sunshine and blithesomeness. He never allows himself to be led away by passion; sticks well to his text; invariably keeps his temper. He wears neither surplice nor black gown in the pulpit, and does quite as well without as with them. For his services he receives about 120 pounds a year and if the times mend he will probably get more. In the chapel there is a harmonium, which is played as well as the generality of such instruments are. The singing is only moderate, and if it were not for the good strong female voice, apparently owned by somebody in the gallery, it would be nearly inaudible - would have to be either gently whispered or "thought out." The services in the main are simple, free from all boisterous balderdash, and if not of such a character as would suit everybody, are evidently well liked by those participating in them.

XXIII

ALL SAINTS' CHURCH.

The calendar of the canonised has come in handy for the christening of churches. Without it, we might have indulged in a poor and prosaic nomenclature; with it, the dullest, as well as the finest, architecture can get into the company of the beatified. Barring a few places, all our churches are associated with some particular saint; every edifice has cultivated the acquaintance of at least one; but that we have now to notice has made a direct move into the general constellation, and is dedicated to the aggregate body. We believe that in church-naming, as in common life, "ALL is for the best," and we commend, rather than censure, the judgment which recognised the full complement of saints when All Saints' was consecrated. A man maybe wrong in fixing upon one name, or upon fifty, or fifty hundred, but if he agglomerates the entire mass, condenses every name into one, and gives something respectable that particular name, he won't be far off the equinoctial of exactness. In this sense, the christeners of All Saints' were wise; they went in for the posse comitatus of saints - backed the favourites as well as "the field" - and their scheme, so far as naming goes, must win. There is, however, not much in a name, and less in a reverie of speculative comment, so we will descend to a lower, yet, perhaps, more healthy, atmosphere.

In 1841, the Rev. W. Walling, son of a yeoman living is Silverdale - one of the prettiest places we know of in the North of England - came to Preston, as minister of St. James's Church. He stayed at the place for about a year, then went to Carlton, in Nottinghamshire, and afterwards to Whitby. Mr. Walling was a man of quiet disposition; during his stay in Preston he was exceedingly well liked; and when he left the town, a vacuum seemed to have been created. He was a missed man; his value was not found out until he had gone; and it was determined - mainly amongst a pious, enthusiastic section of working people - to get him back again if possible. And they went about the business like sensible people - decided not to root out his predecessor at St. James's, nor to exterminate any of the sundry clerical beings in other parts of the town, but to build him a new church. They were only poor men; but they persevered; and in a short time their movement took a distinct shape, and the building, whose erection they had in view, was prospectively called "The Poor Man's Church." In time they raised about 200 pounds; but a sum like that goes only a little way in church building - sometimes doesn't cover those very refreshing things which contractors call "extras;" a number of wealthier men, who appreciated the earnestness of the original promoters, and saw the necessity, of such a church as they contemplated, came to the rescue, and what they and divers friends gave justified a start, on a plot of land between Walker-street and Elizabeth-street. On the 21st of September, 1846, the foundation-stone of the church - All Saints - was laid by the late Thomas German, Esq., who was mayor of Preston at that time. The building, which cost about 2,600 pounds, was not consecrated till

December, 1856, but it was ministerially occupied by the Rev. W. Walling on the 23rd September, 1848, and he held his post, earning the respect and esteem of all in the discharge of its duties, till October 10th, 1863, when death suddenly ended his labours. When the church was consecrated there was a debt of about 750 pounds upon it; but in a few years, by the judicious and energetic action of the trustees, it was entirely cleared off. The present trustees of the church are Dr. Hall, Messrs. J. R. Ambler, F. Mitchell, and W. Fort. The successor of the Rev. W. Walling was the Rev. G. Beardsell, who still occupies the situation; but before saying anything to the point concerning him we must describe the church and its concomitants.

All Saints' is a good substantial-looking church. It is built in the Ionic style of Greek architecture; has a massive pillared front; is railed round, has an easy and respectable entrance, and - getting worse as it gets higher - is surmounted with a small bell turret and a chimney. Other things may be put upon the roof after a while, for space is abundant there. The church has a square, respectable, capacious interior - is roomy, airy, light; doesn't seem thrown together in a dim foggy labrynth like some places, and you feel as if you could breathe freely on taking a seat in it. It is well-galleried, and will accommodate altogether about 1,500 human beings. The pews are good, and whilst it is impossible for them to hold more people than can get into them, they are charged for as if one additional person could take a seat in each after being full! This is odd but quite true. In the case of pews which will just accommodate five persons, six sittings are charged for; those holding four are put down in the rent book for five; and this scale of charges is kept up in respect to all the pews, whether big or little. The rents go into the pocket of the incumbent. At the southern end there is a small chancel, which was erected at the expense of the late J. Bairstow, Esq. It is ornamented with several stained glass windows, and has an inlaid wooden canopy, but there is nothing startling nor remarkable about the work. Beneath the windows there is painted in large, letters the word "Emmanuel;" but the position of it is very inconvenient. People sitting above may see the name fairly; but many below have a difficulty in grasping it, and those sitting in the centre will never be able to get hold of more letters than those which makeup the mild name of "Emma." Names-particularly great ones - should never be put up anywhere unless they can be seen. On each side of the chancel arch then is a small tablet; one being to the memory of the Rev. W. Walling, and the other to that of the late W. Tuson, Esq., who was one of the original wardens. The church is clean and in good condition; but the windows would stand re-painting. There are about 400 free seats in the building, and they are pretty well patronised. The general attendance is tolerably large; between 700 and 800 people frequent the church on the average; but the congregation seems to be of a floating character, is constantly changing, and embraces few "old stagers." Formerly, many who had been at the church from the first might be seen at it; numerous persons recognised as "fixtures" were there; but they have either gone to other churches or died off, and there is now a strong ebb and flow of new material at the place.

The congregation is of a complex description; you may see in it the "Grecian bend" and the coal scuttle hood, the buff waistcoat and the dark moleskin coat; but in the main the worshippers are of a quiet well-assorted character - partly working class, partly middle-class, with a sprinkling of folk above and below both. The humble minded and the ancient appear to have a liking for the left side range of seats; the swellishly-young and the substantially-middle class take up a central position; people of a fair habilimental stamp occupy the bulk of the seats on the other side; whilst the select and the specially virtuous approximate the pulpit - one or two in the excelsior category get even beyond it, and like both the quietude and the dignity of the position. The galleries are used by a promiscuous company of worshippers, who keep good order and make no undue noises. The tale-tellers and the gossips - for they exist here as in the generality of sacred places - are distributed in various directions. It would be advantageous if they were all put in one separate part; for then their influence would not be so ramified, and they might in the end get up a small Kilkenny affair and mutually finish off one another. Late attendance does not seem to be so fashionable at All Saints' as at some churches; still it exists; things would look as if they were getting wrong if somebody didn't come late and make everybody turn their heads. When we visited the church, the great mass were present at the right time; but a few dropped in after the stipulated period; one put in an appearance 30 minutes late; and another sauntered serenely into the region of the ancient people just 65 minutes after the proceedings had commenced. At a distance, the reading desk and the pulpit look oddly mixed up; but a close inspection shows that they are but fairly associated, stand closely together, the pulpit, which is the higher, being in the rear. There is no decoration of any sort in the body of the church; everything appears tranquil, serious, straightforward, and respectable. The singing is of a very poor character, - is slow, weak, and calculated at times to make you ill. Pope, in his Essay on Criticism, says -

Some to church repair,
Not for the doctrine, but the music there.

Probably they do; but nobody goes to All Saints' for that purpose. No genuine hearty interest seems to be taken in the singing by anybody particularly. The choir move through their notes as if some of them were either fastened up hopelessly in barrels, or in a state of musical syncope; the organist works his hands and feet as well as he can with a poor organ; the members of the congregation follow, lowly and contentedly, doing their best against long odds and the parson sits still, all in one grand piece, and looks on. The importance and influence of good music should be recognised by every church; and we trust in time there will be a decided improvement at All Saints'. A church like it - a building of its size and with its congregation - ought to have something superior and effective in the matter of music.

We have already said that the Rev. George Beardsell is the minister of All Saints'. He has been at the church, as its incumbent, about five years. Originally Mr. Beardsell was a Methodist; - a Methodist preacher, too, we believe; but in time he changed his notions; and eventually flung himself, in a direct line, into the arms of "Mother Church." Mr. Beardsell made his first appearance in Preston as curate of Trinity Church. He worked hard in this capacity, stirred up the district at times with that peculiar energy which poor curates longing for good incumbencies, wherein they may settle down into security and ease, can only manifest, and with many he was a favourite. From Trinity Church he went to St. Saviour's, and here he slackened none of his powers. Enthusiasm, combined with earnest plodding, enabled him to improve the district considerably. He drew many poor people around him; he repeatedly charmed the "unwashed" with his strong rough-hewn orgasms; the place seemed to have been specially reserved for some man having just the perseverance and vigorous volubility which he possessed; he had ostensibly a "mission" in the locality; the people of the district liked him, he reciprocated the feeling, and more than once intimated that he would make one or two spots, including the wild region of Lark-hill, "Blossom as the rose." But the period of efflorescence has not yet arrived; a "call" came in due season, and this carried the ministerial florist to another "sphere of action." Mr. Beardsell was translated to the incumbency of All Saints', and he still holds it. When Mr. Walling was at this church the income was about 260 pounds a year; taking everything into account, it is now worth upwards of 400 pounds.

Mr. Beardsell is not a beautiful, but a stout, well-made, strong-looking man, close upon 40, with a growing tendency towards adiposity. He has a healthy, bulky, English look; is not a man of profound education, but, makes up by weight what he may lack in depth; thinks it a good thing to carry a walking-stick, to keep his coat well buttoned, and to arrange his hair in the high-front, full-whig style; has a powerful, roughly eloquent voice; is rather sensational in the construction of some of his sentences; bellows a little at times; welters pathetically often; is somewhat monotonous in tone; ululates too heavily; behaves harshly to the letter "r" - sounds it with a violent vigour, and makes it fairly spin round his tongue end occasionally; can sustain himself well as a speaker; is never at a loss for words; has a forcible way of arranging his subjects; is systematic in his style of treatment; and can throw into his elucidation of questions well-coined and emphatic expressions. He likes perorations - used to imitate Punshon a little. He has a good analogical faculty; takes many of his illustrations from nature, and works them out exceedingly well; is a capital explainer of biblical difficulties; is peculiarly fond of the travels of St. Paul; piles up the agony easily and effectively; many times gets into a groove of high-beating, fierce-burning enthusiasm, as if he were going to take a distinct leap out of his "pent-up Utica," and revel in the "whole boundless continent" of thought and sacred sensation; is a thorough believer in the "My brethren" phrase - we recently heard him use it nineteen times in twenty minutes, and regretted that he didn't make the numbers equal; delights in decking out his discourses with couplets and snatches of hymns; has a full-blown determined style of speaking; reads with his gloves on, and preaches with them off, like one or two other parsons we have seen; makes his sermons too long; is a good platform man, and would make a fair travelling lecturer; has a great predilection for open-air preaching, and has spells of it to the Orchard; might with advantage work more in and less out of his own district; wouldn't commit a sin if he studied the question of personal visiting; shouldn't think that his scripture reader - a really good, hard-working man - can perform miracles, and do nearly everything; can talk genuine common sense if he likes, and make himself either very agreeable or pugnacious; is an Orangeman, with a holy horror of Popery; can give deliciously passionate lectures about the Reformation; considers money a very important article, and is inclined to believe that all people, particularly parsons, should stick to it very firmly; will have his own way in church matters; likes to fight with a warden; has had many a lively little brush over sacrament money; might have got on better with many of the officials if he had been more conciliatory; is a man of moderate ability, of fair metal, of strong endurance, but would be more relished if he were less dogmatic, were given less to wandering preaching, and threw himself heart, soul, purse, and clothes into his own district. Near the church, and occupying good relative positions on each side of a beerhouse, called "The Rising Sun," are All Saints' schools. One of them - that now occupied by the boys - was, according to a tablet at the outside, erected several years ago by our old friend Captain German "as an affectionate tribute to the memory of Thomas German, Esq." About five years since, two class-rooms were attached to it, at the expense of J. Bairstow, J. Horrocks, R. Newsham, and T. Miller, Esqrs. The other school, set apart for the girls, was erected after that built by Captain German. Both of the schools are very good ones - are large, lofty, and commodious. That used for the boys is, scholastically, in a superior condition. The master is sharp, fully up to his duties; and, according to a report by the government inspector, his school is one of the best in the district. The average day attendance at the boys' school is 150; whilst at the girls school the regular attendance may be set down at 330. The schools are used on Sundays, and their average attendance then is 800. Much might be written concerning them; but we must close; we have said enough; and can only add that if all are not saints who go to All Saints' they are about as good as the rest of people.

XXIV

UNITED METHODIST FREE CHURCH AND POLE-STREET BAPTIST CHAPEL.

We have two places of worship to struggle with "on the present occasion," and shall take the freest yet most methodistical of them first. The United Methodist Free Church - that is a rather long and imposing name - is generally called "Orchard Chapel." The "poetry of the thing" may suffer somewhat by this deviation; but the building appears to smell as sweetly under the shorter as the longer name, so that we shall not enter into any Criticism condemnatory of the change. This chapel is the successor, in a direct line, of the first building ever erected in the Orchard. Its ancestor was placed on precisely the same spot, in 1831. Those who raised it seceded from the Wesleyan community, in sympathy with the individuals who retired from the "old body" at Leeds, in 1828, and who adopted the name of "Protestant Methodists." For a short time the Preston branch of these Methodists worshipped in that mystic nursery of germinating "isms" called Vauxhall-road Chapel; and in the year named they erected in the Orchard a building for their own spiritual improvement. It was a plain chapel outside, and mortally ugly within. Amongst the preaching confraternity in the connexion it used to be known as "the ugliest Chapel in Great Britain and Ireland." In 1834 a further secession of upwards of 20,000 from the Wesleyans took place, under the leadership of the late Dr. Warren, of Manchester. These secessionists called themselves the "Wesleyan Association," and with them the "Protestant Methodists," including those meeting in the Orchard Chapel, Preston, amalgamated. They also adopted the name of their new companions. In 1857 the "Wesleyan Association" coalesced with another large body of persons, who seceded from the original Wesleyans in 1849, under the leadership of the Rev. James Everett and others, and the two conjoined sections termed themselves the "United Methodist Free Church." None of the separations recorded were occasioned by any theological difference with the parent society, but through disagreement on matters of "government."

The ministers of the United Methodist Free Church body move about somewhat after the fashion of the Wesleyan preachers. They first go to a place for twelve months, and if they stay longer it has to be through "invitation" from one of the quarterly meetings. As a rule, they stop three or four years at one church, and then move off to some new circuit, where old sermons come in, at times, conveniently for new hearers. The various churches are ruled by "leaders" - men of a deaconly frame of mind, invested with power sufficient to enable them to rule the roost in ministerial matters, to say who shall preach and who shall not, and to work sundry other wonders in the high atmosphere of church government. The "members" support their churches, financially, in accordance with their means. There is no fixed payment. Those who are better off, and not stingy, give liberally; the less opulent contribute moderately; those who can't give anything don't. After an existence of about 30 years, the old chapel in the Orchard was pulled down, in order to make way for a larger and a better looking building. During the work of reconstruction Sunday services were held in the school at the rear, which was built some time before, at a cost of 1,700 pounds. The new chapel, which cost 2,600 pounds, was opened on the 22nd of May, 1862. It has a rather ornamental front - looks piquant and seriously nobby. There is nothing of the "great" or the "grand" in any part of it. The building is diminutive, cheerful, well-made, and inclined, in its stone work, to be fantastical.

Internally, it is clean, ornate, and substantial. Its gallery has stronger supports than can be found in any other Preston chapel. If every person sitting in it weighed just a ton it would remain firm. There are two front entrances to the building, and at each end red curtains are fixed. On pushing one pair aside, the other Sunday, we cogitated considerably as to what we should see inside. We always associate mystery with curtains, "caudle lectures" with curtains, shows, and wax-work, and big women, and dwarfs with curtains; but as we slowly, yet determinedly, undid these United Methodist Free Church curtains, and presented our "mould of form" before the full and absolute interior, we beheld nothing special: there were only a child, two devotional women, and a young man playing a slow and death-like tune on a well-made harmonium, present. But the "plot thickened," the place was soon moderately filled, and whilst in our seat, before the service commenced, we calmly pondered over many matters, including the difficulty we had in reaching the building. Yes, and it was a difficulty. We took the most direct cut, as we thought, to the place, from the southern side - passed along the Market-place, into that narrowly-beautiful thoroughfare called New-street, then through a yet newer road made by the pulling down of old buildings in Lord-street, and reminding one by its sides of the ruins of Petra, and afterwards merged into the Orchard. To neither the right nor the left did we swerve, but moved on, the chapel being directly is front of us; but in a few moments afterwards we found ourselves surrounded by myriads of pots and a mighty cordon of crates - it was the pot fair. Thinking that the Orchard was public ground, and seeing the chapel so very near, we pursued the even tenour of our way, but just as we were about sliding between two crates, so as to pass on into the chapel, a strong man, top-coated, muffled up, and with a small bludgeon in his hand, moved forward and said "Can't go." "Why?" said we; "Folks isn't allowed in this here place now," said he. "Well, but this is the town's property and we pay rates," was our rejoinder, and his was "Don't matter a cuss, if you were Lord Derby I should send you back." We accused him of rudeness, and threatened to go to the police station, close by; but the fellow was obstinate; his labours were concentred in the virtuous guardianship of pots, he defied the police and "everybody;" and feeling that amid all this mass of crockery we had, for once, unfortunately, "gone to pot," we quietly walked round to the bottom of the ground, for the crates and the pots swamped the whole place, came up to the chapel door, within four yards of the Lord-Derby-defying individual, and quietly went into the building.

There are about 300 "members" of the church. In the Preston circuit, which until recently included Croston, Cuerden, Brinscall, Chorley, and Blackpool, and which now only embraces, Cuerden and Croston - the other places being thought sufficiently strong to look after themselves - there are about 400 "members." What are termed "Churches" have been established at all the places named; Preston being the "parent" of them. A branch of the body exists at Southport, and it was "brought up" under the care of the Preston party. Orchard Chapel will accommodate between 700 and 800 persons; but, like other places of worship, it is never full except upon special occasions; and the average attendance may be put down at about 400. In the old chapel the father of the late Alderman G. Smith preached for a time. The first minister of the chapel, when rebuilt, was the Rev. J. Guttridge - an energetic, impetuous, eloquent, earnest man. He had two spells at the place; was at it altogether about six years; and left the last time about a year ago. Mr. Guttridge, who is one of the smartest ministers in the body, is now residing at Manchester, connected regularly with no place of worship, on account of ill health, but doing what he can amongst the different churches. The congregation of Orchard Chapel consists principally of well-dressed working people - a quiet, sincere-looking class of individuals, given in no way to devotional hysteria, and taking all things smoothly and seriously. They are a liberal class, too. During the past two years they have raised amongst themselves about 800 pounds towards the chapel, upon which there is still a debt, but which would have been clear of all monetary encumbrances long since if certain old scores needing liquidation had not stood in the way. The members of the choir sit near the pulpit, the females on one side and the males on the other. They are young, good-looking, and often glance at each other kindly. A female who plays the harmonium occupies the centre. The music is vigorous and, considering the place, commendable. On Sundays there are two services at the chapel - morning and evening; and during the week meetings of a religious character are held in either the chapel or the adjoining rooms.

The present minister of the chapel is the Rev. Richard Abercrombie. He has only just arrived, and may in one sense be termed the "greatest" minister in Preston, for he is at least six feet high in his stocking feet. He is an elderly gentleman, - must be getting near 70; but he is almost as straight as a wand, has a dignified look, wears a venerable grey beard, and has quite a military precision in his form and walk. And he may well have, for he has been a soldier, Mr. Abercrombie served in the British army upwards of twenty years. He followed Wellington, after Waterloo, and was in Paris as a British soldier when the famous treaty of peace was signed. His grandfather was cousin of the celebrated Sir Ralph Abercrombie, who defeated Napoleon's forces in Egypt, and his ancestors held commissions in our army for upwards of four generations. Tired of military life, Mr. Abercrombie eventually laid down his arms, and for 33 years he has been a minister in the body he is now connected with. It is worthy of remark that, before leaving the army, he occasionally sermonised in his uniform, and 35 years ago he preached in his red jacket, &c., in the old Orchard Chapel. Mr. Abercrombie is a genial, smooth-natured, quiet man - talks easily yet carefully, preaches earnestly yet evenly; there is no froth in either his prayers or sermons; he never gets into fits of uncontrollable passion, never rides the high horse of personal ambition, nor the low ass of religious vulgarity - keeps cool, behaves himself, and looks after his work midly and well. He has two or three sons in the United Methodist Free Church ministry, and one of them, called after the general who defeated the Napoleonic forces, is the only man belonging the body who has a university M.A. after his name.

Very good schools are connected with Orchard Chapel. The average day attendance is 140; and on Sundays the average is about 350, In the last place, we may observe that the people belonging Orchard Chapel are, generally, getting along comfortably in all their departments. Formerly they had feuds, and fights, and church meetings, at which odd pieces of scandal were bandied about - they may have morsels of unpleasantness yet to encounter; but taking them all in all they are moving on serenely and well.

Passing not "from pole to pole," but from the Orchard to Pole-street, we come to the Baptist Chapel in that, thoroughfare - a rather dull, strongly-railed-off place, which seems to be receding from public sight altogether. About 45 years ago, a small parcel of Preston people, enamoured of the Calvinistic Methodism which the Countess of Huntingdon recognised, worshipped in a building in Cannon-street. In 1825 they built, or had raised for them, a chapel in Pole-street, which was dedicated to St. Mark. At this time, probably on account of its novelty, the creed drew many followers - the new chapel was patronised by a somewhat numerous congregation, which kept increasing for a period. But it gradually dwindled down, and a total collapse finally ensued. In 1855 a number of General Baptists, who split from their brethren worshipping in the old Leeming-street chapel, struck a bargain with the expiring Lady Huntingdon section for their building in Pole-street, gave about 700 pounds for it, forthwith shifted thereto, and continue to hold the place. There is nothing at all calling for comment as to the exterior of the chapel; and not much as to the interior. It will accommodate about 900 persons. The pews are high, awkward to sit in, and have a grim cold appearance. The building is pretty lofty, and is well galleried. The pulpit is at the far end, and the singers sit on a railed platform before it. The congregation seems both thin and poor. Very lately we were in it, and estimated the number present at 84 - rather a small party for a chapel capable of holding 900.

The building possesses about the best acoustical properties of any place of worship in Preston. The late Mr. Samuel Grimshaw, of Preston, who, amongst many other things, had a special taste for music, used to occupy it at times, with his band, for the purposes of "practising." He liked it on account of its excellent sounding qualities. Once, after some practice in it, Mr. Grimshaw offered a "return" - said he would give the brethren a musical lift with his band during some anniversary services to be held in the chapel. His promise was accepted, and when the day came there was a complete musical flood. The orchestra, including the singers, numbered about 50, and the melodious din they created was something tremendous. "Sam" had the arrangement of it. There were tenors, baritones, bass men, trebles, alto-singers, in the fullest feather; there were trumpeters, tromboners, bassooners, ophicleideans, cornet-a-piston players, and many others, all instrumentally armed to the very teeth, and the sensation they made, fairly shook and unnerved the more pious members of the congregation, who protested against the chapel being turned into a "concert-hall," &c. The music after all, was good, and if it were as excellent now there would be a better attendance at the place. The present orchestra consists of perhaps a dozen singers, including a central gentleman who is about the best shouter we ever heard; and they are helped out of any difficulties they may get into by a rather awkwardly-played harmonium.

The Rev. W. J. Stuart is the minister of the chapel, and he receives from 70 to 80 pounds a year for his duties. He has a gentlemanly appearance; looks pretty well considering the nature of his salary; is getting into the grey epoch of life; is not very erudite; but seems well up in scriptural subjects; is sincere, mild, primitive in his notions; has fits of cautiousness and boldness; is precise and earnest in expression; has an "interpretational" tendency in his sacred utterances; is disposed to explain mysteries; likes homilising the people; can talk much; and can be very earnest over it all. He has fair action, and sometimes gets up to 212 degrees in his preaching. We won't say that he is in any sense a wearying preacher; but this we may state, that if his sermons were shorter they would not be quite so long. And from this he may take the hint. We are told that the attendance at the chapel is slightly increasing; but as compared with the past it is still very slender. The admission to either the platform or pulpit of the chapel, not very long ago, of a wandering "Indian chief," and a number of Revivalists, who told strange tales and talked wildly, has operated, we believe, against the place - annoyed and offended some, and caused them to leave. The minister, no doubt, admitted these men with an honest intention; but everybody can't stand the war-whooping of itinerant Indians, nor the sincere ferociousness of Revivalists; and awkward feelings were consequently generated in some quarters by them. In the main, Mr. Stuart is a kindly, quiet, gentlemanly person, and barring the little interruption caused by the dubious Indian and the untamed Revivalists, has got on with a small congregation and a bad salary better than many parsons would have been able to do.

XXV

CHURCH OF THE ENGLISH MARTYRS.

To this church a name which is general property has been given. Each of our religious sects can number its martyrs. In the good old times cruelty was a reciprocal thing amongst professing Christians; it was a pre-eminently mutual affair amongst the two great religious parties in the land - the Protestants and the Catholics, - for when one side got into power they slaughtered their opponents, and when the other became paramount the compliment was returned. The church we have here to describe is dedicated to those English Catholics who, in the stormy days of persecution, were martyred. It is situated on the northern side of the town, in a new and rapidly increasing part of Preston, at the extreme south-western corner of what used to be called Preston Moor, and on the very spot where men used to be hanged often, and get their heads cut off occasionally. "Gallows Hill" is the exact site of the Church of the English Martyrs. And this "hill" is associated with a movement constituting one of the rugged points in our history. The rebellion of 1715 virtually collapsed at Preston; many fights and skirmishes were indulged in, one or two breezy passages of arms even took place within a good stone-throw of the ground occupied by the Church of the English Martyrs; but the King's troops finally prevailed. According to an old book before us there were "taken at Preston" - amongst the rebels - "seven lords, besides 1,490 other, including the several gentlemen, officers, and private men, and two clergymen." And the book further says, in a humorously sarcastic mood, "There was a Popish priest called Littleton among them; but having a great deal of the Jesuit he contrived a most excellent disguise, for he put on a blue apron, went behind an apothecary's counter, and passed for an assistant or journeyman to the apothecary, and so took an opportunity of getting off." But all the captured rebels did not escape so adroitly as our Jesuitical friend Littleton; for several of them were either hanged or beheaded, and the fate of many was sealed on the site of the Church of the English Martyrs. On the 5th of January, 1715, we are told that sixteen rebels "were hanged upon Gallows Hill, for high treason and conspiracy." In the following year "42 condemned prisoners of all religions were hanged and decapitated at Preston;" and amongst them were five belonging Preston and the neighbourhood. They were "Richard Shuttleworth, of Preston, Esq.; Roger Moncaster, of Garstang, attorney; Thomas Cowpe, of Walton-le-Dale; William Butler, of Myerscough, Esq.; William Arkwright, of Preston, gentleman;" and all of them were put to death on Gallows Hill the cost being for "materialls, hurdle, fire, cart, &c.," and for "setting up" Shuttleworth's head, &c., 12 pounds 0s 4d. There can be no doubt that Gallows Hill derives its name directly from the transactions of 1715-16. Prior to that time it was a simple mound; after that period it became associated with hangings and beheadings, and received the name of "Gallows Hill," which was peculiarly appropriate.

In May, 1817, "Gallows Hill" was cut through, so that

"the great north road to Lancaster" might be improved. Whilst this was being done two coffins were found, and in them there were discovered two headless bodies. Local historians think they were the remains of "two rebel chieftains;" they may have been; but there is no proof of this, although the fair supposition is that they were the decapitated remnants of two somebodies, who had assumed a rebellious attitude in 1715. It is probable that the heads of these parties were "exposed on poles in front of our Town-hall," for that was an olden practice, and was considered very legitimate 154 years ago. We have spoken of the "discoveries" of 1817, and in continuing our remarks it may be said that "near the spot" some timber, supposed to have been the gallows, was once found, and that a brass hand-axe was dug up not far from it, at the same time. The Moor, which amongst other things embraced the "hill" we have mentioned, was a rough wildish place - a rude looking common; but it seems to have been well liked by the people, for upon it they used to hold trade meetings, political demonstrations, &c.; and for 65 years - from 1726 to 1791 - horse races were annually run upon it. The Corporation and the freemen of the borough once had a great dispute as to their respective claims to the Moor, and the latter by way of asserting their rights, put upon it an old white horse; but the Corporation were not to be cajoled out of their ownership by an argument so very "horsey" as this; they ordered the animal off; and Mr. J. Dearden, who still obeys their injunctions with courteous precision, put it into a pinfold hard by.

The Church of the English Martyrs was erected not long ago upon that part of the Moor we have described. Originally the promoters of the church treated for a plot of land about 20 yards above the present site; but the negotiations were broken off, and afterwards they bought Wren Cottage and a stable adjoining, situated about a quarter of a mile northwards. The house was made available for the priest; the stable was converted into a church; and mass was said in it for thc first timc on Christmas morning, 1864. On the 21st of January, 1865, it was formally "opened;" the Revs. Canon Walker, T. Walton, and F. Soden taking part in the services of the day. During 1865 preparations were made for erecting a new church upon the same site; but some of the gentlemen living in the immediate neighbourhood took offence at the movement, and insisted upon certain stipulations contained in the covenants, which barred out the construction of such a building as a church or a chapel, being carried out. There was a considerable amount of Corporation discussion in respect to the question, and eventually the idea of erecting a church upon the land was abandoned. Directly afterwards, "Gallows Hill," in which both the Corporation and Mr. Samuel Pole Shaw had rights, was purchased as a site for it. Operations, involving the removal of an immense quantity of earth - for the place was nothing more than a high, rough, sandy hillock, - were commenced on the 26th of March, 1866. On the 26th of May, in the same year, the foundation-stone was laid, with great ceremony, by Dr. Goss, and on the 12th of December, 1867, the church was opened. Mr. E. W. Pugin designed the building, which externally does not look very wonderful at present; but, when completed, it will be a handsome place. The original design includes a beautiful steeple, surmounted with pinnacles; but want of funds precludes its erection.

The church is a high double-roofed edifice - looks like two buildings, one placed above the other; and, owing to the absence of a steeple, it seems very tall and bald. It has a pretty western gable, which can only be fully appreciated by close inspection. The centre of this gable is occupied by a fine eight-light window, and the general work is surmounted by pinnacles and ornamental masonry. Two angels, cut in stone, originally formed part of the ornamentation; but during a strong gale, early in 1868, they were blown down. These "fallen angels" have never regained their first estate; and as they might only tumble down if re-fixed, and perhaps kill somebody, which would not be a very angelic proceeding, we suppose they will not be interfered with.

The church has an imposing, a noble interior. It is wide, lofty, has a fine calm majestic look, and is excellently arranged. The nave, which is 69 feet high, is supported by 14 stone pillars. From nearly any point every part of the building may be seen; the nave pillars, do not, as is the case in some churches, obstruct the vision; and everything seems easy, clear, and open. In the daytime a rich shadowy light is thrown into the church by the excellent disposition of its windows; at eventide the sheen of the setting sun, caught by the western window, falls like a bright flood down the nave, and makes the scene beautiful. The high altar is a fine piece of workmanship; is of Gothic design, is richly carved, is ornamented with marbles, has a canopy of most elaborate construction, and is in good harmony with the general architecture. Two small altars are near it. One of them, dedicated to St. Joseph, and given by Mr. J. Pyke, of this town, is particularly handsome; the other, dedicated to the Blessed Virgin, is of a less costly, though very pretty, character. Near one of the pillars on the north-eastern side there stands a square wooden frame, which is called the pulpit. It is a deliciously primitive and remarkably common-place concern; but it is strong enough, and will have to stop where it is until money for something better is raised. There are sittings in the church for 850 persons. On Sundays there are masses at eight, and half-past nine; a regular service at eleven, and another at half-past six in the evening. The aggregate attendance during the day is about 1,350. The assemblage at the first mass is thin; at the second it is good - better than at any other time; at eleven it is pretty numerous; and in the evening it is fair. Adults and children from the union workhouse, of the Catholic persuasion, attend the eleven o'clock service; and they come in tolerable force - sometimes they number 100.

The general congregation consists nearly altogether of working class people, and it includes some of the best sleepers we have seen. The members of the choir sit in a gallery at the western end. Their performances are of a curious description. Sometimes they sing very well - are quite exact in their renderings and decidedly harmonious; at other times they torture the music somewhat. But then they are young at the business, haven't had so much experience, and have nothing to rely upon in the shape of instrumental music except the hard tones of an ordinary harmonium. Organ accompaniments help up good choirs and materially drown the defects of bad ones. With better instrumental assistance, the singers at the Church of the English Martyrs would acquit themselves more satisfactorily, and with additional practice they would still further improve matters.

There are two priests stationed at the church - the Rev. James Taylor and the Rev. Joseph Pyke. Father Taylor, the principal, is a blooming, healthy, full-spirited gentleman. He is a "Fylde man;" has in him much strong straight-forwardness; looks as if he had never ailed anything in his life; doesn't appear to have mortified the flesh very acutely; seems to have taken things comfortably and well since the day of his birth; has not allowed his creed to spoil his face - a trick which some professors of religion are guilty of; and is, on the whole, a genuine specimen of the true John Bull type. Father Taylor's first mission was at Lancaster, under the late Dean Brown; afterwards he came to St. Augustine's, Preston, where he remained four and a half years; then he was appointed Catholic chaplain at the House of Correction; and subsequently he took charge of his present mission. He is an active man, and works very hard in his district. As a preacher he is energetic, impetuous, and practical - speaks plainly and straight out, minces nothing, and tries to drive what he considers to be the truth right home. He has very little rhetorical action, hardly moves at all in the pulpit, stirs neither head nor hand except upon special occasions; but he has a powerful voice, he pours out his words in a strong, full volume, and the force he has in this respect compensates for the general immobility he displays during his discourses.

His colleague - the Rev. J. Pyke - is a small, mild gentleman, unassuming in manner, cautious, careful, quiet, precise, and, whilst attending to his duties regularly, he makes no bluster about them. He was ordained at the Church of the English Martyrs, in September, 1868. In the pulpit he is earnest, clear, and regular in his remarks. He makes no repetitions, flings himself into no attitudes, assumes no airs, but proceeds on to the end steadily and calmly. Both the priests named live close to the church, in a building which forms part of the property of the mission. It is intended some time to have a proper presbytery, near the church: one is included in the original plan; but shortness of funds bars its erection. The work thus far executed - the church, vestries, &c. - has cost about 8,000 pounds, and there still remains upon the buildings a debt of about 4,000 pounds. There are no schools in connection with the church; but it is expected that there will be by and bye. The land formerly used as the cattle market, and situated near the church, has been bought for this purpose, and collectors are now engaged in raising money towards the erection of the schools. The church has two or three "guilds," the female members thereof numbering about 200, and the males 100. In the "district" there are about 3,000 Catholics, including 700 children under 10 years of age; so that the priests in charge of it have quite enough on hand for the present. A mission in debt to the tune of 4,000 pounds; a church to internally complete - for much yet remains to be finished in the one described; a church tower which will cost 2,000 pounds to raise; a presbytery to begin of; schools, which are primarily essential, to erect; and 7,000 human beings to look after, constitute what may fairly be termed "no joke."

XXVI

ST. SAVIOUR'S CHURCH.

Few districts are more thoroughly vitiated, more distinctly poverty-struck, more entirely at enmity with soap and water than that in which this church stands. Physically, mentally, and spiritually, it is in a state of squash and mildew. Heathenism seethes in it, and something even more potent than a forty-parson power of virtue will be required to bring it to healthy consciousness and legitimate action. You needn't go to the low slums of London, needn't smuggle yourself round with detectives into the back dens of big cities if you want to see "sights" of poverty and depravity; you can have them nearer home - at home - in the murky streets, sinister courts, crowded houses, dim cellars, and noisy drinking dens of St. Saviour's district. Pass through it, move quietly along its parapets - leaving a tour through its internal institutions for some future occasion - and you will see enough to convince you that many missionaries, with numerous Bibles and piles of blankets, are yet wanted at home before being despatched to either farthest land or the plains of Timbuctoo. The general scene may be thus condensed and described: Myriads of children, ragged, sore-headed, bare-legged, dirty, and amazingly alive amid all of it; wretched-looking matrons, hugging saucy, screaming infants to their breasts, and sending senior youngsters for either herring, or beer, or very small loaves; strong, idle young men hanging about street corners with either dogs at their feet, or pigeon-baskets in their hands; little shops driving a brisk "booking" business with either females wearing shawls over their heads or children wearing nothing at all on their feet; bevies of brazen-faced hussies looking out of grim doorways for more victims and more drink; stray soldiers struggling about beer or dram shops entrances, with dissolute, brawny-armed females; and wandering old hags with black eyes and dishevelled hair, closing up the career of shame and ruin they have so long and so wretchedly run.

Anybody may see the sights we have just described. We mention this not because there is anything pleasing in it, but because it is something which exists daily in the heart of our town - in the centre of St. Saviour's district. No locality we know of stands more in need of general redemption than this, and any Christian church, no matter whatever may be its denominational peculiarities, which may exist in it, deserves encouragement and support. The district is so supremely poor, and so absolutely bad, that anything calculated to improve or enlighten it in any way is worthy of assistance. A Baptist chapel was built in the quarter we are now describing - it was erected in Leeming-street, at the corner of Queen-street - in 1783. Fifty years afterwards it was enlarged; subsequently the Baptists couldn't agree amongst themselves; the parties to the quarrel then separated, some going to Pole-street Chapel, others forming a new "church" - that now in Fishergate; and on the 10th of August, 1859, the old building was bought by certain gentlemen connected with the Church of England. A young man, named William Dent Thompson, strong in constitution, greatly enamoured of Reformation principles, keenly polemical, and brought up under the aegis of the Rev. Geo. Alker, was appointed superintendent of the place. He stayed awhile, then went away, and was succeeded by the Rev. Geo. Donaldson, who in turn left for Blackburn, and was followed by the Rev. Geo. Beardsell, the present incumbent of All Saints' in this town. Mr. Beardsell did an excellent business in the district - worked it up well and most praiseworthily; but he, in time, left.

For seven months after this, there was no regular minister at the place; still it didn't go down; several energetic, zealous laymen looked after it and the schools established in connection with it, and, considering their calibre, they did a good work. But they couldn't keep up a full and continuous fire; a properly stationed minister was needed; and Mr. Thompson, who had in the meantime entered holy orders, was summoned from Blackenall, in Staffordshire, to take charge of the church and district. In 1863 he came; under his ministrations the congregation soon augmented; and in a short time a movement was started for a new church; the old building being a ricketty, inconvenient, rudely-dismal place, quite insufficient for the requirements of the locality. The principal friends of the new movement were R. Newsham, the late J. Bairstow, J. Horrocks, and T. Miller, Esqrs., and what they subscribed constituted a substantial nucleus guaranteeing the commencement of operations. In 1866, the old edifice was pulled down to make way for a new church, and during the work of reconstruction divine service was performed in Vauxhall-road schools, which were, sometime after Mr. Thompson's appointment, transferred by the Rev. Canon Parr from the Parish Church's to St. Saviour's district. R. Newsham, Esq., laid the corner-stone of St. Saviour's Church on the 26th of November, 1866; the building was consecrated by the Bishop of Manchester, on the 29th of October, 1868; on the 9th of December in that year, the Rev. W. D. Thompson was licensed to its incumbency; and on the 16th of April, 1869, the district was "legally assigned" by the Ecclesiastical Commissioners.

St. Saviour's - designed by Mr. Hibbert, architect, of this town - is one of the handsomest and best finished churches we have seen. It almost seems too good for the district in which it is situated. The style of it is Gothic. Externally its most striking feature is the tower. We thought at one time, when the tower had been run up a considerable distance, that it was positively "going to the dogs." At each of its angles there is a strange arrangement of dogs; they bristle out on all sides, and are not over good looking - are thin, hungry, weird-looking animals, appear to have had a hard time of it somewhere, and to be doing their best to escape from the stone whence they are protruding. But the pinnacles placed above have completely taken away their grotesqueness, their malicious, suspicious appearance, and the tower now looks beautiful. There are three entrances to the church - one at the back, another at the north-western corner, and the third beneath the tower on the south-western side. If you please we will enter by the door on the last-named side.

We are within the building - just within; and here we have on the right a glass screen, on the left a multiplicity of warm water pipes, and in the centre of the spot a handsome substantial baptismal font, the gift of Sir T. G. Fermor-Hesketh, M.P. This font can't be too highly praised; its workmanship is excellent; its material is most durable; and with care it will last for at least four thousand years. Behind it are two stained glass windows; one being in memory of the father of the incumbent's wife; the other in remembrance of the architect's mother. Adjoining is a plain window which will shortly be filled in with stained glass, at the expense of Mr. W. B. Roper, in memory of a relative. Leaving the font, and the water pipes, and the windows, we move forward, and are at once struck with the capaciousness, the excellent disposition, and the handsome finish of the interior. Directly in front there is a magnificent five-light chancel window - beautifully coloured, well arranged, containing in the centre a representation of our Saviour, and flanked by figures of the four evangelists. We have seldom seen a more exquisite, a more elegantly artistic window than this. Edward Swainson, Esq., whose works are in the district, presented it. Still looking eastward, but taking a nearer view and one of less altitude, we notice the pulpit - a piece of fine carved oak-work, resting upon a circular column of stone, and given by Mrs. Newsham; then we have a lectern, of the eagle pattern, presented by the Rev. R. Brown; and to the left of this there is a most excellently finished, carved-oak, reading desk, given by R. Newsham, Esq. The communion plate - most choice and elaborate in design - was, we may observe, given by the same gentleman. Turning round, we notice a pretty four-light window in the western gable. This was also presented by R. Newsham, Esq., in memory of the late J. Bairstow, Esq. The church consists of a nave and a northern aisle. If an aisle could be constructed on the southern side the building would assume proportions at once most complete and imposing. But space will not permit of this. Land constitutes a difficulty on that side; and the general building is considerably deteriorated in appearance at present through "associations" in this part. At the south-eastern end there is a small wretched-looking beershop, and near it a dingy used-up cottage. These two buildings are a nuisance to the church; they spoil the appearance of the building at one end completely, and they ought to be pulled down and carted off forthwith.

Reverting to the interior of St. Saviour's, we observe that the northern side is supported by four arches, the central one depending upon double columns of polished granite, and all of them having highly ornamented capitals. A couple of stone angels support the primary principal of the chancel roof, and they bear the weight put upon them very complacently. The northern aisle is occupied below with free seats; and above, in a gallery, with ditto. At the western end there is a continuation of the gallery, filled with free seats. The church will hold 800 people, and more than half the seats are free. All the pews are strong, open, and good to sit in. The central ones on the ground floor are very lengthy - perhaps thirty feet in extent.

The congregation, considering the capacity of the church, is large, and consists almost absolutely of working people. We noticed during our visit to this place what we have seen at no other church or chapel in the town, namely, that many of the worshippers put in an early appearance - several were in their seats at least a quarter of an hour before the service commenced. We further noticed that the congregation is a pre-eminently quiet and orderly one. At some places you are tormented to death with stirring feet, shuffling, rustling clothes, coughing, sneezing, &c.; here, however, you have little of these things, and at times, a positive dead calm prevails. It may also be worthy of mention that we saw fewer sleepers at St. Saviour's than in any other place of worship yet visited by us. Only one gentleman got fairly into a state of slumber during the whole service; a stout girl tried to "drop over" several times, and an old man made two or three quiet efforts to get his eyes properly closed, but both failed. All the other members of the congregation appeared to be wide awake and amazingly attentive. The free seats are well patronised by poor people, and it is to such a class as this that the place seems really advantageous.

The music at the church is simple, hearty, and quite congregational. The tunes are plain, and the worshippers, instead of looking on whilst the choir perform, join in the music, and get up a very full volume of respectable melody. The regular singers have their quarters at the north-eastern end, on the ground floor, and they acquit themselves with a very good grace. Near them is a small, poor-looking organ; it is played well, but its music is not very consolatory, and its tame, infantile appearance throws it quite out of keeping with the general excellence of the church. Some money has, we believe, been promised towards a new organ, and if somebody else would promise some more, a seemly-looking instrument might be obtained.

Two or three "classes" meet every Sunday for instruction in the church. Formerly, owing to defective accomodation, the members of them had to assemble in two public-house rooms, where the education was in one sense of the "mixed" kind, for whilst virtue was being inculcated above, where the members met, the elegant war-whooping of pagans below, given over to beer, tobacco, and blasphemy, could be heard. This wasn't a thing to be desired, and as soon as ever the church was ready, a removal to it was effected. Educational business in connection with St. Saviour's is carried on in various parts of the district. In Vauxhall-road there are day schools with an average attendance of 220. On Sundays, the work of education is carried on here; also at the Parsonage-house (which adjoins Lark-hill convent), where a mother's class is taught by Mrs. Thompson; in Shepherd-street, where a number of poor ragged children meet; and likewise, as before stated, in the church; the aggregate attendance being about 900. The Parsonage-house was purchased and presented to St. Saviour's by the late J. Bairstow, Esq. Handsome new schools are being built (entirely at the expense of R. Newsham, Esq., who has been a most admirable friend to St. Saviour's) near the church. They will accommodate about 400 scholars, and will, it is expected, be ready by the end of the present year. The entire cost of the church, parsonage house, &c., has been about 10,000 pounds; and not more than 50 pounds will be required to clear off all the liabilities thus far incurred.

The incumbent of St. Saviour's is plain, unpoetical, strong-looking, and practical. He was reared under the shadow of Ingleborough. We have known him for 30 years. On coming to Preston he was for sometime a mechanic; then he became missioner in connection with the Protestant Reformation Society, first at St. Peter's in this town, - and next at St. Mary's. Afterwards he left, studied for the ministry, and six years since, as already intimated, came to St. Saviour's as its incumbent. For a time after the church was erected, he had nothing to depend upon but the pew rents, which realised about 70 pounds a year: but fortune favours parsons: the Ecclesiastical

Commissioners subsequently increased his stipend, then 1,000 pounds was left by J. Bairstow, Esq., and the income is now equal to about 300 pounds per annum. Mr. Thompson is not a brilliant man, and never will be. He is close-shaven, full-featured, heavily-set, slow is his mental processes, but earnest, pushing, and enduring. He is an industrious parson, a striving, persevering, roughly-hewn, hard-working man - a good visitor, a willing worker, free and kindly disposed towards poor people, and the exact man for such a district as that in which he is located. If a smart, highly-drawn, classical gentleman were fixed as minister in the region of St. Saviour's, the people would neither understand him nor care for him. If he talked learnedly, discussed old cosmogonies, worked out subtle theories of divinity, and chopped logic; if he spiced up big homilies with Plato and Virgil, or wandered into the domain of Hebrew roots and Greek iambics, his congregation would put him down as insane, and would be driven crazy themselves. But Mr. Thompson avoids these things, primarily because he doesn't know much about them, and generally because plain words and practical work are the sole things required in his district.

The gentleman under review used to be a tremendous anti-Popery speaker, and more than once thought well of the Reformation perorations of Henry Vincent; but he has toned down much in this respect, like Panjandrum the Grand, under whose feathers he originally nestled. He is still, and has a right to be, if that way inclined, a strong believer in the triumph achieved at Boyne Water; only he doesn't make so much stir about it as formerly. Mr. Thompson is a determined and aspiring man; is earnest, windy, and clerically "large;" knows he is a parson without being told of it; has a somewhat ponderous and flatulent style of articulation; has not the faculty of originality much developed, but can imitate excellently; could sooner quote than coin a great thought; believes in stray polemical struggles with outsiders; used to have a Byronic notion that getting hold of other people's thoughts, and passing them off for those of somebody else, was not a very great sin; is a better anecdote teller than reasoner; can be very solemn and most virtuously combative; could yet, though he seems to have settled down, get up, on the shortest notice, any amount of "immortal William" steam, and throw every ounce of it into a good ninth-rate jeremiad. Still he has many capital points; he is a most indefatigable toiler in his own district, and that covers all his defects; he is not too proud nor too idle to visit everybody, however wretched or vile, requiring his advice and assistance; he is homely, sincere, and devoted to the cause he has in hand, and the locality he has charge of; he does his best to improve it; he has not laboured unsuccessfully; and no better minister could be found for such a place. He can adapt himself to its requirements; can level himself to its social and spiritual necessities; does more good in it every day than a more polished, or brilliant, or namby-pamby parson would be able to accomplish in a year; has an excellent wife, who takes her share of the district's work; attends to the varied wants of the locality - and there are many in a godless district like his, with its 5,000 souls - in a most praiseworthy manner. He is the right man is the right place, and it is a good job that he is not too learned, for that would have interfered with his utility, would have dumfounded those in his keeping, and operated against his success. Mr. Thompson, adieu, and good luck to you.

XXVII

CHRISTIAN BRETHREN AND BROOK-STREET PRIMITIVE METHODISTS.

All over, there are many who consider themselves Christian brethren; but the number taking up the name specifically, with a determination to stick to it denominationally, is small. In all large towns a few of this complexion may be found; and in Preston odd ones exist whose shibboleth is "Christian Brethren." We had a spell with them, rather unexpectedly, on a recent "first day" - "Christian Brethren" always call Sunday the first day. And it came about in this way: we were on the point of entering a Dissenting place of worship, when a kindly-natured somewhat originally-constituted "pillar of the Church" intercepted our movements, and said, "You mustn't come here today." "Why?" we asked, and his reply was, that a fiftieth-rate stray parson, whom "the Church doesn't care for" would be in the pulpit that day, and that if we wished for "a fair sample" we must "come next Sunday." We didn't want to be hard, and therefore said that if "another place" could be found for us, we would take it instead. Violent cogitation for five minutes ensued, and at last our friend, more zealous than erudite, conjured up what he termed, "them here new lot, called Christians."

We had heard of this section before, and at our request he accompanied us to a small, curiously-constructed building in Meadow-street. At the side of the doorway we observed a strangely-written, badly-spelled sign, referring to the different periods when the "Christian Brethren" met for worship, &c.; and above it another sign appeared, small and dim, and making some allusion to certain academical business. Hurrying up fourteen steps we reached a dark, time-worn door, and after pausing for a moment - listening to some singing within - our guide, philosopher, &c., opened it, and we entered the place with him. The room was not "crowded to suffocation;" its windows were not gathering carbon drops through the density of human breathing ; there were just fourteen persons in the place - four men, three women, two youths, a girl, and four children. A Bible and a hymn book - the latter, according to its preface, being intended for none but the righteous - were handed to us, and our friend want through the singing in a delightfully-dreadful style. He appeared to have a way of his own in the business of psalmody - sang whatever came into his head first, got into all manner of keys, and considering that he was doing quite enough for both of us, we remained silent, listening to the general melody, and drinking in its raptures as placidly as possible.

Prior to describing either the service we witnessed, or the principles of those participating in it, we must say a word in reference to the building. It stands on the northern side of Meadow-street, between sundry cottage houses, retiring a little from the general frontage, and by its architecture seems to be a cross between a small school and a minute country meeting-house. It was originally built in 1844 by Mr. John Todd of this town. He started it as a chapel on his own account - for at that time he had special theological notions; and probably considered that he had as much right to have a place of worship as anybody else. We have been unable to ascertain the primal denominational character of the building; the founder of it is unable to tell us; all that we have been able to get out of him is, that the place "had no name," and all that we can, therefore, fairly say is, that he built it, and did either something or nothing in it. Mr. Todd did not occupy it very long; he struck his colours in about a year; and afterwards it was used by different Dissenting bodies, including some Scotch Baptists, on whose behalf the building was altered. Originally it was only one story high; but when the Baptists went to it a second story was added, and, having either aspiring notions or considering that they would be better accommodated in the higher than the lower portion of the building, they went aloft, leaving the ground floor for individuals of more earthly proclivities. Two years ago Mr. Todd sold the building, and about six months since certain Christian Brethren hired the top room for "first day" purposes, week day work being carried on in it by an industrious schoolmaster.

Like the Quakers, Christian Brethren are a "peculiar people." They believe more in being good and doing good than in professing goodness formally. They recognise some forms and a few ceremonies; but vital inherent excellence - simple Christianity, plain, unadorned, and earnest - is their pole-star. They claim to be guided in all their religious acts solely by the Scriptures; consider that as "the disciples were first called Christians at Antioch," their followers have no right to assume any other name; think, baptismally speaking, that whilst there may be some virtue in sprinkling and pouring, there can be no mistake about absolute immersion, inasmuch as that will include everything; think baby baptism unnecessary, and hold that none except penitent believers, with brains fairly solidified, should be admitted to the ordinance; maintain that, as under the apostolic regime, "the disciples came together on the first day of the week to break bread," Christians should partake of the sacrament every Sunday; call their ministers "evangelists;" hold that at general meetings for worship there should be full liberty of speech; that worship should be perfectly free; and that everything should be supported on the voluntary principle. Those now worshipping in Meadow-street are the first "Christian Brethren" we have had, regularly organised, in Preston. How they will go on we cannot tell; but if present appearances are any criterion, we are afraid they will not make very rapid progress. They have about ten "members" at present; when the "baker's dozen" will be reached is a mystery.

The executive business of Christian Brethren is managed by deacons; but the diaconal stage has not yet been reached in Preston. There are branches of the body in Blackburn, Southport, Bolton, &c.; but none exist in Lancashire north of Preston. The brethren here have no Sunday-school; but the establishment of one is contemplated, and it may be in time fairly attended. What the number of attendants will be we can't tell, but this may be fairly said - that if each of the ten members happens, in the lapse of time, to have 12 children, and if all are sent to school, 120 scholars will be raised, and that this would constitute a very good muster for a small denomination. But we must return to the subject.

After the singing, which our friend so improved - and he continued "in the werry same tone of voice," as poor Sam Cowell used to say in his "Station Porter's" song, through every hymn - a bearded, mustached, and energetic young man (Mr. W. Hindle), originally a Methodist town missionary, at one time connected with Shepherd-street Ragged School, Preston, and now an "Evangelist" belonging the Christian Brethren, labouring at Southport, Blackburn, &c., but generally engaged for Sunday service at Preston, read several verses from the Bible; then be prayed, his orison being of a free and wide-spreading type; and afterwards he asked if any "brother" would read from Holy Writ. A pause followed, doubt and bashfulness apparently supervening; but at length a calm, thoughtful gentleman got up, and went through sundry passages in Isaiah. The singing of a hymn succeeded, and Mr. Hindle then asked if "another brother" would read. A gentleman, spectacled, with his hair well thrown back, and very earnest, here rose, and having put a small Bible upon a little table in front, and taken up a larger volume which the minister had been perusing, diced into Corinthians, and gave a tolerably satisfactory reading. The minister then commenced discussing certain antithetical points in St. Paul's writings, and next asked if "two or three brethren" would engage in prayer. Thirty seconds elapsed, and then one of the brethren made a prayer. The sacrament - bread and wine - directly followed, and after a purse, suddenly pulled out from some place by the minister, had been sharply handed round for contributions, a serious young man gave out a hymn, which the company genially sung. More speaking ensued: but the minister had it all to himself. He said - "Will any brother speak; now is the time; if you have anything to state utter it; lose no time, but say on." Never a brother spoke; eye-squeezing and thumb-turning, and deep introspection followed; and in the end the minister rose, took his text from three or four parts of the Bible, and gave a lengthy discourse, relieved at intervals with genuine outbursts of eloquence, relative to Christian action and general duty. He seemed to have a poor notion of many Christians, and somewhat fantastically illustrated their position by saying that they were, spiritually troubled with consumption and apparently with diabetes! - were continually devouring good things, constantly wasting away, and doing no particular good amongst it at all. We felt the force of this; but we didn't ejaculate; quietness, except on very excited occasions, being the rule here. His discourse lasted about 30 minutes, and it was well and forcibly delivered. At the conclusion two or three of the Brethren came out of their circle - they were all round a table before the parson - and shook hands with us.

We shortly afterwards retired, leaving our "musical" friend engaged in a hot discussion with the parson as to the propriety of certain observations he had made in his sermon. How the matter was fought out we cannot tell. The Brethren assemble every Sunday morning and evening in the building; sometimes they have a Bible class meeting on a Sunday afternoon; and occasionally a week night service. They are a calm, devout, forlorn-looking class; are distinctly sincere; have strong liberal notions of Christianity; seem to love one another considerably, and may at times greet each other with a holy kiss; but they don't thrive much in Preston. In time they may become a "great people," but at present their status is small. Ten Christian Brethren up 14 steps may grow potent eventually; but they may, figuratively speaking, fall down the steps in the meantime, and so injure the cause as to defy the influence of theraputics.

A few words now as to Brook-street Primitive

Methodist Chapel, which we visited the same day. This is a tiny building, and appears to stand in a dangerous region. On one side all the windows are continually shuttered, so as to prevent the mischievous action of stones, and in front the door is railed in closely so as to frustrate the efforts of those who might be inclined to kick it. The chapel, which is also used for Sunday school purposes, was built in 1856. It is a very humble, plain-looking edifice externally; and internally it is equally unassuming. You get to it collaterally, through a pair of narrow doors, which bang about very much in stormy weather. The roof is supported by two iron pillars, with which a tall stove pipe keeps company. In the centre there are 16 pews, each capable of holding three persons, and a large pew which will accommodate six. Rows of small forms run down each side. Those on the left are used by men and boys; those on the other side are principally patronised by women and little children, some of whom are too young to engage in anything but lactary pursuits. Green is a favourite colour here. The inside of the pews are green; portions of the walls are green; some of the windows are similarly coloured at the base; the music stands in the orchestra are green; and there is a fine semi-circular display of green at the back of the pulpit. At the south-eastern corner there are sundry pieces of old timber piled up; at the opposite side there is a cupboard; and over the entrance numerous forms, colour poles, and a ladder are placed. These constitute all the loose ornaments in the chapel. About 150 persons can be accommodated in the place. When we visited it - the time was rather unfavourable, owing to the roughness of the weather - sixty-six persons, exclusive of the choir and the parson, were in it.

The congregation is a very poor one, but it is singularly

sincere and orderly - is not refined but devout, is comparatively unlettered but honest. There is neither silk, nor satin, nor diamond rings, nor lavender kids, in the place; a hard working-day plainness, mingled with poverty, pervades it; but there is no sham seen: if the people are poor, commonly dressed, noisy - if they effervesce sometimes, and shout "Hallelujah" with a fiery joyfulness, and pray right out, as if they were being ship-wrecked or frightened to death, why let them have their way, for they are happy amongst it. Their convictions are strong, and when they are at it they go in for a good thing - for something roughly exquisite, hilariously pious, and consumingly good. They don't mince matters; are neither dainty nor given to cant, but shout out what they feel at the moment whatever may become of it afterwards. Sunday services, prayer meetings, and class meetings are held in the chapel regularly. The pulpit is occupied by various persons.

The minister stationed at the place is the Rev. J. Hall - colleague of the pastor at Saul-street Chapel - but he only takes his turn in it. A strong-built man, plainly attired, earnest, and not so given to flights of violent fancy as some preachers, had charge of the pulpit during our visit. His style was homely, and in his easier periods he had a knack of putting his left hand into his breeches pocket, and talking in a semi-conversational Lancashire dialect style. He dilated for thirty minutes upon the horn-blowing at Jericho, the siege, the wall-falling, and the sin of Achan; and then wound up by telling his hearers - drawing the moral from Achan's fate - that if they did wrong they would be sure to be found out. The sermon was quite equal to the bulk of homilies given in Primitive Methodist Chapels, and it seemed to go right home to the congregation. The plundering of Achan was well told, and when it was announced that he was stoned with stones, and then burned, the congregation sent up a mild, half-sighing groan, shaking their heads a little, and apparently determining to do right as long as ever they lived.

The music at the chapel was strong, and, remembering the nature of the place, satisfactory. Three men, three young women, and a boy managed it. The women sometimes drowned the men; the boy often got into a shrill mood; but the men finally reached the surface, the women quietly subsided, the boy toned down his forces somewhat; and on the whole the singing was well done. After the sermon there came a prayer meeting. We determined to see it out, preserving that quietude and respect which one ought always to evince towards those believing in the great cardinal points of Christanity, however peculiar may be, the modes of their expression. Only about twenty-five, who assembled on the southern side of the chapel, joined the prayer meeting. The proceedings were of a most enthusiastic, virtuous, hot, and bewildering character. Singing, feet-beating, praying, hand-clapping, and reciprocal shouting constituted the programme. One elderly man went fairly wild during the business. He shook his head, doubled his fists, threw his arms about, ejaculated with terrible rapidity and force, and appeared to be entirely set on fire by his feelings. A thorough craze - a wild, beating, electrifying passion - got completely hold of him for a few minutes, and he enjoyed the stormy pulsations of it exceedingly. At the end somebody said, "Now, will some of the women pray?" Instantly a little old man said, "God bless the women;" "Aye," said another, while several gave vent to sympathetic sighs. But the women were not to be drawn out in this style; none of them were in the humour for praying; they didn't even return the benediction of the little old man by saying "God bless the men;" they kept quiet, then got up, and then all walked out; the last words we remember being from a woman, who, addressing us, said, "Now, draw it mild!"

XXVIII

ST. THOMAS'S CHURCH.

We have made no inquiry as to the original predecessors of those attending this church. They may have been links in the chain of those men who, ages ago, planted themselves on the coast of Malabar, rejoicing in the name of "Christians of St. Thomas," and struggling curiously with Nestorians, Franciscans, Dominicans, and Jesuits; they may have constituted a remnant of the good people whom Cosmas Indicopleustes saw in the East twelve hundred years since; they may have only had a Preston connection, knowing nothing of the Apostle of India - St. Thomas - beyond what anybody knows, and caring more for his creed than his title. Whatever may have been their history and fate, it is certain their successors believe in that most apostolical of unbelievers just mentioned - so far, at least, as the name is concerned. The church they respect is situated at the northern end of Preston, near the junction of Moor-lane and Lancaster-road. It is a small, strong, hard-looking building; seems as if it would stand any amount of rain and never get wet through, any quantity of heat and never have a sunstroke; it is stoical, cold, firm, and very stony; has a bodkin-pointed spire, ornamented with round holes and circular places into which penetration has not yet been effected; and its "tout ensemble" is in no way edifying.

It is neither ornate nor colossal. Strength, plainness, and smallness, with a strong dash of general rigidity, are its outward characteristics.

St. Thomas's is one of the local churches erected through the exertions of the late Rev. R. Carus Wilson; and, like all those churches, it is built in the Norman style of architecture - a massive, severe style, which will never be popularly pleasing, but will always secure endurance for the edifices constructed on its principles. The first stone of this church was laid in August, 1837. The building stands upon a hill, is surrounded by a powerful stone wall, can be approached two ways, and has its front entrance opposite a small street, which has not yet received any name at all. To a stranger, ingress to the building is rather perplexing. A gateway in Lancaster-road, leading to a footpath, fringed with rockery, would appear to be the front way, but it is only a rear road, and when you get fairly upon it you wonder where it will end - whether you will be able to get to the interior by it, or only to some rails on one side and a wall on the other. It, however, eventuates round a corner, at the main entrance. We recommend this back way, for the legitimate front road is much more intricate and harassing; you can only become acquainted with it, if topographically unenlightened, and bashful as to making inquiries, by hovering about an ancient windmill, moving up narrow hilly streets, flanked by angular bye-paths, and then following either the first woman you see with a prayer book in her hand, or the first man you catch a sight of with a good coat on his back. The main entrance is ornamental but diminutive in many respects. There are three doorways here, the collateral ones, which are very low, and quite calculated to prevent people from entering the building with their hats on, being patronised the most - not because there is an offertory box in the central passage, but because the side roads are the handiest. During a second visit to the church we went in by the middle door, the medium course, as the proverb hath it, being the safest, and seeing the offertory box - a remarkably strong, iron-cornered article, fastened to the wall - we remarked to an official, in his shirt sleeves, who was with us, "This will stand a deal of money before falling." The official replied "It will so," and the look, he gave us superinduced the conclusion that the offertory box was not going to fall for some time.

We have seen no more deceptive-looking church than that we are now at. Viewed externally, you would say that scarcely a good handful of people could be accommodated in it; it seems so narrow, so entirely made up of and filled in with stone, that one infers at first sight it will hardly hold the parson and the sacrament-loving "old woman" who invariably exists as a permanent arrangement at all our places of worship; but this is a fallacy, for the building will accommodate about 1,100 people. The interior consists of a nave, two aisles, and a chancel. Everything in the building seems strong, clean, and good; and considering the ponderous character of its architecture a fair share of light is admitted to it. At the entrance, there is a glass screen, ornamentally got up and surmounted with a small lion and unicorn design. Just within this screen there is a curtained pew, and sitting within its enclosure must be a very snug and select thing. It is occupied by Mr. Hermon, M.P., and when he draws the curtains all round - "he sometimes does," said the official accompanying us - no one can see a morsel of him whilst he can see never a one in the building, not even the parson, without a special effort.

The nave is broad and quadrangular, is supported by immensely strong pillars, and has a fine high roof, looking clean and spacious, but considerably spoiled by several commonplace awkwardly fashioned beams. The roof of each aisle is similarily marred. Thc seats are disposed in six parallel ranges, and the generality are quite good enough for anybody. Along each side there is a row of free seats - about 50 altogether - capable of accommodating upwards of 300 persons. There are also many free seats in the gallery.

The present incumbent has an idea that he has made some addition to this accomodation; but people who have known the church ever since it was built say that the extra "free pews" appropriated for the poor by him were never charged for. At the end of each aisle there is a neat stained glass window; that to the right bearing this inscription - "To the memory of W. P. Jones, M.A., ob. January 29, 1864, aged 77 years," and that on the left these words "To the memory of Mrs. Fanny Jones, ob. January 27, 1864, aged 75 years." Mr. Jones was a former incumbent of St. Thomas's. He was a quiet, mild-minded man, devoid of bombast, neither cynical nor meddlesome, and was well liked by all. His wife died just two days before him, and both were interred in one grave in St. Peter's church yard. The pulpit and reading desk at St. Thomas's are good-looking and substantial, but both are rather bad to get into and out of - the steps are narrow and angular, with a sudden descent, which might cause a stranger to miss his footing and fall, if he had not firm hold of the side rail. Right above, perhaps 20 feet high, and surmounting the chancel arch, there is a small ornamental projection, like a balcony. It would make a capital stand for the minister; or might be turned into a conspicuous place of Sunday resort for the wardens;

but, then, they would have to be hoisted to it, for there is no road up, and that would not be seemly. Formerly, we believe, this balcony was used by the singers, but they were subsequently transplanted to the western gallery. The passage to the balcony front is now shut off. A considerable effort at ornamentation has been made on the walls flanking the balcony described. But we don't care much for it. Little pillars, quaint window models, and other architectural devices, are heaped upon each other in curious profusion, and it is difficult to get at their real meaning. They relieve the walls a little, but they do the work whimsically, and you can neither get a smile nor a tear from them. The chancel arch is strong and ornamental; within it there is another arch, the intervening roof being neatly groined and coloured; and beyond there is the chancel - a small, somewhat cimmerian, yet pretty-looking place. There are five windows in it; three having sacred figures painted upon them, and the remaining two being filled in with fancy designs, which don't look over well, owing to the decay of the colours.

The congregation is tolerably numerous, has in it the high, the fair-middling, and the humble - the good-looking, the well-dressed, the rubicund, the mildly mahogany-featured, the simply-dressed, the attenuated, and the indigent. But there is a clear halo of respectability about the place; superior habiliments are distinctly in the ascendant; and orderly behaviour reigns throughout each section of worshippers. The free seats are very fairly patronised, and sometimes very oddly. In one part of them we saw nine persons all near each other, and out of that number five wore spectacles, whilst three could only see with one eye. At the western end of the church there is a beautiful circular window, but it has not met with very good treatment. It has been broken in one part, and every morsel of it is covered up from general view by the organ occupying the gallery. Only the organ blower can see it properly, and having the whole of it to himself, it is to be expected he will derivc some consolation from his special position. If he doesn't, then he neither gets up the wind nor looks through the window properly. The organ is a good one, and it is played with average ability, but it is too big for the place it occupies, and entirely swamps what was once considered a fine gallery. The singers are rather afraid of giving vent to their feelings. They discourse the music tastefully, but they are too quiet, and don't get into a temper, as they ought to do occasionally, over it. Prior to the advent of the present incumbent, the choir, considering its numbers, was, perhaps, as good as any in the town or neighbourhood; but one Sunday morning the gentleman referred to, having apparently been fiercely stung by a Ritualistic wasp, blew the trumpet of his indignation very strongly-got into a whirlwind of denunciation all at once and without the aid of a text, regarding Ritualism; and the organist and singers, whose musical services embraced chants, &c., fancying that the rev. gentleman was either tired of their presence or performances, many of which were voluntary, sent in their resignations. Since then the music has not been very brilliant.

There are religious services every Sunday morning and evening at St. Thomas's, and on Thursday night a small gathering of the faithful takes place in the building. The trustees of the church are - Miss Margaret Ann Beckles, St. Leonard's; Samuel Husband Beckles, Esq., of the Middle Temple; the Rev. Edward Auriol, St. Dunstans; the Rev. Charles F. Close, St. Ann's, Blackfriars; the Rev. W. Cadman, Marylebone; and Sir

Hugh Hill. The Rev. L. W. Jeffrey was the first incumbent of the church; then came the Rev. W. P. Jones, who died, as before stated, in 1884; afterwards the Rev. J. T. Becher was appointed to the incumbency, but he died from typhus fever in five weeks and was succeeded by the Rev. J. P. Shepperd who still holds the post and receives from it about 400 pounds a year.

Mr. Shepperd is a man of middle age, and looks after his sheep fairly, but at times eccentrically. He has a polished, tasteful, clerical contour; attends well to his hair, whiskers, and linen; wears a hat half bishoply and half archidiaconal in its brim; is a good scholar, a clear reasoner, an able-preacher, but repeats himself often, and gets long-winded on Sunday nights; is highly enamelled, touchy, and imperial; is lofty in tone, cream laid and double thick in manner; is full of metal, and there is a stately mystery about him, as if he were a blood relation of the Great Mokanna; he is nearly infallible, and would make a good Pope; he is strongly combative, and would be a vigorous bruiser in stormy ecclesiastical circles. We fancy no parson in Preston has had more officials than Mr. Shepperd. In less than half a dozen years there have been at the place many organists, singers, curates, scripture readers, and eight or nine churchwardens. Either they have been very uneasy people or he has been uniquely antagonistic. Mr. Shepperd resides at a good parsonage some distance north of the church, and he has a pretty garden adjoining, the walls thereof having been built at the expense of Mr. Hermon, who has been a capital friend to the church. In the garden there is a quantity of handsome rockery, purchased by the late Mr. James Carr (who was at one time a warden), out of the church funds. This rockery was originally placed in the church yard, along with that still remaining there; but it was thought by somebody that the yard didn't require so much ornamental stone, so a quantity of it was removed to the place mentioned. If Mr. Shepperd has it set in a circle he may play the Druid amongst it, reserving the biggest block for a cromlech and the smoothest for a seat; if it is concentrated in one mass he may stand upon it, defy all the ex-churchwardens, and quoting Scott, cry out, "Come one, come all, this rock shall fly" &c. Originally, St. Thomas's cost a considerable amount of money, and in consequence of improvements subsequently made, there is still, it is said, a pretty round sum due to the late wardens and the contractors, and they, are much in the dark as to when they will get it. The parson can't see the force of paying it himself, the officers of the church make no move in the matter, the congregation is apathetic on the subject, the beadle keeps quiet, and does his central church walk calmly, never thinking of it. But, if owing, somebody should settle the bill, and the sooner it is liquidated, the more respectable will the affairs of the church become. Bother without end has prevailed at St. Thomas's about money, and until people get their own, and see regular annual statements of accounts - things which seem to be scarce in these times - they will continue to be uneasy and, probably, noisy.

Associated with the church are superior schools - one for infants, in the unchristened street near the church, and two others for boys and girls, in Lancaster-road. The average day attendance is - boys, 250; girls, 220; infants, 240. The average attendance on the Sunday is - boys, 250; girls, 320. The day schools are in a good state of efficiency, and are of great service to the district. They are well managed, and with respect to some of their departments Government reports speak most encouragingly. Worn old grievances with ex-churchwardens are duly squared, when a greater amount of what is called "fixity of tenure" exists in respect to the officials, and when Mr. Sheppard drops his little dogma as to personal immaculacy, and allows other people a trifle more freedom, his flock will be fatter, woollier, and quieter than ever they have been since he came.

XXIX

CROFT-STREET WESLEYANS AND PARKER-STREET UNITED METHODISTS.

In 1827, a little school was opened in a building at the corner of Gildow-street, abutting upon Marsh-lane, in this town. It was established in the Wesleyan Methodist interest, and one of its chief supporters was Mr. T. C. Hincksman, a gentleman still living, who has for a long period been a warm friend of the general cause of Methodism. Although begun tentatively, the school soon progressed; in time there was a good attendance at it; ultimately it was considered too small; and the result was a removal to more convenient premises - to a room connected with the mill of the late Mr. John Furness, in Markland-street: But the little old building did not change so much in its character after being deserted by the Wesleyan scholars; it was still retained for juvenile purposes - still kept open for the edification, if not improvement, of youngsters. Old-fashioned sweets were sold in it, and the place was long known as "Granny Bird's toffy shop." At the mill in Markland-street, which used to be called "Noggy Tow," the school was very prosperous; but the accomodation here at length became defective, and in 1832 the scholars retraced their steps to Gildow-street, - not to the small toffy establishment, where sucklings, if not babes, were cared for, but to a building at the opposite end of the thoroughfare erected specially for them. In 1840 they withdrew from this edifice and went to a new school made in Croft-street, the foundation stone of which was laid by the Rev. John Bedford, a well-known Wesleyan minister, who at that time was stationed in Preston. In 1858 two wings for class and other purposes, principally promoted by the late Mr. T. Meek, costing 700 pounds, and opened clear of debt, were attached to the school, and twelve months ago - scholastic business still proceeding - the central portion of it was set apart for regular religious services on the Sabbath.

The building is large, good-looking, and well-proportioned. There is nothing of an ecclesiastical complexion about either its external or internal architecture. Substantially it is a school, utilised twice every Sunday for devotional purposes. The floor of it is well cared for, and ought to enjoy much fresh air, for there are 18 ventilators, grate shaped, in front of it. When that which formed the nucleus of the school was started, the neighbourhood was open; there was a suburban look about the locality; but entire rows of new dwellings now surround the school; the part in which it stands is densely populated; all grades of men, women, and children inhabit it; "civilisation" - rags, impudence, dirt, and sharpness, for they mean civilisation - has long prevailed in the immediate neighbourhood; a fine new brewery almost shakes hands with the building on one side; the "Sailor's Home" beershop stands sentry two doors off on the other. What more could you desire? A large industrious population, lots of crying, stone-throwing children, a good-looking brewery, a busy beershop, a school, and a chapel, all closely mixed up, are surely sufficient for the most ardent lover of variety and "progress." The room wherein the Wesleyans associated with Croft-street school meet for religious duties is square, heavy-looking, dull, and hazy in its atmosphere. It is ventilated by curious pieces of iron which work curvilinearly up huge apertures covered with glass; its walls are ornamented with maps, painted texts, natural history pictures, &c.; and at the eastern side there is a small orthodox article for pulpit purposes. There are several ways into the room - by the back way if you climb walls, by the direct front if you ascend steps, by the sides of the front if you move through rooms, pass round doorways, and glide past glass screens.

We took the last route, and sat down near a young gentleman with a strong bass voice. In a corner near there was a roseate-featured, elderly man, who enjoyed the service at intervals and slept out what he could not fathom. Close to him was a youth who did the very same thing; and in front there were three females who followed the like example. The service was plain, simple, sincere, and quite Methodistical; it was earnestly participated in by a numerous congregation; the responses were quiet and somewhat internal; an easy respectable seriousness prevailed; nothing approaching either cant or wild-fire was manifested. Working-class people preponderated in the place, as they always do; the singing was clear, and plain, odd lines coming in for a share of melodious quavering; and the sermon was well got-up and eloquent. The Rev. C. F. Hame, who has recently come to Preston in the place of the Rev. W. H. Tindall (Lune-street Circuit), was the preacher on this occasion. He is a little gentleman, with considerable penetration and power; has a good theological faculty; is cool, genial, and lucid in language; and, although he can shout a little when very warm, he never loses either the thread of his argument or his personal equilibrium. There are 120 members at this place of worship; the average attendance at the different services is 250; and the number is gradually increasing.

Regular ministers and local preachers fill the pulpit in turns; there being, as a rule, one of the former at either the morning or evening service every Sunday. Sometimes both kinds may be present and ready for action at the same moment; but they never quarrel as to which shall preach - never get "up a tree," figuratively speaking, and everything is arranged quietly. The school, wherein the services we have referred to are held, has been one of the most useful in Preston; more scholars have probably passed through it than through any other similar place in the town; old scholars - men and women now - who received their religious education here, are in all parts, and there is not a quarter of the globe where some may not be found who have a pleasant recollection of the school. Its average day attendance is 240; its average Sunday morning attendance 275; whilst on a Sunday afternoon the regular number is 425. The school, which is conveniently arranged and well fit up with every sort of ordinary educational contrivance, is in a satisfactory state, and, in conjunction with the "chapel," which it makes provision for, is doing an excellent work in the district, which is open to all comers, and will stand much drilling and spiritual flogging ere it reaches perfection.

"Over the hills and far away" - up the brow of Maudlands, down new streets on the other side, under the canal, up another brow, through narrow, angular roads, flanked with factories, by the edge of a wild piece of land supplying accomodation for ancient horses, brick-makers, pitch and toss youths, and pigeon flyers, and then turning suddenly at a mysterious corner in the direction of mill gates you reach Parker-street United Methodist Free Church. Externally this church is a very simple, prosaic building. Viewed from the front it looks like the second storey bedroom of a cottage; eyed from the side it seems like a long office, four yards from the ground, with a pair of round-headed folding doors below, and at the extreme end a narrow aperture, which apparently leads round the corner. It was built 12 or 13 years ago, for a school, by Messrs. J. and J. Haslam, near whose mill it is situated, and it is still used for educational purposes. During the latter end of 1858 and the beginning of 1859 there was a dispute amongst the United Free Church brethren assembling in Orchard Chapel. Both men and women entered into the disturbance freely; but they did not follow the plan lately adopted by some United Methodist Christians, living at Batley, who, having a grievance at their chapel, "fought it out" in the back yard; what they did, after many a lively church meeting, was to appeal to the authorities of the denomination, state their case quietly, and abide the decision of their superiors. That decision sanctioned a separation and the establishment in Preston of a second United Methodist circuit, totally independent of the Orchard-street people, but responsible to the general executive for its actions. Those forming the new circuit in Preston - about twenty "members" - had not, however, a chapel, so Messrs. Haslam, who sympathised with the movement, permitted them to meet in the school they had built in Parker-street. The course pursued by the secessionists was approved of by some United Methodists at Cuerden Green, where the Orchard brethren had a small chapel, and they left the parent body when the separation already mentioned took place. There was a fair amount of goodly squabbling about the Cuerden Green Chapel. Each side wanted it. For a time the secessionists held it; then the owner of the building died; and, after various movements, the Orchard brethren "went in and won," and they have retained possession of the premises ever since. The second circuit includes no country place except Brindle, where the denomination has a good chapel.

The "full members" of the circuit number about 90, and 75 of them are in Preston. There are 25 "on trial" at the present moment, but as we cannot tell how they will pass through the alembic, it would be out of place to make any absolute statement as to their fate. The circuit is increasing in strength; its finances, notwithstanding bad times, are in a very fair state; a good feeling exists between the members of both circuits; they have become peaceable and pachydermatous, thin-skinnedness being considered an evil; and altogether affairs are satisfactory. The system under which ministers are appointed to Parker-street chapel is the same as that prevailing amongst the general body, and as we described at in a previous article no allusion need now be made to it. The first parson at the chapel in Parker-street was the Rev. Robert Eltringham; since then the following have been at it - the Revs. J. Nettleton, J. Shaw, J. Mara (who is now a missionary in China for the United Methodist body), W. Lucas, C. Evans, J. W. Chisholm, and the Rev. T. Lee. The names show that there has been a new parson at the chapel almost every year. The present pastor (Rev. T. Lee) only came in August last; his predecessor (Mr. Chisholm), who is a sharp, shrewd , liberal-minded gentleman , having been removed to Manchester.

Not long ago, after struggling through many far-away streets, we found ourselves at the corner of a little opening at the top of Parker-street. "This is the place," said a friend who was with us. We knew it was, for several yards before reaching the building, the torrents of a strong voice came impetuously through an open window, and the burthen of its strains had reference to a revival of "our connexion." Such a noise as this we thought ought to have aroused the whole neighbourhood; but we could see nobody about except a woman right opposite, who was engaged in the serious business of front step washing, and who seemed to take no notice whatever of the strong utterances coming through the window. She washed on, and the good man above prayed on. It was rather difficult to find the way to the chapel. It could not, we fancied, be by the front door of a shop which we saw beneath; it could not, we were certain, be through a window above, for whilst there was a pulley roller in front of it there was neither rope nor block visible for regular lifting purposes; neither, we thought, could it be through a large double-door at the side, for that was bolted, and seemed to have been made for something taller and broader than the human form. After sauntering about, the grand rush of words through the window still continuing, in the interests of "our connexion," we moved towards a corner at the far end of the side opening, passed up twelve narrow steps, rushed past a charity box, seventeen hats and caps, and a small umbrella stand, and then sat down.

We were surprised at the cleanness and neatness of the building, and at the large number of people within it. Rumour had conveyed to us a notion that about three persons visited this chapel; but we found between 100 and 200 - all well-dressed, orderly, and pleasant - in attendance. We also noticed a policeman amongst the company. He was present, not to keep the peace, but to get some good, for Heaven knows that policemen need much of the article, and that they have very little Sunday time to find it in. The policeman behaved himself very well during the whole service. The building will accommodate about 200 persons, and the average attendance at the Sunday services is 120. Three or four middle-class persons, several good-looking young women, a number of men, including the policeman; a wedding party, and a numerous gathering of children, made up the congregation we saw. The service was simple and heartily joined in; the singing, supported by a small harmonium, went off well; and the minister preached a fair sermon. But he is far too excitable to last out long. The speed he goes at would kill a man directly if he were made of cast-iron.

Mr. Lee, the preacher, is a ten times breezier man than his vivacious namesake at the Parish Church; he is small like him, dark-complexioned like him, wears spectacles like him; but he travels at the rate of 1000 miles an hour, and his namesake has never yet got beyond 500. The gentleman under review is a pre-eminently earnest man. We never saw any minister throw himself, head, arms, shoes, and shirt, so intensely into the business of praying and preaching as he. Nothing seems to impede his progress. He rushes into space with terrible vehemence; prays until the veins on his forehead swell and throb as if they would burst; and when he sits down he pants as if he had been running himself to death in a dream, whilst sweat pours off him as if he had been trying to burn up the sun at the equator. In his preaching he is equally intense and earnest. He puts on the steam at once, drives forward at limited mail speed; stops instantly;

then rushes onto the next station - steam up instantly; stops again in a moment without whistling; is at full speed forthwith, everybody holding on to their seats whilst the regulator is open; and in this way he continues, getting safely to the end at last, but driving at such a frightfully rapid speed that travellers wonder how it is everything has not been smashed to atoms in readiness for coroners, and juries, and newspaper reporters. As to his sincerity there cannot be a question. He is not profound, but is very honest; he has nothing strongly ratiocinative in him, but he has for ever of earnestness in his composition - indeed he burns himself up in a great blaze of zeal and blows himself to pieces in a self-generated whirlwind. If he were quieter he would be more persuasive; and if he expended less of his vital energy in trying to brew forty storms in one tea pot he would live longer. "Easy does it" is a phrase plucked from the plebeian lexicon of life, which we recommend for his consideration. If he doesn't attend to it we shall have a case of spontaneous combustion to record; and we want to avoid that if possible. There is not a more sincere man, not a man more anxious to do good in Preston than Mr. Lee, only he piles Ossa upon Olympus too stiffly, and that was a job which the gods couldn't manage properly.

The building where the Parker-street brethren meet is used for school purposes regularly - barring the periods when worship is being conducted in it. On week days about 100 scholars attend it; and on Sundays about 150. The school and the chapel have done much good in the locality, and we wish both prosperity. Whatever maybe the character of the building, and however difficult it may be for strangers to get to it, those living in the neighbourhood know its whereabouts, many having derived improvement from it, and if more went to it, pigeon-flying, gambling, Sunday rat hunting, tossing, drinking, and paganism generally - things which have long flourished in its locality - would be nearer a finish.

XXX

GRIMSHAW-STREET INDEPENDENT CHAPEL

Long before two-thirds of the people now living were born there was a rather curious difficulty at the Unitarian Chapel in this town. In 1807, the Rev. W. Manning Walker, who at that time had been minister of the chapel for five years, changed his mind, became "more evangelical," could not agree with the doctrines he had previously preached, got into water somewhat warm with the members, and left the place. He took with him a few sympathisers, and through their instrumentality a new chapel was built for him in Grimshaw-street, and opened on the 12th of April, 1808. It was a small edifice, would accommodate about 850 persons, and was the original ancestor of the Independent Chapel in that street. In 1817 the building was enlarged so as to accommodate between 500 and 600, and Mr. Walker laboured regularly at it till 1822, when declining health necessitated his retirement. The Rev. Thomas Mc.Connell, a gentleman with a smart polemical tongue, succeeded him. Mr. Mc.Connell drew large congregations, and for a time was a burning and a shining light; but in 1825 be withdrew; became an infidel or somcthing of the sort, and subsequently gave lectures on theological subjects, much to the regret of his friends and the horror of the orthodox.

On the 23rd of July, 1826, the Rev. R. Slate began duty as regular minister of the chapel, and remained at his post until April 7th, 1861, when through old age and growing infirmity he resigned. Mr. Slate was a tiny, careful, smoothly-earnest man, consistent and faithful as a minister, made more for quiet sincere work than dashing labour or dazzling performance; fond of the Puritan divines, a believer in old manuscripts, disposed to tell his audiences every time he got upon a platform how long he had been in the ministry, but in the aggregate well and deservedly respected. No clergyman in Preston has ever stayed so long at one place as Mr. Slate; and Grimshaw-street Chapel since it lost him has many a time had a "slate off" in more respects than one.

After Mr. Slate retired from his post at Grimshaw-street Chapel, the Rev. J. Briggs, a young and vociferous gentleman, fresh from college, given to Sunday evening lecturing, Corn Exchange serenading, virtuous speech-making, and other - we were going to say evils - labours of love, appeared upon the stage. Soon after he arrived a new black gown was presented to him, and if one of the local papers which recorded the event at the time tells the truth, he had it donned in the vestry, after which there was a procession round the church, Mr. Briggs leading the way, whilst the deacons, including some mythological "Mr. Clinkscales" - that was the name given - and others brought up the rear. If the town's beadle and mace-bearer had been present, the procession would have been complete. In October, 1866, Mr. Briggs retired, with the gown, and he has since, like Brother Clapham, formerly minister of Lancaster-road Independent Chapel - "par nobile fratrum" - gone over to "mother church."

On the 20th of January, 1867, the Rev. Evan Lewis became minister of Grimshaw-street Chapel, but after staying about a year and a half, he, on account of ill health, resigned, went south, and died there. Mr. Lewis was a cautious, cultured person, had very many letters, which were always coming in a row to the surface, after his name, was a man of ripe and polished intellect, was clever in brain work, had good strategic skill, could manage an ill-natured church meeting well, and would have been a power in his own denomination and in the town if he had been physically stronger. He was an invalided intellectualist, well up in everything, but defective in stamina, muscle force, and lung strength. For about nine months after the retirement of Mr. Lewis no fixed minister occupied the pulpit. Sunday "supplies" were tried in the meantime; finally the Rev. G. F. Newman was selected, and about two months ago he commenced his ministerial labours.

The building as enlarged in 1817 remained without molestation for years; but in 1850 it was thought that a better place was needed; in 1856 it was decided to have a better place; soon afterwards the old edifice was pulled down; and in 1859 the Congregational Chapel we now see was opened. It stands upon the original site, but is extended nearer the street than its predecessor. There used to be a considerable portion of the graveyard in front, but owing to the enlarged character of the new chapel it was mainly covered over - built upon; and only a remnant of the old burial ground can now be seen in this quarter. Two small upright tombstones, immediately adjoining the chapel, and a few flat slabs on the ground below, are the only sepulchural indications remaining here. On the southern side of the building there is a dull and dreary square piece of ground, railed round, which constituted a portion of the old burial-yard, and which now contains a few forsaken-looking tombstones. The new church cost between 3,000 and 4,000 pounds, and it is not entirely finished yet. At the front it has a one-sided irregular look; and this is owing to the non-completion of a collateral spire. In the original design the facade consists of a central elevation with two flanking towers and spires; but one of the towers, whilst being constructed, gave way, got seriously out of the perpendicular, and it was decided to pull it down rather than allow the stone-work to fall of its own accord. New foundations, ten feet deep, had to be sunk into the old front burial ground for it, and during the excavations 33 coffins were taken up and conveyed to a more peaceable place of sepulture. They literally couldn't stand the pressure of the tower, and for their sake; as well as the safety of the building, a change was necessary. Afterwards the tower was raised to its former elevation, but it is still without a spire. The re-erection of the tower coat 380 pounds, which was raised by a weekly offertory.

The chapel, barring the incomplete masonry mentioned, is a well made, neat-looking building. In front there is a large four-light window, which had to be taken right out when the tower was being re-made; on each side there is a long and very narrow window, more for ornament than use; and below there are two small triangular apertures of a similar character. Strong rails, intended to prevent people from approaching the building too closely on week-days, surround the chapel. There are three arched doorways immediately adjoining one another at the front, and on a Sunday you are at perfect liberty to use any of them - to try all of them if so disposed - and pass through that which appears most agreeable. The chapel has a large and remarkably clean interior. It is well lighted with numerous windows bordered with coloured glass, and has a fine arched roof, supported by four principals, and filled-in centrally with elaborate designs. Around the building there is a large octagonal gallery; and whilst all the seats in it run up to a pretty fair height, those at the western end approach quite an aerial altitude. It is almost a question of being "up in a balloon, boys," when you are perched in the loftiest of them.

All the pews are plain, strong, and without doors. The central ones on the ground-floor are very uniform in design; those at the sides are, of various shapes, and are whimsically disposed - seem to be up and down, straight, diagonal, and semi-circular. The first pew on the right side was occupied, when we last saw it, with three brushes, an elderly shovel, and two gas-meters, one of them being a very full-grown fatherly affair - a sort of deacon amongst ordinary meters, and looking very authoritatively upon its smaller colleague and the brushes. The pulpit, at the eastern end of the chapel, is neatly made, but when the parson sits in it you can't see him from the front. When we went the other Sunday evening, we could see no one in it; but after a hymn had been sung, a spring seemed to be touched, and up jumped the parson, who had been reclining on his dorsal vertebra for eight minutes at the rear. The pulpit formerly stood about a foot-and-a-half higher than it does now; Mr. Slate, who was a little man, would have it a good height; but a hole was afterwards made in the platform supporting the pulpit, and it was dropped through it to the level of the ordinary floor, where it now stands. Six chairs, in Gothic design, with cushions of rich velvet, are placed upon the platform near the pulpit; in the centre there is a more patriarchal-looking seat - a sort of pastoral throne; and in the front of the whole there is a strong table. The deacons and the minister sit here periodically, feeling grand and furzy all over, weighing up the universe on special occasions, but endeavouring always to discharge their executive duties with due propriety and gravity. We have seen them once or twice on this platform - on those silk velvet-bottomed chairs, resting upon Brussels carpet - and they looked majestic. One old gentleman we know, who used to be a deacon here, never would sit in any of these chairs. He seemed to have either a dread of the eighteen-inch elevation they conferred, or a fear that the platform would give way, or a dislike of the conspicuousness caused by it, and on all occasions when his official brethren took possession of the chairs, he sat upon an open bench adjoining.

An ancient-looking organ, of Gothic pattern, and formerly used in a Blackburn chapel, is placed within an archway in the eastern gallery. It is a moderately fair instrument, and is decently played, but it is not good enough for the place, and it is quite time to sell it to some other chapel, and get a better. The choir contains about the usual complement of smiling young men and maidens, with a central gentleman "bearded like the pard," who sits in state in an elaborately backed chair, and conducts the proceedings with legitimate authority. The singing of the choir is pretty exact and melodious; but it is too weak - needs more harmonic energy and general strength. The congregation do their duty mildly in the singing portion of the proceedings, and at times, when some good old tune is started, they rush to the rescue with much dexterity and thoracic power. There are about 200 "members of the Church" at this place of worship, and several young people are now, we believe "ready for admission." The average congregation will be about 300 - not a large number considering the size of the building; but then, through ministerial changes, &c., the place has had much to contend with, and it has not had a chance for some time of getting into proper working order. Peacefulness prevails now at the chapel.

Prior to the advent of the late Mr. Lewis, there were many storms at the place. The parson never got to literal fighting with any of the members; the members never threatened to hit him; but one or more of them have been heard to say that they would put him "behind the fire" in the vestry, and he in turn has been heard to remark that he would return the compliment. But all this sort of Christian courtesy has disappeared - let us hope forever; and the members now nestle in their seats lovingly, casting calm glances at each other betimes, and attending duly to the parson, who eyes them placidly, and encourages their affection. If they had to nestle upon each other's bosoms during the intervals - properly, and without falling asleep over the job - he would not grow sullen and angry. On Sundays, there are a couple of services - morning, and evening - at the chapel; and every Wednesday evening there is a prayer meeting, but it is not a very savage gathering; men and women seldom lash themselves into a foam at it; and nothing is uttered during its proceedings out of the ordinary run of Queen's English.

The Rev. G. F. Newman, a south of England gentleman, who, during the past seven or eight years, through delicate health, has spent much of his time in France, is the minister. He has an income independent of his clerical stipend. From Grimshaw-street Chapel he gets about 3 pounds per week. It is derived from pew rents, which range from 1s. to 2s. 11d. per seat per quarter, so that its increase will depend upon the manner he fills the place. Mr. Newman is about 34 years of age, is of middle stature, has nothing physically ponderous or irrelevant about him; is a dark complexioned, moderately-sized person, of gentlemanly taste, deportment, and expression; knows manners - "they order this matter better in France," as Sterne would say; his commingling with our lively neighbours has evidently given him the direct cue to them; has a temperament of the nervous-bilious order; is more perceptive than reflective; but has a calm, clear intellect notwithstanding; is rather fond of the sublime, and likes a strong dash of the beautiful; believes in good music, and understands notes a little himself; is an excellent reader - one of the best we have heard; is an average preacher; has nothing flashy or terrific in his style, but goes on quietly, tastefully, and with precision; cares more for short than long sermons; repeats himself rather often; likes to give his own experience during illustrations; talks much of France, and never forgets to let his hearers know that he has been there; takes long, careful pauses in his sermons, as if he were elaborating his conceptions, or selecting the exact words in which to convey them most definitely; has a special regard for the gas pendant on the left side of the pulpit, which he handles affectionately as a rest; dislikes being interrupted when either reading, or praying, or preaching; can't stand coughing; doesn't like a Preston cough - it has a half-harsh half-oily sound, which he could detect if in London or Paris; believes more in faith than good works, but respects both; is scrupulous as to punctuality, and is almost inclined to emulate the incumbent of Christ Church, who once threatened to lock the doors of that building at a certain time after business commenced, if all were not in their places; particularly objects to a lady coming late, because, as a rule, she makes a great noise with her dress on entering a place of worship, and, in addition, induces all the other ladies present to turn round, or look on one side, for the purpose of seeing what she is wearing; is more of a conversationalist than a speaker; likes chit-chat; would be at home in a conversazione or al fresco tea party, where the attendants walk about, gossip merrily, and, whilst holding a tea cup in one hand, poise with two fingers a piece of delicately-buttered toast in the other - a continental style quite aesthetic and refined in comparison with our feeding, and gormandising, and sweating exhibitions. Mr. Newman promises to be a good minister. His commencement has been, satisfactory, and his prospects are encouraging. He is a bachelor, and seems mildly happy; but his bliss might be consummated - let no lady prick her ears too highly, for Mr. Newman has cautiousness largely developed - if he would study and practically carry out that notion expressed at a meeting over which he recently presided; the lecturer on that occasion saying that "marriage is essential to the true happiness of man."

The young men at Grimshaw-street are pretty intelligent and controversial. They have a mutual improvement class, which is one of the best of its kind in the town, and they discuss the laws of life, - mental, physical, political, and spiritual - like embryonic philosophers bent upon rectifying all creation. Their class is prosperous, and is calculated, if correctly managed, to be of much importance to those visiting it. All such classes ought to encouraged, and we hope the Grimshaw-street essayists will go on rectifying creation - never forgetting themselves at the same time. For a long period there has been a Sunday school in connection with the chapel. Several years, in the earlier stages of the denomination's career, the scholars were taught in the vestry and in pews at the chapel; but in 1836 a school was erected for them upon a plot of land adjoining, and in 1846 it was enlarged to its present size. The average Sunday attendance is about 300. In January, 1868 a day school for boys, girls, and infants was opened in the same building, under the conductorship of Mr. J. Greenhalgh. So far it has been very successful. Its average attendance is about 190. Government reports speak very hopefully of the place; more prizes have been awarded to it by the Science and Art Department, South Kensington, than to any other school in the town; and its present status indicates a prosperous future. An unsectarian night school is also held in the building, and its average attendance is about 120. In addition there is a band of hope society at the place, and it is better attended than any other similar association in Preston. All that Grimshaw-street Chapel wants is a fuller congregation. That would develope every department of it; and energy, combined with continuity of service, would secure this. Mr. Newman who understands French, must adopt as his motto, and have it embossed on the buttons of his own and his deacons' coats, and on the backs of the seven chairs they use in the chapel, the words "Boutez en avant."

XXXI

ST. PAUL'S CHURCH.

There are nearly 13,000 people in the "district" of this church. What a difference time makes! At the beginning of the present century the greater portion of the district was made up of fields; whilst lanes, with hedges set each side, constituted what are now some of its busiest streets. Volunteers and militiamen used to meet for drill on a large piece of land in the very heart of the locality; troops of charwomen formerly washed their clothes in water pits hard by, and dried them on the green-sward adjoining; and everything about wore a rural and primitive aspect. St. Paul's Church is situated on a portion of land which, 50 years ago, was fringed with trees and called "The Park;" and this accounts for the name still given by many to the sacred edifice - namely "Park Church." The sisters of the late J. Bairstow, Esq., kept a school at one time on, or contiguous to, this park. A road, starting opposite the Holy Lamb, in Church-street, and ending near the top of High-street, formerly passed through "The Park." Years ago a ducking or cucking stool was placed at the northern side of it, adjoining a pit, and at the edge of the thoroughfare known as Meadow street. This ducking stool was intended for the special benefit of vixens and scolding wives. It consisted of a strong plank, at the end of which was a chair, the centre working upon a pivot, and, after the person to be punished had been duly secured, she was ducked into the water. If this system were now in force, it would often be patronised, for there are many lively termagants in the land, and lots in Preston.

The first stone of St. Paul's Church was laid on Tuesday, 21st October, 1823. Out of the million pounds granted by Parliament for the erection of churches, some time prior to the date given, Preston, through Dr. Lawe, who was then Bishop of Chester, got 12,500 pounds. It was originally intended to expend this sum in the erection of one church - St. Peter's; but at the request of the Rev. R. Carus Wilson, vicar of Preston, the money was divided, one half going to St. Peter's, and the other to St. Paul's. Some people might consider this like "robbing Peter to pay Paul," but it was better to halve the money for the benefit of two districts, than give all of it for the spiritual edification of one, and leave the other destitute. The land forming the site of St. Paul's was given by Samuel Pole Shawe, Esq. The full cost of the building was about 6,500 pounds. Around the edifice there is a very large iron-railed grave yard, which is kept in pretty good order. St. Paul's is built entirely of stone, in the early English style of architecture. It has a rather elegant appearance; but it is defective in altitude has a broad, flat, and somewhat bald-looking roof, and needs either a good tower or spire to relieve and dignify it. In front there are several pointed windows, a small circular hole above for birds' nests, two doorways with a window between them, a central surmounting gable, and a couple of feathery-headed perforated turrets, one being used as a chimney, and the other as a belfry. There is only a single bell at the church, and it is pulled industriously on Sundays by a devoted youth, who takes his stand in a boxed-off corner behind one of the doors. At the opposite end of the church there are two turrets corresponding in height and form with those is front. Two screens of red cloth are fixed just within the entrance and, whilst giving a certain degree of selectness to the place, they prevent people sitting near them from being blown away or starved to death on very windy days when the doors happen to be open.

The interior consists of a broad, ornamentally roofed nave (resting upon twelve high narrow pillars of stone), and two aisles. The pillars seriously obstruct the vision of those sitting at the sides; indeed, in some places so detrimental are they that you can see neither the reading-desk nor the pulpit. Above, there is a very large gallery, set apart on the west for the organ and choir, and on each side for general worshippers, school children, as a rule, being in front, and requiring a good deal of watching during the services. In some parts of the gallery seeing is quite as difficult as in the sides beneath, owing to the intervening nave pillars. Efforts have been made to rectify this evil, not by trying to pull down the pillars, but by removing the pulpit, &c, so that all might have a glance at it. The pulpit is situated on the south-eastern side, near the chancel, and one Sunday it was brought into the centre of the church; but it could be seen no better there than in its old position, so it was carried back, and has remained unmolested ever since. If it were put upon castors, and pushed slowly and with becoming reverence up and down the church during sermon time, all would get a view of its occupant; but we believe the warders have an objection to pulpits on castors, so that there is no hope in this respect. The reading-desk stands opposite the pulpit, and looks very broad and diminutive. The chancel is plain. A large, neatly designed stained glass window occupies the end. On each side there is a mural monument - one being to the memory of Samuel Horrocks, Esq., Guild Mayor in 1842, and son of S. Horrocks, Esq., of Lark-hill, who for twenty-two years represented Preston in Parliament; and the other, raised by public subscription, to the memory of the Rev. Joseph Rigg, who was minister of St. Paul's for nineteen years, and who died in 1847. The general fittings and arrangements of the church indicate plainness of design, combined with medium strength and thorough respectability. In no part of the building is there any eccentric flourishing or artistic meandering. The roof, the walls, and the base of the window niches, which have become blackened with rain, need cleaning up; and some day, when money is plentiful, they will no doubt be renovated. The seats are strong, broad, and regular in shape. All of them, except one, are let, and it would speedily be tenanted if more conveniently located. There is a pillar in it, and, in order to get a proper view of the officiating minister, you must stand up, lean forward, and glance with a rolling eye round the corners of the obstruction - a thing which many of the more bashful of our species would not like to do.

The church will accommodate about 1,200 persons, and the average Sunday attendance may be calculated at 800. The gallery is patronised extensively by the "million"; the ground floor pews are occupied by more select and fashionable individuals. The great majority of the worshippers sit above, and few vacant spaces can as a rule be seen there. Down stairs the crush is less severe. The congregation is a mixture of working and middle class people; the former kind being preponderant. At the sides there are long narrow ranges of free seats; but they are not often disturbed. On two successive Sundays we gave them a passing look, and they appeared to be almost deserted. A couple of little boys seated in the centre, and engaged in the pleasing juvenile businsss of swinging their legs, were the only occupants we saw on the right side during our first inspection; and when we viewed the range on the other side, the Sunday after, we could only catch tender glimpses of three females, all very quiet, and each belonging the antique school of life. "Where will you sit?" said a large-hearted young man, when we made our second appearance. "There," was our reply, pointing at the same time to a well-cushioned and genially sequestered seat at the north-west corner, and we were ushered into it with becoming decorum. In two minutes afterwards five women and a festive infant, dressed in a drab cloak, and muffled all over to keep the cold out, stopped at the pew door. We stepped out; three of the females, with the baby, stepped in; the remainder went into the next pew; and after condensing our nerve power, we settled down in the corner from which we had been disturbed, quietly lifting one hand over the door and latching it firmly at the same moment, our idea being than an environment of five females, with a baby thrown into the bargain, was quite enough for the remainder of the morning. After an inquiry as to the christening arrangements at the church, for we fancied this was a christening gathering, we got nearer the baby, and, in a delicately sympathetic whisper said - "How old is it?" The maiden who was holding it blushed, and laconically breathed out the words, "Three months." We subsequently found out that the seat we were in was the incumbent's, and that the blessed baby, whose lot we had been contemplating with such interest, was his, too.

Six minutes before the commencement there were only nine persons in the body of the church; but nearly 300 were congregated there when the service began, whilst the gallery was well filled with worshippers of all ages and sizes. All the responses here are "congregational" - none of them being in any way intoned. We believe that St. Paul's is the only Protestant church in Preston wherein this system is observed. The effect, when compared with the plans of intonation now so universal, is very singular; and it sometimes sounds dull and monotonous - like a long, low, rumbling of irregular voices, as if there were some quaint, oddly-humoured contention going on in every pew. But the worshippers seem to like the system, and as they have a perfect right to be their own judges, other people must be silent on the subject. The music is not of an extraordinary sort; it is plain, and very well joined in by the congregation. But the choir, like many others, lacks weight and symphony. Mrs. Myres, the wife of the incumbent, is a member of the choir, and if all the other individuals in it had her musical knowledge, an improvement would soon follow. The organ is a very good one. It was given by the late T. Miller, Esq., and H. Miller, Esq., and placed in the church in 1844. Recently it has been put in first-rate condition, for organs, like the players of them, get worse for wear, by T. H. and W. P. Miller, Esqrs. The organist knows his work, and is able to perform it with ability.

At St. Paul's there is morning and evening service on a Sunday; and every Wednesday evening there is a short service, but like the bulk of mid-week devotional exercises it is not much cared for, only about 150 joining it on the average. On the second Sunday in each month there is an early sacrament at St. Paul's. At no other place of worship in the town, that we know of, save Christ Church, is there a similar sacramental arrangement. Since St. Paul's was opened, there have been five incumbents at it. The first was the Rev. Mr. Russell; then came the Rev. J. Rigg, who was a most exemplary clergyman; next the Rev. S. F. Page, who was followed by the Rev. J. Miller; the present incumbent being the Rev. W. M. Myres, son of Mr. J. J. Myres, of Preston. Mr. Myres came to St. Paul's at the beginning of 1867, and when he made his appearance fidgetty and orthodox souls were in a state of mingled dudgeon and trepidation as to what be would do. It was fancied that he was a Ritualist - fond of floral devices and huge candles, with an incipient itching for variegated millinery, beads, and crosses. But his opponents, who numbered nearly two-thirds of the congregation, screamed before they were bitten, and went into solemn paroxysms of pious frothiness for nothing. Subsequent events have proved how highly imaginative their views were. No church in the country has less of Ritualism in it than St. Paul's. Its services are pre-eminently plain; all those parts whereon the spirit of innovation has settled so strongly in several churches during the past few years are kept in their original simplicity; and in the general proceedings nothing can be observed calculated to disturb the peace of the most fastidious of show-disliking Churchmen.

Mr. Myres is about 30 years of age, is corporeally condensed, walks as if he were in earnest and wanted to catch the train, has a mild, obliging, half-diffident look, wears a light coloured beard and moustache, each of which is blossoming very nicely; is sharp, yet even-tempered; bland and genial, yet sincere; has keen powers of observation, has a better descriptive than logical faculty, is not very imaginative, cares more for prose than poetry, more for facts than sallies of the fancy, more for gentle devotion, and quiet persevering labour in his own locality than for virtuous welterings and sacred acrobatism in other districts. He has endeavoured, since coming to Preston, to mind his own business, and parsons often find that a hard thing to accomplish. Polished in education, he is humble and social in manner. He will never be an ecclesiastical show-man, for his disposition is in the direction of general quietude and good neighbourship. If he ever gets into a sacred disturbance the fault will be through somebody else dragging him into it, and not because he has courted it by natural choice. He is more cut out for sincere labour, pleasantly and strenuously conducted, than for intellectual generalship or lofty theological display. His brain may lack high range and large creativeness; but he possesses qualities of heart and spirit which mere brilliance cannot secure, and which simple cerebral strength can never impart. We admire him for his courteousness, his artless simplicity of nature, his earnest, kindly-devotedness to duty, and his continual attention to everything affecting the welfare of those he has to look after. Mr. Myres is greatly respected by all in his district; he has transmuted the olden ritualistic horror which prevailed in the district, into one of love and reverence; and all his sheep have a genial and affectionate bleat for him.

The Rev. C. G. Acworth, a learned young man, whose facial capillary forces are coming gradually into play, and who seems to have the entire Book of Common Prayer off by heart, is the curate of St. Paul's. He is a good reader, a steady, sententious, epigrammatic preacher, and with a little more knowledge of the world ought to make a clever and most useful minister. Something, which we do not think exists in connection with any other Preston church for the management of affairs, is established here. It is a "Church Committee." It consists of the ministers, the churchwardens, and a dozen members of the congregation. They discuss all sorts of matters appertaining to the district, smooth down grievances when any are nursed, and keep everything in good working order. The outside machinery for mentally and religiously improving the district is very extensive and varied. There are five day and Sunday schools under the auspices of St. Paul's. They are situated in Pole and Carlisle streets, and are under the guidance of four superintendents and fifty-seven teachers. Mrs. Myres (wife of the incumbent), who is a great favourite throughout the district, is one of the teachers. The day or national schools are the largest in the town; they have an average attendance of 934; and that in which boys are taught is the only one of its kind in Preston which is self-supporting. The average attendance of Sunday scholars is 800.

Night schools also form part of the educational programme, and they are well attended. A mutual improvement class - the oldest in the town - likewise exists in connection with St. Paul's. It was established by the Rev. S. F. Page, and is conducted on principles well calculated to regulate, illumine, and edify the youths who mar and make empires at it. A temperance society, in which the Rev. Mr. Acworth, who is a "Bright water for me" believer, has taken praiseworthy interest, has furthermore got a footing in St. Paul's, and beyond that there is a band of hope society in the district, which does its share of work. Every Monday afternoon, a "Mother's Meeting," conducted by Mrs. Myres, Mrs. Isherwood, Miss Wadsworth, and the Bible woman, is held in a room of the Carlisle-street school. The mothers are pretty lacteous and docile. In various parts of the district, cottage lectures, conducted by the curate and a number of energetic teachers, are held weekly. The district of St. Paul's is great in missionary work. There are about four-and-twenty collectors in the field here, and by the penny a week system they raise sums which periodical efforts would never realise. By the way, we ought to have said that there are a good many collections in St. Paul's church - 16 regular ones and 14 on the offertory principle - every year. Those who consider it more blessed to give than receive should be happy at St. Paul's. The sums collected at the church range from about 12 to 50 pounds. The Irish Church Missionary Society receives much of its Preston support from this district. Lastly, we may remark that there is a good staff of tract distributors, supervised by a ladies' committee, in connection with St. Paul's. The distributors are chiefly young women belonging the schools. Owing to the vastness of the district it is contemplated to erect as early as possible a school chapel as an auxiliary of the church. It will be built near the railway bridge in St. Paul's-road. R. Newsham, Esq., has offered to give a handsome sum towards the edifice, which is much needed. When opened a second curate will be required, and towards the stipend of such gentleman, E. Hermon, Esq., M.P., has offered to contribute liberally. The salary of the incumbent is about 280 pounds per annum. The generality of the officials connected with the church and schools have been long at their posts - a proof of even action and good harmony; everything seems to be progressing steadily in the district; and if St. Paul himself had to give it a visit he would shake hands warmly with Mr. Myres, the incumbent, praise Mrs. Myres and the baby, and throw up his hat gleefully at the good work which is being done amongst the people.

XXXII

ST. MARY'S-STREET AND MARSH-END WESLEYAN CHAPELS, AND THE TABERNACLE OF THE REVIVALISTS.

"When shall we three meet again?" We can't tell - don't care about knowing; you have met now; and keep quiet, if possible, whilst being vivisected. There are worse companions, so shake hands, and sigh for universal bliss. We shall use the dissecting knife with a kindly sharpness. The first of the places named is situated in St. Mary's-street, opposite a very high wall, which we believe is intended to prevent men from scaling it, and is closely associated with the arrangements of the House of Correction. One hundred yards off, it looks like a high, modernised, seaside hotel; fifty yards off, it seems like a well-arranged gentleman's residence, in the wrong place; two yards off, it indicates its own mission, and clearly shows that something embracing both education and religion is carried on within it. It is a large, well-built, quadrangular building, with two round-headed ranges of windows in front, and a good roof above, surmounted with an iron rail, put up apparently for imaginary purposes. Nobody has yet got over that rail so far as we have heard; and if the job is ever attempted, nothing will be found on the other side worth carrying home. The foundation stone of this building - it is really a school chapel - was laid on Good Friday, 1866, and the place was opened in the same year. The place cost 2,500 pounds, and it is nearly out of debt. Internally, it is full of rooms. On the ground floor there are nine apartments - all well disposed, appropriately fit up, and set apart for general scholastic and class purposes. On week days, some of them are used as school-rooms, the average attendance of pupils, who are carefully looked after, being about 120; and on Sundays they are devoted to "class" business. In a large room above, children are also taught on Sundays: the general attendance on those days throughout the place being about 450. This school-chapel owes its existence to the cotton famine. During that trying period, when people had nothing else to do but think, live on 2s. a week, and grow good, Messrs. Wilding and Strachan generously opened a room connected with their mill in New Hall-lane, for secular and religious instruction. It was attended mainly by those belonging the Wesleyan persuasion; in time it became too little; and the result was the erection of a school-chapel in St. Mary's-street. We have never seen a better arranged nor a more commodious place of its kind than this. Its class, and ordinary scholastic departments we have alluded to. Let us now proceed above-into the room used for worship. You can reach it from either the northern or the southern side, but from neither can you make headway without ascending a strong, winding series of steps, which must be trying and troublesome to heavy and asthmatic subjects, if any of that sort ever show themselves at the building. The room is large, lofty, clean, and airy, and will hold about 400 persons. Just within each doorway there is a box, intended for contributions on behalf of "sick and needy scholars." But both have been put too near the side; they often catch people's clothes, on entering, and as everybody is not disposed to stop and exercise the organ of benevolence, whilst the remainder wish to be judicious about the business and save their dresses, it has been decided to shift them inwards a little. From the centre of the ceiling, gas burners, in star-shaped clusters, are suspended, and when the taps are on they give good lights.

The congregation, which is generally constituted of working-class people, numbers about 350. The people attending this place are a quiet, devoted lot, with patches of pride and self-glorification here and there about them, but, on the whole, kindly-looking and sincere. Some of them are close-minded and intensely orthodox; but the majority are wide-awake, and won't pray for fair weather until it has given over raining. The members of the choir sit on the eastern side, and if not so refined and punctillious in their musical performances, they are at least pretty strong-lunged and earnest. They are located near the wall. The harmonium-player enjoys a closer proximity to it. He manipulates with fair skill, has a clock right above him, and ought, therefore, to keep "good time." If he doesn't, then let the clock be condemned as a deceiver and incumberer of the wall. The pulpit is a broad, neatly-arranged affair - fixed upon a platform at the southern end, and environed with rails of blue and gold colour. Just within, and on its immediate left, there is a small paper nailed up with four nails, and containing, is written English, these words, as a reminder for each preacher during his "supplications" - "Pray for God's ancient people of Israel." "Does this mean the Jews?" said we to an elderly man near us, whilst we were scrutinizing with a plaintive eye, the pulpit, and he replied, "Bleeve it does." That, we thought, was a bad speculation for a chapel containing two subscription boxes for "sick and needy scholars." The man who wrote out that exhortation in the interests of Petticoat-lane men and their kindred, and the patriot who drove with a fierce virtue the four nails into it didn't, we are afraid, know clearly how much it costs to convert a genuine Jew, else more caution would have been exercised by each of them. A Jew's eye is a costly thing; but a Jew's conversion is much more expensive; you can't get at the thing fairly for less than 10,000 pounds; and as five good Wesleyan Chapels could be built, in ordinary districts, for that sum, we advise Wesleyans to go in for chapels and not for Jews.

If the pulpit had not been a broad and accommodating one, in St. Mary's-street Chapel, we should have been inclined to think that the parson might have had a "walk round." There is just space enough in front of the pulpit for a medium-sized gentleman to pass between it and the front rails. In a moment of high dudgeon, a thin preacher with a passion for "action" might easily flank off and traverse it frontally; but an easy-minded individual would find plenty of room in the pulpit, and if he did not, presuming he were stout, he would have to "crush" considerably in order to accomplish a full circular route. Beyond and in the immediate front of the pulpit rails there is a circular seat. This we fancied, during our inspection, was the "penitent form" - it seemed close and handy during a season of stern excitement and warm eruption; but in a moment we were told it was for "sacrament people," who patronise it in turns, on particular Sundays. Two services are conducted on Sundays here by regular and itinerent preachers; the former coming from Lune-street Chapel, and the latter being furnished out of the general lay body. Nearly every night throughout the week, class meetings, &c., are held in the building, and they are conducted with much rapture and peacefulness. How the Jew-converting business gets on we cannot tell - badly, we imagine; but in respect to the ordinary operations of the place they are successful and promise to be still more so. A chapel whose members branched off from this place has been established at Walton. About 12 months ago it was opened. A cottage situated on the road side leading to the church constitutes the walhallah of Methodism there, and the support accorded to it is increasing. We have no more to say as to the St. Mary's-street mission. We hope it will go on and agreeably grapple with the people in its own district whatever may become of the Jews.

A mile and a half distant, on the other side of the town, and quietly resting amongst the desolate premises once occupied by the Preston Ship Building Company, at the Marsh End, there is a small preaching place, wherein the Scriptures are expounded and the doctrines of John Wesley duly inculcated. About two and a half years ago a couple of cottages in this locality were "thrown into one," and arranged so as to moderately accommodate those caring about religion, and willing to have it in a "good old Methodist" style. There was considerable briskness of trade hereabouts at that time, ships were made in the adjoining yards, the bubble of speculation was being strongly blown, large numbers of strong-armed men, caring more for ale in gallon jugs than either virtue in tracts or piety in sermons, resided in the district, the population was rapidly increasing, a new section of the town's suburbs was being strongly developed, and there being drinking houses, skittle grounds, and other accompaniments of a progressive age visible, it was considered prudent to mix up a small Wesleyan preaching room and school with the general confraternity of institutions in the locality. At the beginning of this year, owing to the insufficient accomodation of the premises, a portion of the pattern room of the Ship Building Company, which in the meantime had resolved its organisation into thin air and evaporated, was secured, and arranged in a homely fashion for the required business. After passing through a small door in the centre of a large one, leading to the shipyard, then turning to the right, then mounting 18 steep awkward steps, and then turning again to the right, you arrive at the place.

The moment we saw it we knew it. It was in this very room where grand champagne luncheons used to be given after ship launches, and where dancing and genteel carousing followed. The last time we had business at this place we saw twenty-three gentlemen alcoholically merry in it, six Town Councillors helpless yet boisterous in it, thirty couples of ladies and gentlemen dancing in it, four waiters smuggling half-used bottles of champagne rapidly down their throats in it, an ex-Mayor with his hat, thrown right back, looking awfully jolly, and superintending the proceedings, in it, and in an adjoining room, now used for vestry purposes, three ladies in silk velvet, wine-freighted, and just able to see, blowing up everybody because their bonnets were lost. The place where all this "fou and unco happy" work was transacted is now the school chapel of the Wesleyans. The room wherein the congregation meet is bare, plain, and primitive-looking, with an open roof, whitewashed all round, and boarded off from a workshop at the southern end. Its "furniture" consists of eleven forms, three stoves, a pulpit with no back, and a chair. A strip of wood is placed across a window at the rear of the chair, which is used by the officiating parson, and this wood prevents him from breaking the glass if he should happen to throw his head back sharply. On one side of the room there are 19 hat hooks, and on the other 24. There are seats in the place for about 100. The members number about 20, and the average congregation, entirely working people, and of homely, orderly character, will range from 80 to 100. The room is connected with the Wesley circuit; every Sunday there are two services in it; a meeting for religious purposes is held each Thursday night; and the preaching is done by "locals" and "regulars." The singing is neither good, nor bad, nor indifferent; but a mixture of the whole three qualities. It is accompanied by a small harmonium, played by a young lady in moderately tasteful style. The services are simple and hearty, and whilst there may be a little plaintive noisiness now and then in them - a few penitent flutterings - they are generally, and remembering the complexion of the congregation, respectably conducted.

"It's a regular bird nest, and you'll never get to it, unless you ask the neighbouring folk," said a friend to us whilst talking about the Revivalists' tabernacle. To the bottom of Pitt-street we then went, and seeing two or three females and a man dart out of a dim-looking passage beneath one of the side arches of the railway bridge there, we concluded that we were near the "nest." Having sauntered about for a few moments, and assured ourselves that this was really the place we were in search of, we went to the arch, walked six or seven yards forward, looked up a dark, tortuous, narrow passage on the right, and entered it. In the centre of the passage there was a hole, through which you could see telegraph wires and the sky, on one side a grim crevice running narrowly to the top of the railway bridge, and ahead a shadowy opening like the front of an underground store, with a wooden partition, in the centre of which was a small square of glass. Theseus, who got through the Labyrinth, would have been puzzled with this mystic passage. We never saw such a time-worn and dumfounding road to any place, and if those who patronise it regularly had done their best to discover the essence of dinginess and intractibility, they could not have hit upon a better spot than this. A warm air wave, similar to that you expect on entering a bakehouse, met us just when we had passed the wooden partition. In the centre of the room there was a stove, almost red-hot. This apartment, which was filled with small forms, was, we ascertained, a Sunday-school. At the bottom end there were some narrow steps, leading through a large hole into a room above - the "chapel." A fat man could never get up these steps, and a tall one would injure his head if he did not stoop very considerably in ascending them.

The chapel is about five yards wide, 15 yards long, very low on one side, and moderately high on the other. It is plain, ricketty, and whitewashed. The side wall of the railway bridge forms one end of it. On the northern side, there is a door fastened up with a piece of wood in the form of a large loadstone. This door leads to the top of a pig-stye. The "chapel" will hold about 70. When we visited it, the congregation consisted of 35 children of a very uneasy sort, 11 men, and five women. Every now and then railway goods trains kept passing, and what with the whistling of the engines, the shaking caused by the waggons, the barking of a dog in a yard behind, the grunting of a pig in a stye three yards off, and the noise of the 35 children before us, we had a very refreshing time of it.

The congregation - a poor one - consists of a remnant of the Revivalists who were in Preston last year, and it has a kind of nominal connection with the Orchard United Methodists. The building we have described was formerly a weaving shop or rubbish store. Its present tenants have occupied it about twelve months. They are an earnest body, seem obliging to strangers, are not as fiery and wild as some of their class, and might do better in the town if they had a better room. They have no fixed minister. The preacher we heard was a stranger. He pulled off his coat just before beginning his discourse. After a few introductory remarks, in the course of which he said he had been troubled with stomach ache for six hours on the previous day, and that just before his last visit to Preston he had an attack of illness in the very same place, a lengthy allusion was made to his past history. He said that he had been "a villain, a gambler, a drunkard, and a Sabbath breaker" - we expected hearing him say, as many of his class do, that he had often abused his mother, thrashed his wife, and punished his children, but he did not utter a word on the subject. The remainder of his discourse was less personal and more orthodox. At the close we descended the steps carefully, groped our way out quietly, and left, wondering how ever we had got to such a place at all, and how those worshipping in it could afford to Sabbatically pen themselves up in such a mysterious, ramshackle shanty.

XXXIII

ST. MARY'S AND ST. JOSEPH'S CATHOLIC CHAPELS.

In this combination the past and the present are linked. Into their history the elements of a vast change enter. One is allied with "saintly days," followed by a reactive energy, vigorous and crushing; the other is amalgamated with an epoch of broadest thought and keenest iconoclasm; both are now enjoying a toleration giving them peace, and affording them ample room for the fullest progress. Unless it be our Parish Church, which was originally a Catholic place of worship, no religious building in Preston possesses historic associations so far-reaching as St. Mary's. It is the oldest Catholic chapel in Preston. Directly, it is associated with a period of fierce persecution. Relatively, it touches those old times when religious houses, with their quaintly-trimmed orders, were in their halcyon days. After the dissolution, caused by Henry VIII, it was a dangerous thing to profess Catholicism, and in Preston, as in other places, those believing in it had to conduct their services privately, and in out-of-the-way places. In Ribbleton-lane there is an old barn, still standing, wherein mass used to be said at night-time. People living in the neighbourhood fancied for a considerable period that this place was haunted; they could see a light in it periodically; they couldn't account for it; and they concluded that some headless woman or wandering gnome was holding a grim revel in it. But the fact was, a small band of Catholics debarred from open worship, and forced to secrete themselves during the hours of devotion, were gathered there.

When the storm of persecution had subsided a little, Catholics in various parts of the country gradually, though quietly, got their worship into towns; and, ultimately, we find that in Preston a small thatched building - situated in Chapel-yard, off Friargate - was opened for the use of Catholics. This was in 1605. The yard, no doubt, took its name from the chapel, which was dedicated to St. Mary. There was wisdom in the selection of this spot, and appropriateness, too - it was secluded, near the heart of the town, and very close to the old thoroughfare whose very name was redolent of Catholicity. Friargate is a word which conveys its own meaning. An old writer calls it a "fayre, long, and spacious street;" and adds, "upon that side of the town was formerly a large and sumptuous building belonging to the Fryers Minors or Gray Fryers, but now [1682] only reserved for the reforming of vagabonds, sturdy beggars, and petty larcenary thieves, and other people wanting good behaviour; it is now the country prison . . . and it is cal'd the House of Correction." This building was approached by Friargate, and was erected for the benefit of begging friars, under the patronage of Edward, Earl of Lancaster, son of Henry III. The first occupants of it came from Coventry, "to sow," as we are, told by an ancient document, "the seeds of the divine word, amongst the people residing in the villa of Preston, in Agmounderness, in Lancashire."

Primarily it was a very fine edifice, was built in the best style of Gothic architecture, and had accomodation for upwards of 500 monks. Upon its site now stands the foundry of Mr. Stevenson, adjoining Lower Pitt-street. The Catholics of Preston satisfied themselves with the small building in Chapel-yard until 1761, when a new place of worship, dedicated to St. Mary, was erected upon part of the site of the convent of Grey Friars. Towards this chapel the Duke of Norfolk gave a handsome sum, and presented, for the altar, a curious painting of the Lord's Supper. But this building did not enjoy a very prosperous career, for in 1768, during a great election riot, it was pulled down by an infuriated mob, all the Catholic registers in it were burned, and the priest - the Rev. Patrick Barnewell - only saved his life by beating a rapid retreat at the rear, and crossing the Ribble at an old ford below Frenchwood. Another chapel was subsequently raised, upon the present site of St. Mary's, on the west side of Friargate, but when St. Wilfrid's was opened, in 1793, it was closed for religious purposes and transmuted into a cotton warehouse. The following priests were at St. Mary's from its opening in 1761 until its close in 1793:- Revs. Patrick Barnewell, Joseph Smith, John Jenison, Nicholas Sewall, Joseph Dunn, and Richard Morgan. The two last named gentleman lived together in a cottage, on the left side of the entrance to the chapel, behind which they had a fine room commanding a beautiful view of the Ribble, Penwortham, &c., for at that time all was open, on the western side of Friargate, down to the river. Whittle, speaking of Father Dunn, says he was "the father of the Catholic school, the House of Recovery, and the Gasworks," and adds, with a plaintive bathos, that "on the very day he left this sublunary world he rose, as was his custom, very early, and in the course of his rambles exchanged a sovereign for sixpences, for distribution amongst the indigent."

In 1815 the chapel was restored; but not long afterwards its roof fell in. Nobody however was hurt, just because nobody was in the building at the time. The work of reparation followed, and the chapel was deemed sufficient till 1856, when it was entirely rebuilt and enlarged. As it was then fashioned so it remains. It is a chapel of ease for St. Wilfrid's, and is attended to a very large extent by Irish people. The situation of it is lofty; it stands upon higher ground than any other place of worship in the town; but it is so hemmed in with houses, &c., that you can scarcely see it, and if you could get a full view of it nothing very beautiful would be observed about the exterior. The locality in which this chapel is placed is crowded, dark-looking, and pretty ungodly. All kinds of sinister-looking alleys, narrow yards, dirty courts, and smoky back streets surround it; much drinking is done in each; and a chorus of noise from lounging men in their shirt sleeves, draggle-tailed women without bonnets, and weird little youngsters, given up entirely to dirt, treacle, and rags, is constantly kept up in them. The chapel has a quaint, narrow, awkward entrance. You pass a gateway, then mount a step, then go on a yard or two and encounter four steps, then breathe a little, then get into a somewhat sombre lobby two and a half yards wide, and inconveniently steep, next cross a little stone gutter, and finally reach a cimmerian square, surrounded by high walls, cracked house ends, and other objects similarly interesting. The front of the chapel is cold-looking and devoid of ornament. Upon the roof there is a square perforated belfry, containing one bell. It was put up a few years ago, and before it got into use there was considerable newspaper discussion as to the inconvenience it would cause in the morning, for having to be rung at the unearthly hour of six it was calculated that much balmy quietude would be missed through it. Some people can stand much sleep after six, and on their account early bell-ringing was dreaded. But the inhabitants have got used to the resonant metal, and those who have time sleep on very excellently during its most active periods.

The chapel has a broad, lofty, and imposing interior; but it is rather gloomy, and requires a little extra light, which would add materially to the general effect. There is considerable decorative skill displayed in the edifice; but the work looks opaque and needs brightening up. The sanctuary end is rich and solemn, has a finely-elaborate and sacred tone, and combines in its construction elegance and power. At the rear and rising above the altar there is a large and somewhat imposing picture, representing the taking down of our Saviour from the cross. It was painted by Mr. C. G. Hill, after a picture of Carracci's, in Stonyhurst College, and was originally placed in St. Wilfrid's church. St. Mary's will accommodate about 1,000 persons. All the pews have open sides, and there are none of a private character in any part of the church. The poorest can have the best places at any time, if they will pay for them, and the richest can sit in the worst if they are inclined to be economical.

Large congregations attend this chapel, and the bulk, as already intimated, are of the Milesian order. At the rear, where many of the poor choose to sit, some of the truest specimens of the "finest pisantry," some of the choicest and most aromatic Hibernians we have seen, are located. The old swallow-tailed Donnybrook Fair coat, the cutty knee-breeches, the short pipe in the waistcoat pocket, the open shirt collar, the ancient family cloak with its broad shoulder lapelle, the thick dun-coloured shawl in which many a young Patrick has been huddled up, are all visible. The elderly women have a peculiar fondness for large bonnets, decorated in front with huge borders running all round the face like frilled night-caps. The whole of the worshippers at the lower end seem a pre-eminently devotional lot. How they are at home we can't tell; but from the moment they enter the chapel and touch the holy water stoops, which somehow persist in retaining a good thick dark sediment at the bottom, to the time they walk out, the utmost earnestness prevails amongst them. Some of the poorer and more elderly persons who sit near the door are marvellous hands at dipping, sacred manipulation, and pious prostration. Like the Islams, they go down on all fours at certain periods, and seem to relish the business, which, after all, must be tiring, remarkably well. Considering its general character, the congregation is very orderly, and we believe of a generous turn of mind. The chapel is cleanly kept by an amiable old Catholic, who may, if there is anything in a name, be related to the Grey Friars who formerly perambulated the street he lives in; and there is an air of freedom and homeliness about it which we have not noticed at several places of worship. Around its walls are pictures of saints. They make up a fine family group, and seem to have gathered from every Catholic place of worship in the town to do honour to the edifice.

There are sundry masses every Sunday in the chapel, that which is the shortest - held at half-past nine in the morning - being, as usual, best patronised. The scholars connected with St. Wilfrid's attend the chapel every Sunday. Each Wednesday evening a service is also held in the chapel, and it is most excellently attended, although some who visit it put in a rather late appearance. When we were in the chapel, one Wednesday evening, ten persons came five minutes before the service was over, and one slipped round the door side and made a descent upon the holy water forty-five seconds before the business terminated. Of course it is better late than never, only not much bliss follows late attendance, and hardly a toothful of ecstacy can be obtained in three-quarters of a minute. The singing is of an average kind, the choir being constituted of the school children; whilst the organ, which used to be in some place at Accrington, is only rather shaky and debilitated. During the past ten years the Rev. Thomas Brindle, of St. Wilfrid's, has been the officiating priest at St. Mary's. Father Brindle is a Fylde man, is about 45 years of age, and is a thoroughly healthy subject. He is at least 72 inches high, is well built, powerful, straight as a die, good looking, keeps his teeth clean, and attends most regularly to his clerical duties. He is unassuming in manner, blithe in company, earnest in the pulpit. His gesticulation is decisive, his lungs are good, and his vestments fit him well. Not a more stately, yet homely looking, honest-faced priest have we seen for many a day. There is nothing sinister nor subtle in his visage; the sad ferocity glancing out of some men's eyes is not seen in his. We have not yet confessed our sins to him, but we fancy he will be a kindly soul when behind the curtain, - would sooner order boiled than hard peas to be put into one's shoes by way of penance, would far rather recommend a fast on salmon than a feast on bacon, and would generally prefer a soft woollen to a hard horse hair shirt in the moments of general mortification. Father Brindle! - Give us your hand, and may you long retain a kindly regard for boiled peas, soft shirts, and salmon. They are amongst the very best things out if rightly used, and we shouldn't care about agonising the flesh with them three times a week.

St. Joseph's Catholic Church stands on the eastern side of Preston, and is surrounded by a rapidly-developing population. The district has a South Staffordshire look - is full of children, little groceries, public-houses and beershops, brick kilns, smoke, smudge, clanging hammers, puddle-holes, dogs, cats, vagrant street hens, unmade roads, and general bewilderment. When the new gasometer, which looks like the skeleton of some vast colosseum, is finished here, an additional balminess will be given to the immediate atmosphere, which may be very good for children in the hooping-cough, but anything except pleasant for those who have passed through that lively ordeal. In 1860, a Catholic school was erected in Rigby-street, Ribbleton-lane. Directly afterwards divine service was held in the building, which in its religious character was devoted to St. Joseph. But either the walls of the edifice were too weak, or the roof of it too strong, for symptoms of "giving way" soon set in, and the place had to be pulled down. In 1866, having been rebuilt and enlarged, it was re-opened. In the meantime, religious services and scholastic training being essential, and it being considered too far to go to St. Ignatius's and St. Augustine's, which were the places patronised prior to the opening of St. Joseph's mission, another school, with accomodation in it for divine worship, was erected on a plot of land immediately adjoining. Nearly one half of the money required for this building, which was opened in 1864, was given by Protestants. At the northern end of it, there is a closed-off gallery, used as a school for boys. The remainder of the building is used for chapel purposes. The exterior of the edifice is neat and substantial; the interior - that part used for worship - is clean, spacious, and light. At the southern end there is a small but pretty altar, and around the building are hung what in Catholic phraseology are termed "the stations." There is not much ornament, and only a small amount of paint, in the place.

The chapel will hold 560 persons; it is well attended; and the congregations would be larger if there were more accomodation. Masses are said here, and services held, on the plan pursued at other chapels of the same denomination. The half-past nine o'clock mass on a Sunday morning is a treat; for at it you can see a greater gathering of juvenile bazouks than at any other place in the town. Some of the roughest-headed lads in all creation are amongst them; their hair seems to have been allowed to have its own way from infancy, and it refuses to be dictated to now. The congregation is a very poor one, and this will be at once apparent when we state that the general income of the place, the entire proceeds of it, do not exceed 100 pounds a year. Nearly every one attending the chapel is a factory worker, and the present depressed state of the cotton trade has consequently a special and a very crushing bearing upon the mission. A new church is badly wanted here; in no part of the town is a large place of worship so much required; but nothing can be done in the matter until the times mend. A plot of land has been secured for a church on the western side of the present improvised chapel, and close to the house occupied by the priests in charge of the mission; but until money can be found, or subscribed, or borrowed without interest, it will have to remain as at present.

The first priest at St. Joseph's was the Rev. R. Taylor; then came the Rev. R. Kennedy; next the Rev. W. H.

Bradshaw, who was succeeded by the Revs. J. Walmsley and J. Parkinson - the priests now at the place. Father Walmsley, the superior, who originally came from Brindle, is a placid, studious-looking, even-tempered gentleman. He is slender, but wirey; is inclined to be tall, and has got on some distance with the work. He is thoughtful, but there is much sly humour in him; he is cautious but free when aired a little. He knows more than many would give him credit for; whilst naturally reticent and cool he is by no means dull; he is shrewd and far-seeing but calm and unassuming; and though evenly balanced in disposition be would manifest a crushing temper if roughly pulled by the ears. His first mission was at the Church of the English Martyrs in this town; then he went to Wigan, and after staying there for a time he landed at St. Joseph's. Father Parkinson is a native of the Fylde, and he has got much of the warm healthy blood of that district in his veins. He has a smart, gentlemanly figure; has a sharp, beaming, rubicund face; has buoyant spirits, and likes a good stiff tale; is full of life, and has an eye in his head as sharp as a hawk's; has a hot temper - a rather dignified irascible disposition; believes in sarcasm, in keen cutting hits; can scold beautifully; knows what he is about; has a "young-man-from-the-country-but-you-don't-get-over-me" look; is a hard worker, a careful thinker, and considers that this world as well as the next ought to be enjoyed. He began his clerical career at Lancaster in 1864; attended the asylum whilst at that town; afterwards had charge of a workhouse at Liverpool; is now Catholic chaplain of Preston House of Correction, and fills up his spare time by labouring in St. Joseph's district. Either the House of Correction or the poor mission he is stationed at agrees with him, for he has a sparkling countenance, and seems to be thriving at a genial pace. Both Father Walmsley and Father Parkinson have been in Spain; they were, in fact, educated there. Both labour hard and mutually; consoling each other in hours of trial, tickling one another in moments of ecstacy, and making matters generally agreeable. The schools attached to St. Joseph's are in a good condition. They are well attended, are a great boon to the district, and reflect credit upon those who conduct them. All the district wants is a new church, and when one gets built we shall all be better off, for a brighter day with full work and full wages will then have dawned.

XXXIV

ST. MARK'S CHURCH.

Not very far from the mark shall we be in saying that if this Church were a little nearer it would not be quite so far off, and that if it could be approached more easily people would not have so much difficulty in getting to it. "A right fair mark," as Benvolio hath it, "is soonest hit;" but you can't hit St. Mark's very well, because it is a long way out of ordinary sight, is covered up in a far-away region, stands upon a hill but hides itself, and until very recently has entailed, in its approach, an expedition, on one side, up a breath-exhausting hill, and on the other through a world of puddle, relieved by sundry ominous holes calculated to appal the timid and confound the brave. We made two efforts to reach this Church from the eastern side; once in the night time, during which, and particularly when within 100 yards of the building, we had to beat about mystically between Scylla and Charybdis, and once at day time, when the utmost care was necessary in order to avoid a mild mishap amid deep side crevices, cart ruts two feet deep, lime heaps, and cellar excavations. We shall long remember the time when, after our first visit, we left the Church, All the night had we been in a sadly-sweet frame of mind, listening to prayers and music, and drinking in the best parts of a rather dull sermon; but directly after we left a disheartening struggle amid mud ensued, and all our devotional sentiment was taken right out of us. An old man, following us, who had been manifesting much facial seriousness in the Church, stepped calmly, but without knowing it, into a pile of soft lime, and the moment he got ankle deep his virtue disappeared amid a radiation of heavy English, which consigned the whole road to perdition. For several months this identical road spoiled the effect of numerous Sunday evening sermons; but, it is now in a fair state of order. St. Mark's Church, is situated on the north-western side of the town, between Wellington-terrace and the Preston and Wyre Railway, and was opened on the 22nd of September, 1863. For some time previously religious services were held on Sundays in Wellfield-road school, which then belonged Christ Church, but the district being large and of an increasing disposition, a new church was decided upon. The late Rev. T. Clark, incumbent at that time of Christ Church, promoted its erection very considerably; and when the building was opened those worshipping in Wellfield-road school (which was afterwards handed over for educational purposes to St. Mark's) went to it. St. Mark's cost about 7,000 pounds - without the steeple, which is now being erected, and will, it is expected, be finished about the beginning of March next. It will be a considerable architectural relief to the building, and will be some guide to strangers and outer barbarians who may want to patronise it either for business purposes or piety. The late J. Bairstow, Esq., left 1,000 pounds towards the steeple, which will cost about 1,250 pounds. In the district there are upwards of 6,000 persons, and not many of them are much better than they ought to be.

St. Mark's is built in the cruciform style, is mildly elaborate, and moderately serene in outline; but there is nothing very remarkable about any part of it. Rails run round it, and on the roof there are eight boxed-up, angular-headed projections which may mean something, but from which we have been unable to extract any special consolation. At each end of the church there are doors; those at the back being small and plain, those in front being also diminutive but larger. The principal entrance possesses some good points, but it lacks capaciousness and clearness - has a covered-up, hotel doorway aspect which we don't relish. It seems also to be very inconveniently situated: the bulk of those attending the church come in the opposite direction, and, therefore, if opposed to back door business, which is rather suspicious at a church, have to make a long round-about march, wasting their precious time and strength considerably in getting to the front. The church, which is fashioned externally of stone, has a brick interior.

A feeling of snugness comes over you on entering; small passages, closed doors, and an amplitude of curtains - there are curtains at every door in the church - induce a sensation of coziness; but when you get within, a sort of bewildering disappointment supervenes. The place seems cold and unfinished, - looks as if the plasterers and painters had yet to be sent for. But it has been decided to do without them: the inside is complete. There may be some wisdom in this style of thing; but a well-lined inside, whether it appertains to men or churches, is a matter worthy of consideration. There is an uncomely, fantastical plainness about the interior walls of St. Mark's, a want of tone and elegance all over them, which may be very interesting to some, but which the bulk of people will not be able to appreciate. If they were whitewashed, in even the commonest style, they would look better than at present. Bands of cream-coloured brick run round the walls, and the window arches are bordered with similar material. The roof is amazingly stocked with wood, all dark stained: as you look up at it a sense of solemn maddlement creeps over you; and what such a profuse and complex display of timber can mean is a mystery, which only the gods and sharp architects will be able to solve. The roof is supported by ten long, thin, gilt-headed iron pillars, which relieve what would otherwise in the general aspect of the church amount to a heavy monotony of red brickwork and sombre timber. On each side of the body of the church there are four neat-looking three-light windows; at the western end there is a beautiful five-light window, but its effect is completely spoiled by a small, pert-looking, precocious organ, which stands right before it. At each end of the transept there are circular lights of condensed though pleasant proportions.

The chancel is spacious, lofty, and not too solemn looking. The base is ornamented with illumined tablets, and above there are three windows, the central one bearing small painted representations of the "Sower" and the "Good Shepherd," whilst those flanking it are plain. This chancel, owing to its good architectural disposition, might, by a little more decoration and the insertion of full stained glass windows, be made very beautiful. The Church is an extremely draughty one; and if it were not for a screen at the west end and a series of curtains at the different doors, stiff necks, sore throats, coughs, colds, and other inconveniences needing much ointment and many pills would be required by the congregation. Just within the screen there is a massive stone font, supported by polished granite pillars, and surrounded at the base by a carpet upon which repose four small cushions bearing respectively on their surface a mystic injunction about "thinking" and "thanking."

The Church will accommodate about 1,000. There are 500 free sittings in it, the bulk being in the transept, which is galleried, and is the best and quietest place in the building, and the remainder at the extreme western end. All the seats are small, open, and pretty convenient; but the backs are very low, and people can't fall asleep in them comfortably. The price of the chargeable sittings ranges from 8s. to 10s. each per year. The average congregation numbers nearly 600; is constituted of working people with a seasoning of middle-class individuals; is of a peaceable friendly disposition; does not look black and ill-natured when a stranger appears; is quite gracious in the matter of seat-finding, book-lending, and the like; and is well backed up in its kindness by a roseate-featured gentleman - Mr. Ormandy, one of the wardens - who sits in a free pew near the front door, and does his best to prevent visitors from either losing themselves, swooning, or becoming miserable. In this quarter there is also stationed another official, a beadle, or verger, or something of the sort, who is quite inclined to be obliging; but he seems to have an unsettled, wandering disposition, is always moving about the place as if he had got mercury in him, can't keep still for the life of him more than two minutes at a time, and disturbs the congregation by his evolutions. We dare say he tries to do his best, and thinks that mobility is the criterion of efficiency; but we don't care for his perpetual activity, and shouldn't like to sleep with him, for we are afraid he would be a dreadfully uncasy bed-fellow.

The organ gallery appears to be a pleasant resort for a few hours' gossip and smirking. The musical instrument in it is diminutive, rather elegant in appearance at a distance, and is played with medium skill; but somehow it occasionally sounds when it should not, sometimes gives a gentle squeak in the middle of a prayer, now and then is inclined to do a little business whilst the sermon is being preached; and a lady member of the congregation has put this question to us on the subject, "Would it sound if the organist kept his hands and feet off it, and attended to the service?" That is rather a direct interrogation from so fair a source, and lest we might give offence we will allow people to answer it for themselves in their own way, after which they may, if inclined, communicate with the vivacious beadle, and tell him to look after the organ as well as the doors, &c. The singers in the gallery are spirited, give their services, like the organist, "gratisly" - one of the wardens told us so - and, if not pre-eminently musical, make a very fair average ninth-rate effort in the direction of melody. They will mend, we have no doubt, eventually - may finally get into the "fastoso" style. In the meantime, we recommend careful reading, mingled with wise doses of sal-prunel and Locock's wafers. On the first Sunday in every month, sometimes in the morning and sometimes in the evening, the sacrament is partaken of at St. Mark's church; and, comparatively speaking, the number of participants is considerable. The business is not entirely left, as in some churches, to worn-out old men and sacredly-snuffy old women - to a miserable half-dozen of fogies, nearly as ignorant of the vital virtues of the sacrament as the Virginian old beldame who took it to cure the rheumatism. At St. Mark's the sacrament takers consist of all classes of people, of various ages, and, considering the district, they muster very creditably.

The first incumbent of St. Mark's was the Rev. J. W. Green, who had very poor health, and died on the 5th of October, 1865. Nineteen days afterwards the Rev. T. Johnson was appointed to the incumbency which he continues to retain. Mr. Johnson is apparently about 40 years of age. He was first ordained as curate of St. Peter's, Oldham; stayed there two years and five months; then was appointed curate of Pontefract Parish Church, a position he occupied for nearly two years; subsequently took sole charge of a church at Holcombe, near Bury; four months afterwards came to Preston as curate of the Parish Church; remained there a considerable time; then went to Carnforth, near Lancaster; stayed but a short period in that quarter; and was afterwards appointed incumbent of St. Marks in this town. Although not very aged himself be lives in a house which is between 700 and 800 years old, and which possesses associations running back to the Roman era. This is Tulketh Hall, an ancient, castellated, exposed building on an eminence in Ashton, and facing in a direct line, extending over a valley, the front door of St. Mark's Church. With a fair spy-glass Mr. Johnson may at any time keep an exact eye upon that door from his own front sitting room. Nobody can tell when the building, altered considerably in modern times and now called Tulketh Hall, was first erected. Some antiquaries say that a body of monks from the monastery of Savigny, in Normandy, originally built it in 1124; others state that the place was made before that time; but this is certain, that a number of monks from the monastery named occupied it early in the twelfth century, and that they afterwards left it and went to Furness Abbey. On the south-west of Tulketh Hall the remains of a fosse (ditch or moat) were, up to recent times, visible; some old ruins adjoining could also be seen; and it has been supposed by some persons that there was once a Roman stronghold or castle here. Tulketh Hall has been occupied by several ancient families, and was once the seat of the Hesketh, of Rossall, near Fleetwood. The Rev. T. Johnson has lived in it for perhaps a couple of years, and seems to suffer none from either its isolation or antiquity. He thrives very well, like the generality of parsons, and will be a long liver if careful. He has what a phrenological physiologist would call a vitally sanguine constitution - has a good deal of temper, excitability, and determination in his character. You may persuade him, but he will be awkward to drive. He has a somewhat tall, gentlemanly, elastic figure; looks as if he had worn stays at some time; is polished, well-dressed, and careful; respects scented soap; hates the smell of raw onions; is scrupulous in his toilet; is sharp, swellish, and good-mannered; rather likes platform speaking; is inclined to get into a narrow groove of thought politically and theologically, when crossed by opponents; is eloquent when earnest; talks rubbish like everybody else at times; has a strong clear voice; is a good preacher; is moderate in his action; has never, even in his fiercest moments, injured the pulpit; has a refined, rather affected, and at times doubtful pronunciation; gets upwards of 300 pounds a year from the Church; has been financially lucky in other ways; has a homely class of parishioners, who would like to see him at other times than on Sundays; is well respected on the whole, and may thank his stars that fate reserved him for a parson.

His curate - the Rev. C. F. Holt - seems to be only just out of pin feather, is rather afraid of hopping off the twig; and needs sundry lessons in clerical flying before he will make much headway. He is good-looking, but not eloquent; precise in his shaving, but short of fire and originality; smart in features, but bad in his reading; has a very neat moustache, but a rather mediocre mental grasp; wears neat neck-ties and very clean shirts, but often fills you with the east wind when preaching. He is, however, a very indefatigable visitor, works hard and cheerfully in the district, has, by his outside labours, augmented the congregation, and on this account deserves credit. He is neither eloquent in expression nor sky-scraping in thought: but he labours hard amongst outside sinners, and an ounce of that kind of service is often worth a ton of pulpit rhetoric and sermonising bespanglement. At the schools in Wellfield-road the average day attendance is 310; whilst on Sundays it reaches 470. The school is a good one; the master is strong, healthy, and active, and the mistress is careful, antique-looking, and efficient.

XXXV

ZOAR PARTICULAR BAPTIST CHAPEL.

Some good people are much concerned for the erection of new places of worship in our large towns, labour hard for long periods in maturing plans for them, and nearly exhaust their energies in securing that which is held to be the only potent agent in their construction - money. But this is an ancient and roundabout process, and may, as it sometimes has done, terminate in failure. A stiff quarrel is about the surest and quickest thing we are acquainted with for multiplying places of worship, for Dissenters, at any rate; and probably it would be found to work with efficacy, if tried, amongst other bodies. Local experience shows that disputes in congregations invariably end in the erection of new chapels. Show us a body of hard, fiercely-quarrelsome religious people, and although neither a prophet nor the son of one we dare predict that a new place of worship will be the upshot of their contentions. We know of four or five chapels in Preston which here been raised on this plan, and those requiring more need only keep the scheme warm. It is not essential that persons anxious for new sacred edifices should expend their forces in pecuniary solicitations; let them set a few congregations by the ears and the job will be done at once. Deucalion of Thessaly was told by the oracle of Themis that if he wished to renew mankind he must throw his mother's bones behind his back. This was about as irreverent and illogical as telling people that if they want more religious accomodation they must commence fighting; and yet, whilst olden history gives some faint proof that the Grecian prince was successful, in stone if not in bone throwing, modern experience ratifies the notion that a smart quarrel is certain to be followed by a good chapel.

There was a small feud in 1849-50 at Vauxhall-road Particular Baptist Chapel, Preston, concerning a preacher; several liked him; some didn't; a brisk contention followed; and, in the end, the dissatisfied ones - about 50 in number, including 29 members - finding that they had "got up a tree," quietly retired. They hired a place in Cannon-street, which somehow has been the nursery of two or three stirring young bodies given to spiritual peculiarity. Here they worshipped earnestly, looking out in the meantime for a plot of land in some part of the town whereon they could build a chapel, and thus attend to their own business on their own premises. Singular to say they hit upon a site adjoining the most fashionable quarter of the town - hit upon and bought the only piece of land in the Belgravia of Preston whereon they or anybody else could build a place of worship. This was a little spot on the north-eastern side of Regent-street, abutting upon Winckley-square, and freed from the restrictions as to church and chapel building which operated in respect to every other vacant piece of land in the same highly-spiced neighbourhood. Upon this land they raised a small chapel, and dedicated it to Zoar. Whether they did this because Zoar means little, or because it was fancied that they had "escaped," like Lot of old, from a very unsanctified place, we cannot tell. The chapel was opened in 1853, at a cost of 500 pounds, one-fifth of which, apart from previous subscriptions, was raised during the inaugural services.

As to the outward appearance of this chapel, not so much can be said. It is built of brick, with stone facings; at the front there is a gable pierced with a doorway, flanked with two long narrow windows, and surmounted by a small one; above, there is a stone tablet giving to the name of the chapel and the date of its opening; on the left, calmly nestling on the roof, there is a sheet iron pipe; and on the ground, at the same side, there are some good stables. These stables do not belong to the chapel, and never did. There is no bell at the chapel; but the name of Mr. Bell, who rents the stables, is fixed at one side of it; and in this circumstance some satisfaction may be found. The chapel has a microscopical, select, sincere appearance; has no architectural strength nor highly-finished beauty about it; is bashful, clean, unadorned; and looks like what it is - the cornered-up, decorous, tiny Bethel of a particular people. Its internal arrangements are equally sedate, condensed, and snug. A calm homeliness, a Quakerly simplicity runs all through it. Nothing glaring, shining, or artistically complex is visible; neither fresco panellings, nor chiaroscuro contrasts, nor statuary groups adorn its walls: if any of these things were seen the members would scream. All is simple, clean, modest. The walls, slightly relieved on each side by two imitation columns, are calmly coloured; the ceiling, containing a floriated centre piece, is plainly whitewashed; the gas stands have no pride in them; the pulpit is small, durable, unpretentious. There are 22 deep long narrow pews in the chapel, and they will accommodate 200 persons. A small and rather forlorn-looking clock perches over the doorway, and keeps time, when going, moderately well. In the south-western corner of the building there is a mural tablet, in memory of the late Mrs. Caroline Walsh, who gave 50 pounds towards the erection of the chapel. If she had given 100 pounds probably two monuments would have been raised to her memory.

Nearly all who visit the chapel are middle-class people. The average attendance ranges from 70 to 80. There are 34 members at the place. Half of those who originally joined it are dead. They did not die through attending the chapel, but through ordinary physical ailment. The congregation, numerically speaking, is stationary, at present. Those attending the chapel profess the very same principles as the Vauxhall-road Baptists, sing out of hymn books just like theirs, and drink in with equal rapture the Philpottian utterances of the Gospel Standard - the organ of the body. They have four collections a year, and the hat never goes round amongst them in vain. Their pulpit is specially reserved for men after their own heart. They will admit to it neither General Baptists, nor Methodists, nor Independents; and however good a thing any of the preachers of these bodies might have to say, they would have to burst before the Zoar Chapel brethren would find them rostrum accomodation for its expression. All classes, they fancy, ought to mind their own affairs; and preachers they consider should always keep to the pulpits of their own faith. Although touchy as to preachers they are somewhat liberal as to writers, and have a great fondness for several of the works of Church of England divines. They esteem considerably, we are informed, the writings of "Gill, Romaine, Hawker, Parkes, Hewlett, and others belonging that church." There is a debt of 150 pounds upon Zoar Chapel; and if any gentleman will give that sum to square up matters we can guarantee that good special sermons, eulogistic of all his virtues since birth, will be preached, and that a monument will be erected to him in the chapel when he dies.

The first minister the Zoar Chapel people had, after their secession, was Mr. D. Kent, a Liverpool gentleman who came over to Preston weekly, for seven years, and preached every Sunday. He got no salary, was content with having his railway fare paid and his Sunday meals provided, and he gave much satisfaction. In the end he had to retire through ill health. Mr. J. S. Wesson, who evaporated quietly from Preston some time ago, followed Mr. Kent, and preached for the Zoar folk six years. His successor was Mr. Edward Bates, of Darwen, who visited the chapel every Sunday for 12 months, and then withdrew. Since his departure there has been no regular minister at the Chapel; and whenever one does come he will have to be a "Mr." and not a "Rev." Particular Baptists don't believe in "reverend" gentlemen - think none of them are really reverend, and that it is presumption in any man, however sublimated his virtue or learning may be, to sacredly oil up his name with any such prefix.

We have visited Zoar Chapel twice. It was exactly twenty minutes to seven one Sunday evening when we first entered it. The lights were burning, the blinds were drawn, and there were 23 people in the place. In a pew on the left-hand side a little old man was holding forth as to the "prodigal son." It was the first time he had ever talked in the chapel, and he has never said a word since. He had a peculiarly free and easy style. Sometimes he leaned over the pew door, and beat time with one foot whilst talking; at other periods he would stand back a little, push his right arm up to the elbow in his breeches pocket, and scratch his leg quietly; then he would turn half round, and look up; then make to the pew door again; then leave it, and so on to the finish. He was an earnest, plain-spun sort of individual, but he got through his parabolical exposition very satisfactorily. We fancied he would afterwards ascend the pulpit, which was lighted up; but he kept out of it, and nobody ever went near it at all, except at the finish, when a man quietly walked up the steps and put the gas out. We could not exactly see the force of lighting the pulpit when nobody ever went into it; but others in the place might, for there are shrewd men amongst them, and they may have found out some virtue in lighting gas burners when they are not wanted. The music we heard was moderate; the praying which followed was mildly exhilarating.

When we turned into the chapel the second time - this was during a forenoon service - there were located in it an elderly, fatherly, farmerly man, who occupied the pulpit; eleven middle-aged men, with subdued countenances; six young men with their eyes and ears open to every move; nine blushing maidens with their back hair combed up stiffly and their mastoid processes bared all round; nine matured members of the fair sex with larger bonnets and more antique hair arrangements; five little girls; four small boys; and seven singers; making in the aggregate fifty-two. The person in the pulpit was, we learned, a Fylde farmer; but he must at some time have lived in the north, for he said "dowter" for daughter, "gert" for great, "nather" for neither, "natteral" for natural, and gave his "r's" capital good exercise, turning them round well, throughout his entire discourse; and he cared very little for either singular or plural verbs. If he got the sense out he deemed it sufficient. He spoke in a conversational style, was more descriptive than argumentative, was homely, discreet, and neither too lachrymose nor too buoyant. This preacher, we have been told, was Mr. James Fearclough, of Hardhorn, near Blackpool, who was the original organiser of the church.

The singers, who collected themselves around a square, conical-headed table, in a shy-looking corner, gave vent to their feelings without music books. They had hymns before them, and these they held to be sufficient. Their performances were rather of a timid character; but this might be to some extent accounted for by the fact that the conductor was absent. When they started a tune they sighed, blushed, held their heads down, and looked up shyly into their eye lids; but when they had proceeded a little and got the congregation into a sympathetic humour, courage came to them, and they moved on more exactly and courageously. About a dozen preachers have been tried since the pulpit was vacated by the Darwen gentleman; but the exact man has not yet been found, and until his advent the congregation will have to solicit "supplies," and be content with what they can get. None of the members can preach; nobody in the congregation can preach; and their only hope at present consists in the foreign import trade. The congregation has a homely, unpretentious, kindly-hearted, social appearance, and when in the midst of it you feel as if you were at home, and as if the tea things had only to be brought out to make matters complete. There are no loud talkers, no scandal-mongers, no sanguine souls who get into a state of incandescence during prayers or sermons here. A respectable, homely, smoothly-elegant serenity dominates in it.

Two services are held in the chapel on Sundays, and on

a Wednesday evening there is a prayer meeting. A Sunday school, opened in 1855, is held in the building, and is attended by about 50 children. At present, the general business of the chapel is rather dull; and there will be no perceptible improvement in it nor in the number attending it until a regular minister is appointed. Listening to stray sermons is like feeding upon wind - you may get filled with it, but will never get fat upon it. We hope the Zoarists will by and by be successful; that, having escaped to their present quarters, they will keep them, - an effort has been once or twice made to purchase the building for a public-house; and that they will never, like the party who first fled to Zoar, become troglodytes.

XXXVI

ST. LUKE'S CHURCH.

With the district in which this Church is situated we are not much acquainted. With even the Church itself we have never been very familiar. It is in a queer, far-of unshaven region. Aged sparrows and men who like ale better than their mothers, dwell in its surroundings; phalanxes of young Britons, born without head coverings, and determined to keep them off; columns of wives, beautiful for ever in their unwashedness, and better interpreters of the 28th verse of the 1st chapter of Genesis then all the Biblical commentators put together, occupy its district. Prior to visiting St. Luke's Church we had some idea of its situation; but the idea was rather inclined to be hazy when we desired to utilise it; we couldn't bring it to a decisive point; and as we objected to the common business of stopping every other person in order to get a perplexing explanation of the situation, the question just resolved itself into one of "Find it out yourself." Exactly so, we mentally muttered on entering Ribbleton-lane; and we passed the thirty feet House of Correction wall to the right thereof, with an air of triumph, redolent of intrepidity and independence. To the left of the lane entered we knew St. Luke's was located; but doubt overshadowed its precise whereabouts. The first street in that direction down which we looked contained, at the bottom, six coal waggons and a gate. Those unhappy-looking waggons and that serious gate couldn't, we said, be St. Luke's. Another street to the left; but at the end of it we saw only a tavern, some tall rails, and an old engine shed. Convinced that St. Luke's was not here, we proceeded to the head of the third street, and down it were more rails, sundry children, a woman sweeping the parapet, and the gable of a mill. At the extreme end of the next a coal office and a gate met us. Number five street showed up the fading placards of a news shop, and the cold stillness of a Sunday morning factory. Down the sixth avenue we peered eagerly, but "more factory" met us. The termination of its successor consisted of pieces of timber, three arches, and some mill ends. We had hope as to the bottom of the next; but it was blighted and withered in its infancy as we gazed upon 25 tree trunks, a mill, and two tall chimneys. Additional wood, an office, and an entire mill formed the background of the street subsequently encountered. Extra mill buildings closed up the career of the road beyond it; ditto beyond that; partially ditto afterwards, the front of the picture being relieved by a few thirsty souls, looking plaintively at a landlord, who stood with a rolling eye upon door step, anxious to officiate as the "Good Samaritan," but afraid to exercise his benevolence. After this there would surely, we thought, be something like the church we were seeking. But not so; a swampy wide road and more of the irrepressible mill element constituted the whole of the scene presented.

It is, however, a long lane which has no turning, and at last we got to a small corner shop, below which were two clothes props, one being very much out of the perpendicular, an open piece of ground, numerous bricks in a heap, and a railed round edifice rising calmly , sedately , and diminutively. This was St. Luke's - the shrine we had been looking for, the Mecca we had been in search of. Plenty of breathing space has the church now: on three of its sides there is a wide expanse; but the cottage homes of England are steadily approaching it, and in time the building will be tightly surrounded by innumerable dwellings, whose occupants, we hope, will feel the spiritual salubrity of their situation. St. Luke's has a serene, minutely-neat exterior; is proportionate, evenly balanced, and devoid of that tortuous masonry which some architects delight to honour. It is a meekly-conceived, yet substantially-built little church, with a rural placidity and neatness about it, reminding one of goodness without showiness, and use without sugar-coated detail. A modest spire, very sharp-pointed, rises above the tower at the western side. At the angles of the tower there are pinnacles, supported not by monstrosities of the common gargoyle type, but by pleasant featured angels, duly pinioned for flying. There appears to have been a "rage" for windows at this said western end. From top to bottom there are fifteen; four being moderately large, and the bulk of the remainder remarkably small.

The interior of the church is particularly plain; is stone-coloured all round; has an unassuming, modestly-serious, half-rural appearance; has no tablets, no ornaments, and no striking colouring of any kind on its main walls. It consists of a nave (depending upon fourteen arches) and two aisles. The centre is pretty high, has a narrow, open roof, and is moderately crowded with timber. The sides are small, but in sitting in them you do not experience that buried-alive sensation, that bewilderment beneath a heavy ceiling elaborated with hugely awkward prop-work and pillars, which is felt in some church aisles. Here, as at St. Mark's, there is a strong belief in the healthiness of red curtains at the various entrances. The chancel is high and open, and has rather a bare look. Within it there are three windows, filled in with stained glass, of sweet design, but defective in representative effect. The colours are nicely arranged; but with the exception of a very small medallion in the centre, referring to the Last Supper, they give you no idea of anything living, or dead, or yet to be made alive. The windows were put in by the late T. Miller, Esq;, C. R. Fletcher Lutwidge, Esq.; and J. Bairstow, Esq., and they Cost 90 pounds. At the western end there are three stained-glass windows, which look well. The colours are rich, and the designs artistic. Two of them, we believe, were fixed in memory of the late Mrs. Winlaw. The vestry stands on one side of the chancel, and in the doorway of it there is a red curtain, intended to keep out the tail end of whirlwinds and draughts in general. When we looked into this vestry, the idea flashed upon us that its occupant must be a specially studious and virtuous gentleman, for upon the mantelpiece there were 14 large Bibles, surmounted by three sacramental guides. But earth is very nigh to heaven, and when we saw a series of begging boxes flanking the books, and a looking-glass, which must at some time have cost tenpence, we retreated.

From the centre of the chancel, the church looks very imposing: indeed, you get a full view of all its architectural details here, and the conclusion previously arrived at, through what you may have seen from other points - namely, that the edifice is simple, bucolic, and prosaic - is entirely changed. The reading desk is a commendable article, and with care will last a considerable period. The pulpit - circular-shaped, and somewhat small in proportions - has a seemly appearance; but it looks only a homely-built affair when minutely inspected, and might be pulled in pieces quickly by a passionate man. Two or three curious articles are associated with it. At the base, there is quietly lying an aged gutta percha pipe, the object of which we could not make out; and in the pulpit there is another gutta percha pipe, with an elongated, funnel-shaped top, put up, probably, for some very useful purpose - for whispering, or speaking, or sneezing, or coughing - which alone concerns the preacher, and need not be further inquired into by us. There is a thermometer opposite the pulpit, which, probably, is intended to test the atmosphere of the church, but which may, for aught we know, be serviceable to the minister in moments of extreme mental coldness, or in periods of high clerical enthusiasm. If he can regulate the sacred temperature of either the reading desk or the pulpit by this thermometer, and can, in addition, utilise the gutta percha tubes as exhaust pipes, then we think he will derive a tangible advantage from their presence. Near the entrance to the centre aisle there is a somewhat handsome stone font, octagonal in shape, carved on four of its sides, and resting upon a circular pedestal, which is surrounded by eight small pillars. Not far from and on each side of the font there is an official wand, carried at intervals, with a decorum akin to majesty, by the beadle.

St. Luke's Church was opened on the 3rd of August, 1859; the cost of it - land, building, and everything - being 5,350 pounds. The late J. Bairstow, Esq., was an admirable friend of St. Luke's; he gave 700 pounds towards the building fund, and 6,000 pounds for the endowment. The church will accommodate 800 persons. Three-fourths of the sittings are free. The average attendance on Sundays, including school children, is 250. Considering that there are about 5,500 persons in the district, this number is only trifling. When we visited the church there were 280 present, and out of this number 160 were children. We fancied that the weather, for it was rather unfavourable, might have kept many away, but when we recollected that we had passed groups of men standing idly at contiguous street corners, discussing the merits of dogs and ale, as we walked to the church; and saw at least 40 young fellows within a good stone throw of it as we left, hanging about drinking-house sides, in the drizzling rain, waiting for "opening time," and talking coolly about "half gallons," we grew doubtful as to the correctness of our supposition. If men could bear a quiet drenching in the streets, could leave their homes for the purpose of congregating on the sides of parapets, in order to make a descent upon places essentially "wet," we fancied that moderately inclement weather could not, after all, be set down as the real reason for a thin congregation at St. Lukes. The fact is, there is much of that religion professed by the horse of Shipag in this district - working on week days and stuffing on Sundays is the creed of the multitude.

The congregation worshipping at St. Luke's is formed chiefly of working people. In summer the scholars sit in a small gallery at the west end; in winter they are brought into 28 seats below it. They seem to be of a rather active turn of mind, for in their management they keep two or three men and a female hard at work, and continue after all to have a fair amount of their own way - not, perhaps, quite so much of it as three youths who sat before us, who appeared to extract more pleasure out of some verses on a tobacco paper than out of either the hymns or the sermon - but still enjoying a good share of personal freedom, which children will indulge in. There is a service at St. Luke's every Wednesday evening; but it is not much cared for. Only about 30 attend it, and it is not known to what extent they enjoy the Proceedings. The instrumental music of the church has apparently been regulated on the Darwinian theory of "selection." What it was at the very beginning we can-cannot say; but towards the commencement it appears to have been emitted from a small harmonium; then a little organ was procured, and it came from that; then a large organ was obtained, and from that it now radiates. Some day a still larger instrument may be procured; but the present one, which used to do duty in Christ Church, Preston, is a respectable, good-looking, tuneful apparatus; and it is played with ability by an energetic, clerical-looking young gentleman, who receives a small salary for his services. The members of the choir manifest tolerable skill in their performances; but they lack power, and are hampered at line ends by the dragging melody of the scholars.

The incumbent of St. Luke's is the Rev. W. Winlaw - a grave, sharp-featured gentleman, who comes from the north, and, like all his fellow-countrymen, knows perfectly well what time it is. Mr. Winlaw was originally an Independent minister, and he looks like one to this day. He was a fellow-student of the Rev. G. W. Clapham, formerly of Lancaster-road Congregational Chapel, Preston, and now a minister of the Church of England. Mr. Winlaw was the successor of the Rev. J. H. Cuff (father of Messrs. Cuff, of this town), at an Independent Chapel in Wellington. In 1855 he was ordained by the Bishop of Manchester to

St. Peter's, Ashton-under-Lyne. In 1867 he came to Preston, as curate of St. Paul's, and in 1859 he was appointed incumbent of St. Luke's. Mr. Winlaw is a slender, carefully-organised, cute, sharp-eyed man; is inclined to be fastidious, punctillious, and cold; is a ready speaker; talks with grammatical accuracy and laboured precision; is rather wordy and unctuous; can draw out his sentences to a high pitch of solemnity, and tone them off in syllabic whispers; has an active physiognomical expression - can turn the muscles of his face in all directions; shakes his head considerably in the reading-desk and pulpit, as if constantly in earnest; is keenly susceptible, and has strong convictions; couldn't be easily persuaded off a notion after once seeing it in his own light; seems to have smiled but seldom; has sharp perceptive powers - looks into you with a piercing eye; cares little for the odd or the humorous - has a strong sense of clerical dignity; would become sarcastic if touched in the quick; is earnest, cautious, melancholy, and felt-hatted; has good strategic powers; can see a considerable way; is vigorous when roused, maidenly when cool, cutting when vexed, meek when in smooth water; is generally exact in composition, and clear in style; but preaches rather long sermons, and has a difficulty in giving over when he has got to the end. In one of his sermons we heard him say, after a five-and-twenty minutes run, "In conclusion," "Lastly," and "Finally;" and we had almost made up our mind for another sermon after he had "finished," but he decided to give over without preaching it. Mr. Winlaw, in the main, is a fair speaker, with a rather eccentric modulation, is a medium, gentlemanly-seeming, slightly-inflated, polished, precise minister, who has earned the confidence of his flock, and the goodwill of many about him. Like every other parson he is not quite perfect; but he appears to be suitable for the district, and with a salary of 300 pounds per annum is, we hope, happy. Day and Sunday schools adjoin the Church. At the former, there is an average attendance of 180; at the latter of 400. A capital library is attached to the schools. Orange and other societies for the maintenance of Protestantism, and the support of "Our glorious Constitution," exist in connection with the church, and the members, who are rather of the high-pressure type, enjoy the proceedings of them muchly.

XXXVII

EMMANUEL CHURCH AND BAIRSTOW MEMORIAL CHAPEL.

Preston has been developing itself for several years northwards. There was a period, and not very long since, either, when nearly the whole of the land in that direction was a mere waste - a chaos of little hills and large holes, relieved with clay cuttings, modified with loads of rubbish, and adorned with innumerable stones - a barren, starved-out sort of town common, where persecuted asses found an elysium amid thistles, where neglected ducks held high revel in small worn-out patches of water, and upon which rambling operatives aired their terriers, smoked in gossiping coteries, and indulged in the luxuries of jumping, and running and tumbling; but much of this land has been "reclaimed;" many dwellings have been erected upon it; and in the heart of it stands Emmanuel Church - a building which ought to have been opened some time since, which might have been opened 90 days ago if two or three lawyers had exerted themselves with moderate energy in the conveyancing business, and which it is expected will be consecrated and got ready for the spiritual edification of the neighbourhood in a few weeks. The locality assigned to Emmanuel Church used to form part of St. Peter's district; but that church having enough on its hands nearer home, it was decided to slice off a portion of its area, and start a new auxiliary "mission" northwards. Thomas Tomlinson, Esq., of London, gave land at the end of Brook-street sufficient for a new church and schools; subscriptions for the erection of the necessary buildings were afterwards solicited; sums of money were promised; but enough could not be obtained to carry out the entire work, so the building committee, acting upon the sagacious plan that it is easier at any time to lift a pound than a ton, concluded to make a start by constructing schools. This was in 1865. After the lapse of a short time the schools were completed, and up to the present (Dec. 1869) worship has been held in them.

The schools are strong and good; the principal room wherein the religious services are held has a tincture of the ecclesiastical element in its interior architecture; but either those who attend it or those who exercise themselves about its precincts are of too active a disposition, for nineteen squares of glass in its windows are cracked, and this rather "panes" one at first sight. There were about 240 persons, 80 or 90 being children, in the building when we paid our Sunday visit to it.

The congregation was of the working class species. At the north-east corner seven or eight singers, somewhat vigorous and expert in their music, were stationed; a female who played a little harmonium was near them; and in one corner, in a small pulpit run up to the wall as tightly as human skill could devise, was a condensed Irish gentleman, whom nobody seemed to know, but who turned out, in the end, to be an Oswaldtwistle minister, who had exchanged pulpits with the regular clergyman. He was a cute, well-educated little party; but awfully uneasy - was never still - moved his head, arms, and body about at the rate of 129 times a minute (we timed him with a good centre-seconds watch), talked much out of the left corner of his mouth; was full of rough vigour and warm blood; would have been a "boy" with a shillelagh; and yet he got along with his work excellently. We couldn't help smiling when we saw, during the preliminary portion of the service, another surpliced gentleman join him. Just when the lessons came on a stout, plump-featured, and most fashionably-whiskered young man stepped into the pulpit, crushed the little Oswaldtwistle party into the north-eastern Corner of it, and poured out for about twenty minutes a sharp, monotonous volume of sacred verses. The scene underwent further development when, during the singing, both stood up side by side. The pulpit, would hardly hold them; but they stuck well to its inner sides, cast tranquil fraternal glances at each other, once threw a Corsican brother affection into the scene, looked now and then fierce, as if feeling that each had as much right to the pulpit as the other, and finally marched off with a twinly love beaming in their eyes, to the vestry adjoining, from which in a few minutes the Oswaldtwistle minister emerged in a black gown, and entered the pulpit, whilst his companion followed, in a buttoned-up black coat, to the front of the communion rails, where he took a seat and became very quiet. The sermon was briskly condemnatory of unbelief, for ten minutes, then got immensely pungent as to Popery, and ended in a coloured star-shower concerning the excellence of "the good old Church of England." We couldn't help admiring the preacher's eloquence; and a man who sat near us, and at the finish said, "Who is that fellow?" - a rather vulgar kind of query - seemed to be fairly delighted with him.

The Church, in which the services will soon be held, stands close to the school. It is a curious piebald-looking building; is made of brick with intervening stone bands and facings; and is something unique in this part of the country. In the south of England - particularly in the metropolitan districts - such like buildings are not uncommon; but hereabouts architecture of the Emmanuel Church type seems odd. The edifice, although quaint, and rather poor-looking at first sight, owing to its bricky complexion, will bear close examination; indeed, the more you look at it and the better you become reconciled to its proportions. In general contour it is symmetrical and strong; in detail it is neat and compact; and, whilst the colour of it may indicate some singularity, and strike you as being eccentrically variegated, there is nothing in any sense improper about the character of its materials, and as time goes on, and familiarity with them is increased, they will cease to look whimsical and appear just as good as anything else. The general architecture of the building is of the early English type; the design, &c., being furnished by Messrs. Myres, Veevers, and Myres, of Preston. At the west end there is a rather prettily shaped tower, surmounted at each corner with a strong stone pinnacle; the extreme height being 100 feet. A few yards above the centre of the tower there are angular projections - stretched-out, dreadful-looking figures, a cross between vampires and hyenas - and you feel glad that they are only made of stone, and in the next place that they are a good way off. The man who carved them must have tightened up his courage to the sticking point many a time during the completion of these uniquely-unbeautiful figures. The principal entrance to the church is at the western end, where there is a pretty gabled and balconied porchway, elaborated with carvings, some of which are being executed at the expense of patriotic youths, who pay for a yard or two each, as they are in the humour, and expect an apotheosis afterwards. The doors at this end open into an inner vestibule, which is well screened from the main building, and may be used for class purposes, the rendezvousing of christening parties, or the halting plate of sinners, who go late to church, and hesitate until they get desperate or highly virtuous before proceeding further. In a corner at the north-west there is a beautiful baptismal font, made of Caen stone, ornamented with emblematic figures and monograms, and supported by four small columns of Leeds stone. The font is covered up by a piece of strong calico, in the shape of a huge night-cap, and the arrangement suits it, for however closely covered down the cap may be, no grumbling of any sort is ever heard. The building is cruciform in shape, and has a strong, yet tastefully-finished, galleried transept, approached by collateral doers, which also give ingress to the church on the ground floor. The entrances are so arranged that everything in the shape of that most objectionable of all things - a draught - is obviated. It is expected that sufficient wind will be brought to bear upon the question by the organ blower, without admitting additional currents through the doors.

The church has a solid, substantial, well-finished interior, and the only fault which can be found with it is, that it is rather low. If the roof could be lifted a yard or so higher, the general effect would be wonderfully improved; but it would be very difficult to do this now; and we suppose the altitude, which was regulated by the funds in hand during the process of building, will have to remain as at present. But the lowness of the roof may have some compensating advantages. If higher the church might have been colder, and its sounding properties, which are good, might have been interfered with. At present the space is condensed, and this tends to concentrate both warmth, and what acoustical gentlemen term, reverberation. The roof is strongly filled in with diagonally laid, dark-stained timber, is open and semi-circular, but looks rather heavy and gloomy. There are no huge ungainly pillars in the body of the building; an easy, capacious freedom prevails in it; seeing is not a difficult business; the first sensation which increases as you remain in the church, is calmly pleasurable and satisfactory. There is nothing flimsey, nor specious, nor whimsical in the place; evenness and harmony of proportion; simplicity and solidity of style, strength and straightforwardness of workmanship, strike you as its characteristics. The pulpit, which is made of stone, and approached by an internal staircase, adorned on one side with open pillars, is most durable, and handsome in style. Every part of the church can be seen from it; and several parsons might be accommodated in it and the balcony immediately adjoining. The reading desk is of carved oak, and, although rather small, has a tasteful and substantial appearance. T. Tomlinson, Esq., who gave the font, presented both the pulpit and the desk, and has likewise given the ceremonial books. The lectern - strong, ornamental, and weighty - is the gift of M. Myres, Esq. The chancel is tolerably lofty and cheerful-looking. Good windows are inserted in it; but the main one is inferior in design to those in the transept, and that at the western end. Passages of scripture are painted round the arches of the chancel and transept; the expense thereof having been defrayed by Mr. Park, decorator, and Mr. Veevers, of the firm of Myres, Veevers, and Myres. There is a neat dado round the church, which was made at the expense of Mr. J. J. Myres. The seats in the church are most conveniently arranged. They are well fit up, have good sloped backs, and are so constructed as to accommodate either large or small families in separate sections. Emmanuel Church, the foundation-stone of which was laid on the 18th of April, 1868, by Sir T. G. Fermor-Hesketh, M.P., has cost, in round figures, 6,000 pounds. It will accommodate 1,000 people, and all the seats, except 359, are free.

The church, considering its capacity and general finish, is thought to be one of the cheapest buildings for miles round. Some time, when the building fund has been replenished, a parsonage house will be erected at the eastern end of the church. The schools which adjoin are attended, during week days, by upwards of 220 scholars; and on Sundays the attendance, including the various classes, with their teachers, &c., will be about 450. There is a "Conservative Constitutional Association" in connection with Emmanuel Schools. The members meet in a building which was once a farmhouse, near the church; they have for ever of courage; can discuss the great concerns of the empire with ease and eloquence; are prepared at any time to administer remedies for all the grievances of the five divisions of the human race, as classified by Blumenbach; and would be willing to sit daily, from ten till four, on the highest peak of Olympus, and direct the affairs of the universe.

The minister of the church is the Rev. E. Sloane Murdoch; and we dare say if the Cuilmenn of Erin, or the Book of the Uachongbhail, or the Cin Droma Snechta, or the Saltair of Cashel could have been consulted, his ancestors would have been found named therein. Mr. Murdoch is a young man, hails from Derry, possesses a strong constitution, has small, sharp eyes, and a very round head; has remarkably smooth hair, brushed close to the bone, and well parted; and is of a determined, active disposition. Following the example of many other parsons, he likes a closely-buttoned coat and a walking stick. He is sharp, quick in resenting aggressions, would soon have his native blood stirred, is tempted to be a little imperious, considers that he is a power in the district, has much endurance, is systematical in thought, wary in expression, hesitates and flutters a little in some of his sentences, has a strong Hibernian brogue, but is precise with it; throws more recollection than original thought into his utterances, visits his district well, is a fair scholar, is dry and prosaic until warmed up, can feel more than he can express, has little rhetorical display, seems as if he would like to shake himself when at a white heat, gets 195 pounds a year - 135 pounds from Emmanuel Church, and 60 pounds for his services at the workhouse - and would not find any fault whatever if the sum were raised to 300 pounds. Mr. Murdoch was originally ordained curate of a parish in the diocese of Kilmore, the father-in-law of the present incumbent of St. Peter's, Preston, being bishop thereof at the time; he stayed in the parish about a year; then went into the diocese of Derry, taking a curacy near Coleraine, which he held for three years; got a degree at Trinity College, Dublin, in 1858; was then ordained by the late Bishop of Killaloe; came to St. Peter's, Preston, as curate, in the spring of 1863; stayed there upwards of three years; and was then agreeably translated to Emmanuel Church. Mr. Murdoch is a very useful minister in the district, has striven much to illumine the sinners thereof, is bringing them now to a very fair state of enlightenment, and may in time get the whole district into a bright state of sacred combustion.

At the bottom of Fishergate Hill, in Bird-street, there is a small, clean-looking, pleasantly-formed building which, since the 14th of October 1869, has been used as a chapel of ease for Christ church. It cost 1000 pounds, was built conjointly by Mr. R. Newsham, Mr. J. F. Higgins, and Mr. W. B. Roper in memory of the late J. Bairstow, Esq., who left each of them several thousands; will accommodate about 240 persons; is tolerably well attended; and is one of the tidiest little places of worship we have seen. No effort at architectural display has been made in its construction. It has a brick exterior, has a comely little porch at the west end, is surmounted in the centre by a turret, has several yards of iron railing bending in various directions near the front, and will require considerable protection, if its general health has to be preserved. None of the windows have yet been broken, but we dare say they will be by and by, for the neighbourhood possesses some excellent stone-throwers; the Ribble has not yet flowed into it, but it may pay one of its peculiar visits some day, for in this quarter it is no respecter of buildings, whether they be chapels or public houses. The edifice has a light, simple, unassuming interior. Chairs seem to constitute the principal articles of furniture. There are 232 for the congregation, and 232 little red buffets as well, 11 for the choir, one for the organ blower, and two for the parson. At the top of each chair back there is a thick piece of wood on which is plastered a printed paper, requesting the worshippers to kneel during prayers, and to join in the responses. The paper also makes a quiet allusion to offertory business, the defraying of expenses, and the augmentation of the curate's salary. The chairs are planted down the church in two rows, and they look very singular. The organ at the south east corner is a pretty little instrument. A reading desk on the opposite side, standing upon a small platform, suffices for the pulpit. Behind there is a strip of strong blue-painted canvas bearing a text in gilt letters referring to the Sacrament. Above there is a three-light stained glass window. At the western end, just under the doorway, a marble tablet is fixed; and upon it is an allusion to the virtues of the late J. Bairstow, Esq., and to the gentlemen who erected the building. The average congregation consists of about 200 middle and working class people. The services are generally conducted by the Rev. J. D. Harrison, curate of Christ Church - a young gentleman who works with considerable vigour, and never sneezes at the offertory contributions, however small they may be. Mr. Harding, of this town, designed the building, which is a homely, kindly-looking little affair - a bashful, tiny, domesticated creature, a nursling amid the matured and ancient, a baby among the Titans, which may some day reach whiskerdom and manhood.

XXXVIII

ST. MARY'S CHURCH.

"And now, finally, brethren." To the "beginning of the end" have we got. The journey has been long and tortuous. When we have proceeded forty inches further we shall stop. Not with the "last rose of summer," nor with the "last of all the Romans," nor with the "last syllable of recorded time," nor with the "last words of Marmion" - the Mohicans are barred out - have we to deal, but with the last place of worship, fairly coming within the category of "Our Churches and Chapels." St. Mary's Church is situated in a huge, rudely-spun district, known by the name of "New Preston." That district used to be one of the wildest in this locality; "schimelendamowitchwagon" was not known in it; not much of that excellent article is yet known in it; and tons of good seed, saying nothing of manure, will have to be planted in its hard ground before it either blossoms like the rose or pays its debts. This district was originally brought into active existence by John Horrocks, Esq., the founder of the Preston cotton trade. Prior to his time there were a few people in it who believed that 10s. a week was a good wage, and that Nixon's Book of Prophecies was an infallible guide; but not before he planted in the locality a body of hand-loom weavers did it show signs of commercial vivacity, and begin to develope itself. Handloom weaving is now about as hopeless a job as trying to extract sunlight out of cucumbers; but at that time it was a paying air. Weavers could then afford to play two or three days a week, earn excellent wages, afterwards wear top boots, and then thrash their wives in comfort without the interference of policemen. They and their immediate descendants belonged to a crooked and perverse generation. Cock-fighting, badger-baiting, poaching, drinking, and dog-worrying formed their sovereign delights; and they were so amazingly rude and dangerous, that even tax collectors durst not, at times, go amongst them for money. Men of this stamp would be much appreciated at present. The population has thickened, and civilisation has penetrated into the region since then; and yet the "animal" preponderates rather largely in it now. Rats, pigeons, dogs, and Saturday night eye openers - toned down with canary breeding, ale-supping, herb-gathering, and Sunday afternoon baking - still retain a mild hold upon the affections of the people, and many of the youthful race are beginning to imitate their elders admirably in all these little particulars. A pack of hounds was once kept for general enjoyment in "New Preston;" but that pack has "gone to the dogs" - hasn't been heard of for years.

During the past quarter of a century what missionary breakfast men call a "great work" has been done by way of evangelising the people in this quarter of the town; and very much of it has been achieved through St. Mary's Church and schools. For a very long period the schools in connection with St. Mary's have formed an excellent auxiliary of the church. Prior to the erection of the church, scholastic work was carried on in some cottages on the north side of what is now termed New Hall-lane. The scholars were then in the care of the Parish Church. When St. Paul's was erected they were handed over to it. Afterwards, when St. Mary's was raised, a building was provided for them in a street just opposite, which has undergone many alterations and enlargements since, owing to the great increase in the number of scholars. The principal room of the schools is the largest in Preston, with one exception - the assembly room of the Corn Exchange. A little cottage-house looking place, up New Hall-lane, constitutes a "branch" of the schools. The average week-day attendance is about 900; whilst on a Sunday the gathering of scholars is about 1,200. At the schools, on Sundays, there are male and female adult classes; and on week-days a number of earnest mothers meet therein for the purposes of instruction, consolation, and pious news-vending. At the schools - we shall get to the church and Mr. Alker by and by, so be patient, if possible - there is a "Church of England Institute," under whose auspices innocent games are indulged in, and periodicals, &c. read. A Conservative association, established to guard the constitutional interests of Fishwick Ward, also holds its gatherings in one of the rooms. The Rev. Robert Lamb, a very energetic man, and formerly incumbent of St. Mary's, gave the first great impetus to the schools, which are the largest of their kind in Preston. Mr. Lamb is now at St. Paul's, Bennett-street, Manchester, and, singular to say, he has worked up the schools of that church until they have become the greatest in the city. The late T. Miller, Esq., was a warm friend of St. Mary's schools, and, whenever any extensions were made at them, he always, on having the plans and estimates submitted to him, defrayed one-third of the expenses.

St. Mary's Church stands just at the rear of the Preston House of Correction. That is better than standing inside such a grim establishment - any site before the insite (oh) of a prison; and has for its south western support the store-house of the Third Royal Lancashire Militia. It forms one of the churches erected mainly through the exertions of the late Rev. R. Carus Wilson; and like its brethren is built in the Norman style of architecture, the designer being Mr. John Latham. The first stone of the edifice was laid in May, 1836; in 1838 the church was opened; and in 1853 it was enlarged by the erection of a transept at the northern end. The late John Smith, Esq., gave the site for it. The building is surrounded by a graveyard, which might be kept in better order than it is. The Rev. R. Lamb considerably impoverished himself in enclosing the ground; and the Rev. H. R. Smith, one of the incumbents, afterwards spent a sum of money in ornamenting it with shrubs, &c.; but nobody cares much for it now, and Nature is permitted to follow her own unfettered way in it. Formerly there was a road to the church from the west, through some land adjoining the House of Correction; and it was a great convenience to those living on that side of the town; but for some reason it was closed; and one of the most roundabout ways imaginable has been substituted for it. St. Mary's is one of those churches which can be felt rather than seen. Until you get quite to it you hardly know you are at it. Approaching it from the west the first glimmering of it you have is over one end of the House of Correction. At this point you catch what seems to be a cluster of crosses - the surmountings of the tower; visions of a ponderous cruet-stand, of five nine pins, and other cognate articles, then strike you; afterwards the body of the church broadens slowly into view, and having described three-fourths of a wide circle with your feet, and passed through a strong gateway, it is found you are at the building. St. Mary's has a strong, heavy, compact appearance. Its front is arched below and storied above; it has ivy creeping up its walls - trying probably to get to some of the five nondescript ornaments above the tower - and has a half baronial, half old hall look at first sight. Some years ago there was much ivy about the general building; but the "rare old plant" engendered dampness and had to be pulled down. At each side of the front there is a small pinnacle, and flanking the gables of the transept there are four somewhat similar elevations. They are mainly used by sparrows.

The church can be approached by a doorway at the eastern end of the transept; but the bulk of the worshippers pass through those at the southern or front end - three in number, and rather heavy and dim in appearance. The centre one leads into the body of the building, and we may as well take advantage of it. We are just within; above there is a serious looking groined roof, with a lamp suspended from the middle of it; before us there is a screen, filled in with clear glass, through which you can see the worshippers who seem thin and scattered. Formerly the back of a sharply drawn up, dangerous gallery, for scholars, over which careless children might have fallen with the greatest ease, occupied the place of this screen, and a series of hot water pipes - apparently intended for warming the doorway and the churchyard in front, for they could have been of no use to people inside the building - were fixed there. In 1866, when the church was renovated, they were carried about fifteen yards into the edifice, where they may be seen to this day. We sat close to eight of them, with a top coat on, onc Sunday evening, as a compensation for being nearly starved to death in one of the back side wings in the morning, and felt charmingly cooked at the end of the service. On the left side of the central entrance, and near the glass door and the screen, there is an elaborately carved box of Gothic design, intended for missionary contributions; but it is fixed in such a dim corner that nobody can see it. We have recommended the beadle to place this box in a more prominent position, for it is worth looking at as an ornament, even if nothing is put into it. The aperture in the lid might be closed, and the box could then be hung up beside the doorway lamp, so that its proportions might be fairly realised. The interior of the church is broad and lofty, but through its Norman configuration it is stiff and coldly ponderous in effect. Massive bare walls, high narrow windows, and a semi-sexagonal ceiling dependent upon rather ungainly beams and rafters, like a series of hanging frames, chill you a little; but on looking northward, to the end of the building, the chancel and transept arches, which are strong and elegantly moulded, relieve you, and as you advance the place seems to gradually assume a finer and more imposing aspect.

The chancel has a calm, goodly look; is, in fact, the best part of the building, architecturally speaking. At the base, there is an archway of tablets, upon which nobody ever bestows very close attention; above, there are three staple-shaped windows; and surmounting all, there is a round recessed light, which can only be seen through by people who sit in the gallery. On the left side of the chancel, there are two windows. There is no stained glass in the chancel. If the windows were adorned with it, and the walls more cheerfully painted, a very beautiful effect would be produced. Five different kinds of carpetting, all very well worn, deck the floor of the chancel. Within the communion rails, there is a rich carpet, in needlework, made by some of the members of the congregation, At each side there is as antique chair, being part of the furniture in the vestry which adjoins, and which was given by the Rev. H. R. Smith. It consists altogether of ten pieces - including chairs, bookcase, looking-glass, dressing-table, chest, &c., and is about 200 years old. The only stained windows in the building are in the west transept. They are four in number; two being of the merely ornamental type, whilst the remainder are of the memorial order. At the bottom of one of them there are these words - "In memory of Mary Smith, born 1779, died 1845. Erected by Henry Robert Smith." At the base of the other window there is this inscription:- "In memory of John Smith, born 1773, died 1849. Erected by the church, 1855." The deceased persons referred to were the parents of the Rev. H. R. Smith, who, as already said, was a former incumbent of the church. The ends of the transept are very dim, and sometimes you can hardy tell who is sitting in them.

St. Mary's will accommodate 1,450 persons. The pews on the ground floor, excepting a few free ones at the entrance and at the top of the church, are all of the "closed" kind - have doors to them. When the Church was renovated the pews were cut down about eight inches, were remodelled, and thoroughly cleaned. Previously they were painted, and had a gummy, sticky influence rearwards upon peoples clothes. One or two bits of shawl fringe, &c., drawn off by the old gluey paint still remain at the back of some of the seats (notwithstanding the chemical cleansing they got), reminding one of the saying of friend Billings, that "A thing well stuck iz stuck for ever." The gas burners hang far down in pendant clusters from the ceiling, and with their glass reflectors, which would cast off a better light if cleaner, have a lamp-like effect, putting one in mind, when lighted, of some Eastern mosque.

The font is a prettily shaped article, is made of fossil marble, and was given by the Rev. Canon Parr and the wardens of the Parish Church, in which building it once stood. It rests upon a platform of ornamental tiles bordered with stone, and looks well. Above it is a carved wooden canopy surmounted by a dove. The canopy is raised by a descending ball of equal weight. When the ball falls the pigeon rises. In ordinary life the ball rises when the pigeon falls; but this is not the case at St. Mary's, although it amounts to the same thing in the end, for after the pigeon has ascended three feet the ball descends upon its back and settles the question.

At the southern end there is a large gallery, overshadowing the noisiest galaxy of Sunday infants we ever encountered. There are more infants at St. Mary's schools than at any other place in Preston, and trouble, combined with vexation of spirit, must consequently exist there in the same ratio. The bulk are kept from the church; but a few manage to creep in, and when we saw them they were having a very happy time of it. Some whistled a little - but they seemed to be only learners and couldn't get on very well with tunes; others tossed halfpennies about, a few operated upon the floor with marbles, and all of them were exceedingly lively. The gallery above is large, deep, and long; ingress to it is tortuous; and strangers would have to inquire much before properly reaching it. There is an old funeral bier in one part of it, and we have failed to ascertain the precise object of the article. It is not used when fainting fits are in season; it is never taken advantage of in the case of people who fall asleep, and require carrying home to bed; it seems to be neither useful nor ornamental; and it ought to be either taken off to the cemetery and quietly inurned, or sold to one of the sextons there.

In the gallery there is a large organ. It is a very respectable-looking instrument, has a healthy musical interior, and is played moderately. The members of the choir, to whom several people in the bottom of the church look up periodically, as if trying to find out either what they were doing or how they were dressed, are only in embryo. They are new singers; but some of them have fair voices, and in spite of occasional irregularity in tune and time, they get along agreeably. The elements of a good choir are within them, and they have only to persevere, in order to secure excellence, saying nothing of medals, and other tokens of appreciation. The whole of the seats in the gallery, generally used by scholars, are free.

St. Mary's is situated a district containing about 8,000 persons, and as they are nearly entirely of the working class sort, the congregation is naturally made up of similar materials. Including 14 militia staff men, the congregation will number, on an average, without the scholars, about 500. More people appear to come late to this church than to any other in Preston; they keep dropping in at all times - particularly in a morning - up to within twenty minutes of the finish; but they are connected with the schools, visit the church after they have done duty there, and this accounts for their lateness. The beadle of this church has the strongest, if not the longest, official wand in the town, and he is very modest, blushing occasionally, while carrying it.

The first incumbent of St. Mary's was the Rev. James Parker, a relative of Councillor Parker, of Preston, who had to retire through ill health. He exchanged livings with the Rev. W. Watson, of Ellerburne, in Yorkshire, who required a more active sphere, and found it at St. Mary's. Mr. Watson afterwards found higher preferment, and went to the South of England. Then came the Rev. Robert Lamb, who worked most vigorously in the district. He is now rector of St. Paul's, Manchester. His successor was the Rev. Henry Robert Smith, who, after staying a while, retired to St. Paul's, at Grange, where he still labours. The next incumbent was the Rev. George Alker, who came to St. Mary's in December, 1857. He is still at the church; but we dare say he would be willing to leave it for a rectory, if one were offered, with 500 pounds a year. Mr. Alker is an Irishman, and is about 42 years of age. He is rather tall; is genteelly fashioned, has good features, wears an elegantly-trimmed pair of whiskers, has pompous, odorous, Pall Mall appearance, is grandiose and special, looks like a nineteenth century Numa Pompilius, would have made a spicey Pontifex Maximus, ought to have lived in Persia, where he might have worn velvet slippers and been fanned with peacock feathers, would have been a rare general director of either fire-eaters or fire worshippers; is inclined to run when he walks alone, and to be stately, slow, regal, and precise when, like Fadladeen, he is in charge of Lalla Rookh. Is a man of determination, and never sleeps with his clothes on. Is a sharp debater, a briskly-pompous, eloquent talker, has had a good deal of trouble at time and time in putting on his kid gloves, which used to fit so mortally tight that he couldn't stir his thumbs in them; stands with a fine commanding air in the pulpit, as if about to shoulder arms; preaches extempore; says "my brethren" more frequently in his sermons than any minister we ever heard; has a clear, keen intellect; is dexterous, courageous, impassioned, imperious; has a lofty, threepence-halfpenny majesty about him; has been a hard worker, a stiff fighter, and a stinging public lecturer. After leaving Ireland, he took a curacy in Liverpool. In 1857 he accepted a similar post at St. Peter's, Preston. Here he organised a class of young men, 800 strong, and whilst here he set the town on fire with anti-Popery denunciation; and of him it might, at that time, have been said -

He comes from Erin's peaceful shore
Like fervid kettle bubbling o'er
With hot effusions - hot and weak;
Sound Humbug all your hollowest drums,
He comes of Erin's martyrdoms
To Britain's well-fed Church to speak.

Yes, he was a regular Mr. Blazeaway, and what he said was equal to the strongest of the theatre thunder and the most dazzling of forked lightning. Other Irish curates have tried the same game on since then in the town, but they have not been so successful; none of them have yet got into decent incumbencies, and we are afraid they will have to rave on for a yet longer period ere the requisite balm of Gilead is found. After piling up the agony for a few months at St. Peter's, Mr. Alker left for Dublin, stayed there a short time, then retraced his steps to Preston, and in due time got the incumbency of St. Mary's - an event which seems to have toned down all his fury about the "abomination of Rome," and made him nearly quite forget the existence of Pope Pius. Paraphrasing one of his own country's poets, we may say, -

As bees on flowers alighting cease their hum,
So settling at St. Mary's Alker's dumb.

Still be has occasional spells of anti-Popery hysteria; he can't altogether get the old complaint out of his bones; Rome is yet his red rag when in a rage; and he has latterly shown an inclination to wind up the clocks of the Jews and the Mahommedans. He may have a fling at the Calmuck Tartars and a quiet pitch into the Sioux Indians after a bit. When Mr. Alker first went to St. Mary's his salary was small; but it has now reached the general panacea of incumbents - 300 pounds a year. He has also a neat, well-situated parsonage, on the south eastern side of the town, a good garden, which has been the scene of many lovely sights, and a neat patch of ground beyond. In his district Mr. Alker has been an energetic worker, and in connection with the schools particularly he has been most useful. For his services in this respect he deserves much praise, and we tender him our share. His influence is hardly so great as it used to be, still he is the great Brahmin and the grand Lama of the locality. There have been five curates at St. Mary's - the Rev. W. Nesbit M'Guinness, clever and ambitious; the Rev. John Wilson (not of St. James's), an industrious gentleman, who had a row with the congregation in respect to his marriage, and afterwards went away; the Rev. R. Close, a pretentious young man, who appeared to use much hair oil and think well of pious gammon; the Rev. E. M. David, a Welshman, who couldn't speak plainly enough for the congregation, and had to retire; and, lastly, the Rev. Bernard Robinson, who has been at St. Mary's about twelve months, and is evidently working satisfactorily in the district. We have finished: all is over; the lime lights are burning, the coloured fires are radiating their hues, the curtain is falling, and bidding "Adieu" to all our kind readers, we vanish.

www.ingramcontent.com/pod-product-compliance
Lightning Source LLC
LaVergne TN
LVHW050922080826
845145LV00001B/174

* 9 7 8 1 5 9 5 4 0 6 1 0 1 *